James Surowiecki

BEST BUSINESS CRIME WRITING

OF THE YEAR

James Surowiecki writes a business column
for *The New Yorker*.

BEST BUSINESS CRIME WRITING OF THE YEAR

Edited by *James Surowiecki*

ANCHOR BOOKS

A DIVISION OF RANDOM HOUSE, INC.

NEW YORK

AN ANCHOR BOOKS ORIGINAL, NOVEMBER 2002

Copyright © 2002 by James Surowiecki

All rights reserved under International and Pan-American Copyright Conventions. Published in the United States by Anchor Books, a division of Random House, Inc., New York, and simultaneously in Canada by Random House of Canada Limited, Toronto.

Anchor Books and colophon are registered trademarks of Random House, Inc.

Permissions acknowledgments can be found at the end of the book.

Library of Congress Cataloging-in-Publication Data

Best business crime stories / edited by James Surowiecki.
p.   cm.
ISBN 1-4000-3371-3 (trade paper)
1. Commercial crimes—United States.   2. White collar crimes—United States.   3. Journalism, Commercial—United States.
I. Surowiecki, James, 1967–
HV6769 .B47 2002
364.16'8'0973—dc21
        2002514113

Book design by Debbie Glasserman

www.anchorbooks.com

Printed in the United States of America
10 9 8 7 6 5 4 3 2 1

CONTENTS

PART TWO—WHO WATCHES THE WATCHMEN? 137

INTRODUCTION

A COUPLE OF YEARS ago, a book like this one would have been very hard to imagine. To be sure, the 1990s saw their share of corporate fraud and deceit. Sunbeam CEO Al Dunlap deluded investors by shipping backyard grills to empty warehouses. Waste Management executives inflated profits by a tidy $1.7 billion. And managers at direct marketing powerhouse CUC International made up sales and profit numbers whenever it looked like they were going to fall short of Wall Street's expectations. But while all of these scandals were well covered by the business press, at the time they seemed like anomalies, interesting in their own right but not symptomatic of anything bigger. The story of American business at the end of the last century was one of technological innovation, global dominance, and ever rising stock prices. Corporate crooks had no role to play in that tale.

Those were the days. Today, the narrative of productivity and boom has been replaced by one of crime and bust. Corporate heroes are hard to find, with even icons like Jack Welch tarnished, while corporate villains have become the stuff of front-page news. Business writers who three years ago would have been analyzing a hot new Internet company have turned their attention to accounting fraud, tax law, and stock-option shenanigans, and in the process have produced any number of incisive pieces about what was really happening behind boardroom doors. So many good pieces were produced, in fact, that they seemed to demand a book of their own. And so we have this collection, an anthology of the best business crime stories of the year, an anthology whose very existence is testimony to just how much things have changed. From Enron to WorldCom to Adelphia to Tyco to companies that you have probably never heard of, the stories collected here offer a clear view of a time when corporate culture went bad, when the checks and balances of a healthy market system were absent, and the incentives to commit misdeeds were immense. Uniting sharp detail with an unusually sophisticated sense of context and background, they narrate the rise and fall of individual wrongdoers while keeping us aware of the systemic forces that allowed wrongdoing not simply to exist but to flourish. Taken together, they paint as sharp and detailed a collective portrait of corporate America in the bubble and post-bubble years as we will have for some time to come.

EVEN NOW, IT'S REMARKABLE to remember how different that portrait would have looked a year and a half ago. Consider the August 2001 issue of *Business 2.0*. There, on the cover, is former Enron CEO Jeff Skilling, underneath the headline "The Revolution Lives . . . Pass It On." Inside, Skilling talks about how the Internet is transforming the economy. Companies everywhere, he predicts confidently, will soon be following in Enron's footsteps, adopting its business model and mimicking its strategies.

Skilling, of course, left out one thing: Enron's business model was the proverbial house of cards, and he was getting ready to flee before it collapsed all around him. Just a couple of weeks after that issue of *Business 2.0* hit the newsstands, Skilling resigned as CEO, citing the obligatory "personal reasons" for his departure. Two months later, Enron made public a host of secretive transactions that had saddled it with billions in debt. The company's stock price plummeted, and by early December, the firm was bankrupt. In February, Skilling testified before the Senate Commerce Committee, which grilled him for five hours on his role in Enron's collapse. In six months, Skilling went from being an example of all that was right about the American economy to the epitome of all that was wrong with it. Today, *The New York Times* tells us, he sometimes sits in a bar near his Houston home, protesting his innocence and asking people, "Don't you believe me?"

The answer, of course, is "No." No one believes Jeff Skilling, just as no one believes that Bernie Ebbers had nothing to do with the financial shenanigans at WorldCom, and no one believes that Wall Street analysts were really making objective judgments when they slapped "buy" ratings on fly-by-night Internet companies. In one recent poll, two-thirds of Americans said they thought corporate executives had low ethical standards, while another poll showed that Americans were less likely to trust CEOs than the members of any other profession.

BUSINESS CRIME IS NOTHING new. Commerce necessarily brings with it the possibility of fraud, and from the beginning con men have found America a congenial place to operate. The kind of scandalous behavior that corporate CEOs engaged in at the end of the 1990s is, in fact, new only in its magnitude, which is orders greater than anything in the past. When you look at the stories that dominated the headlines over the past year—Enron, WorldCom, Tyco, Adelphia, ImClone—what you see at their core is the same fundamental misdeed: self-dealing. Self-dealing is what you call it when the people running companies line their own pockets instead of those of the companies' owners, and it has plagued American capitalism since the creation of the first modern corporations.

Look, for example, at the story of the Central Pacific Railroad. Started by four merchants from Sacramento—including Leland Stanford—who were known as "the Big Four," the California company owned the right to build the western end of the transcontinental railroad. The Central Pacific was supported by taxpayer subsidies, blessed with immense land grants, and appeared to own a monopoly on rail traffic into California. It was hard to see what could go wrong. Outside investors, most of them British, bought up the company's shares in anticipation of lavish profits and an ever rising stock price. But the profits never materialized. Instead, they ended up in the pockets of the Big Four. They had had the foresight to set up an outside construction firm, which just happened to win the contract to build the Central Pacific's railroad. The construction company charged the Central Pacific about three times as much as it should have. This was good for the Big Four but bad for the shareholders of the Central Pacific. By the time the Golden Spike was finally driven, Leland Stanford and his pals had pocketed, by some estimates, at least $50 million in overcharges alone. In the years that followed, would-be railroad titans across the country did their best to emulate the Big Four. When a British emissary was sent to America in the 1890s to find out what had happened to the money his bosses had put into an American firm, he wrote them that he had asked one of the company's directors where all the invested capital was, and had received this less-than-reassuring reply: "Well, really, Sir, that is what I am always asking, but which I can never get to know."

The problem that this hapless investor was wrestling with was the same problem that hamstrung investors in Enron and WorldCom a century later. Economists call it the "agency problem," and it stems from a simple fact: the people who own corporations aren't the people who run corporations. So a company's shareholders always face the risk that the company's managers (their "agents") will do things that the shareholders wouldn't approve of, like pay themselves high salaries, reward themselves with stock options, lie about the company's earnings, or channel corporate money to outside firms that they own.

Since the days of the Central Pacific, it's been clear that the agency problem needed to be solved. And we've tried a variety of solutions. We have "independent" accounting firms that are supposed to testify to the accuracy of a company's financial statements. We have Wall Street firms that are supposed to vet firms' financial prospects. Since the 1930s, we've had an elaborate system of government regulation—far more elaborate than that of any other country—requiring quarterly reports to shareholders, formal audits, public disclosure of important news, and the protection of shareholder rights. More recently, companies hit on the idea that stock options were the solution to the agency problem. If the problem was that CEOs weren't owners, make them owners by giving them a big stake in the company, and the problem would go away.

But in the late 1990s, as the pieces in this collection document, all of these safeguards failed. Start with stock options. In theory, they were supposed to align the interests of investors and managers. But in practice, stock-option packages actually turned out to facilitate—rather than curb—self-dealing. Issuing more options didn't increase executives' stake in companies. They just cashed in existing options. And the way options were awarded encouraged executives to adopt risky strategies. If stock prices skyrocketed, they got massive options grants as a reward; if stock prices plummeted, they got massive options grants as an incentive, or they had their options repriced. Either way, executives couldn't really lose. If in the old days, investors worried about executives paying themselves high salaries, lavishing perks on themselves, and spending money to redecorate the executive dining room, now they had to worry about executives using deceptive numbers to jack up the stock price in order to dump their stakes and put hundreds of millions in the bank before anyone could figure out what was wrong.

Then there were the investment banks and the accounting firms, which were supposed to serve as a check on corporate malfeasance but instead turned a blind eye to it at best and at worst actively encouraged it. This was disastrous because it threatened the sense of trust that any strong market-driven economy needs if it's going to function smoothly. For capital to flow freely from investors to corporations, investors need to be sure that most deals are not shakedowns or scams. And while the United States has an elaborate system of contracts and a judicial system that will enforce them, it's not enough. If every contract and every bill of sale ended up being haggled over in court, it would simply be too expensive and too time-consuming to do anything.

That's why, in most healthy market-driven societies, you have a host of institutions whose business it is to distinguish between the trustworthy and the trustworthless. These institutions are what economist Daniel Klein calls "independent knowers." The Underwriters Laboratories, for instance, tests electrical equipment, affixing its UL logo to products that meet its standards. The Better Business Bureau measures companies' reputation for fairness and honesty. Companies like Equifax rate people's creditworthiness. When it comes to investing, Wall Street firms, bond-rating agencies, the stock exchanges, and accounting firms are all independent knowers. If Goldman Sachs underwrites a stock offering for a company, it's saying that that company has real value, as is Merrill Lynch when one of its analysts issues a "buy" recommendation. When the New York Stock Exchange lists a company, it's attesting to the fact that the firm is not a fly-by-night operation. And when an accounting firm signs off on an audit, it's telling us that we can trust that company's numbers.

The great thing about these institutions is that because their entire business depends on the reliability of their recommendations, they don't have to be inherently virtuous to work well. They only have to worry about what will happen to their reputations if they stop doing a good job of separating the wheat from the chaff.

There's one problem with this arrangement: it only works if the firms that don't do a good job of separating wheat from chaff are punished for their failure. And in the late '90s, that did not happen. The NASDAQ listed companies that owned little more than an idea and a silly name. White-shoe firms like Goldman Sachs underwrote stock offerings for companies that had no meaningful prospects for future profits. And, most egregiously, accounting firms stopped working in the interests of investors and started working in the interests of CEOs. (Between 1997 and 2000, seven hundred companies were forced to restate their earnings. In 1981, three companies did so.) Yet none of these institutions paid a price for their dereliction of duty. Just look at the most egregious case, Arthur Andersen. In the late '90s, it was auditor of record for accounting disasters like Waste Management and Sunbeam. Yet investors did not look more skeptically on companies—like, say, WorldCom and Enron— that continued to use Andersen as their accountant. So the watchmen did not watch because no one was watching them.

As for the regulations that were supposed to keep us safe, they may in the end have only exacerbated the problem, as P. J. O'Rourke suggests in "How to Stuff a Wild Enron." The Securities and Exchange Commission was clearly underfunded, which meant it didn't have enough people to give corporate 10-Ks and 10-Qs the going-over they obviously deserved. But even so, investors in the United States had and have far more information about the companies they were sinking their money into than investors anywhere else do. When you look back at Enron and Adelphia and Qwest and Global Crossing, in fact, what's striking is not how little information investors had, but how much. CEO compensation packages, for instance, were public information and were the subject of scathing stories long before Jeff Skilling became a household name. ("The Great CEO Pay Heist," *Fortune* called it in 2000.) The cost of stock options was not listed as an actual expense on companies' income statements, but the number of options issued was in every company's annual report, and any money manager with a calculator could easily have figured out how expensive all those options grants were. Even a company like Enron, which was especially adept at dubious financial shenanigans, did not hide the fact that it was hiding stuff. The company was, as it were, openly closemouthed. That should have made investors wary, since the less information is available, the riskier a company is. Instead, mutual fund managers—who are paid to be smarter than this—kept buying the stock. They thought they knew more than they did know.

The willingness of investors to overlook obviously sketchy corporate behavior seems like an excellent example of what psychologist Gerald Wilde has called "risk compensation." The idea behind risk compensation is simple: if a given behavior seems less risky than it once did people compensate by doing it in a riskier fashion. If you improve road lighting, people drive faster and are less attentive. Cars with antilock brakes are driven faster, and are involved in just as many accidents, as cars without them. And a study of floods in the United States over an eighty-year period found that the property damage from floods did not drop at all over those eighty years, even though the government had invested heavily in flood control measures. The measures led people to underestimate the real risk and to build where previously they wouldn't have. In the same way, investors—imagining that the SEC would somehow protect them—happily embraced Enron, willfully disregarding the risks of giving money to people who make a point of not saying what they're doing with it. That doesn't mean that we don't need regulations. It means that investors shouldn't expect regulations to protect them from their own bad judgment, especially since investors exercising their judgment is how all the important decisions get made in a capitalist system.

Like investors, the business media was nowhere near as rigorous as it should have been in interrogating the hype, the myths, and the outright deceptions that helped inflate the stock-market bubble. *Business 2.0* putting Skilling on the cover in August 2001 may be the most extreme example, but even a cursory glance through the back issues of business magazines over the past three years would yield a plethora of decisions that in hindsight appear absurd, from Dennis Kozlowski of Tyco being hailed as the next Jack Welch to Bernie Ebbers of WorldCom being acclaimed as a visionary. That isn't to say that the business press was simply parroting New Economy hype. Alongside the fawning profiles, there were—even in the heyday of the bubble—plenty of serious pieces that pointed to problems ahead. But the role of the business press in fostering the myth of the CEO as hero—a myth that was at the heart of the corporate scandals of the late '90s—cannot be overestimated. In turning CEOs into rock stars, the media provided a deeply flawed picture of the way corporations actually work, contributing to the illusion that having the right person at the top was the real key to corporate success. The deification of CEOs was, in no small part, responsible for the massive pay packages of the 1990s and contributed to the false sense of invulnerability that doomed executives at places like WorldCom and Enron.

Look, for instance, at Alex Prud'homme's biting profile of Sam Waksal, the CEO of struggling biotech company ImClone, in which Waksal compares himself to Bill Gates. Gates' company essentially created the modern computer industry as we know it and permanently altered the way hundreds of millions of people work and communicate. ImClone has made a single drug, which it has yet to bring to market. But in Waksal's mind, the simple fact that he was a CEO made him Gates' equal.

In that sense, it may be telling that nearly all of the corporate scandals recounted in the stories collected here involve people who, for all intents and purposes, created the companies that they eventually helped destroy. Adelphia, Enron, WorldCom, Tyco, ImClone: in each case, the men (and they were all men) at the top had built those companies from nothing (or almost nothing) into corporations that were worth tens or hundreds of billions of dollars.

Now, one might have thought this would make them more responsible, not less. After all, we want people to feel a sense of ownership over the companies they work for, rather than just punch a time card. One of the biggest criticisms levied against American business in the era of the Organization Man was that because employees didn't have any real stake in their companies, they didn't have any real interest in improving their companies' performance.

What the recent scandals suggest is that there's a downside of ownership, too: even after a company goes public, the CEO and top managers may continue to think of it as essentially their property. That was certainly the case with the Rigas family, founders of the cable company Adelphia Communications, as Devin Leonard shows in his devastating piece in *Fortune*. The Rigases used Adelphia as a personal piggy bank, taking and borrowing money from the company to build golf courses, finance the operations of a professional hockey team, and pay for lawn care. Even when they were hauled away in handcuffs, they continued to insist that they had done nothing wrong. More broadly, you can see this in the outrageous compensation packages and option grants that the CEOs at so many of these companies took home during the 1990s. For these executives, the companies they were running were their creations. Without them, there would be no WorldCom or no Enron to talk about. So why should anyone mind if they took home a couple hundred million a year in stock options? If CEOs were the superstars that everyone was saying they were, shouldn't they be paid accordingly? Of course, they were not superstars, and they were not as important to their companies as they imagined. But in the late 1990s, there were not many people willing to stand up and say that.

Of course, this doesn't excuse the looting of corporate America by greedy CEOs. But as many of the stories in this collection make clear, what happened in the late 1990s was as much a failure of the system as it was a failure of individuals. Capitalism works best not when virtue is its own reward but when virtue is rewarded. In the bubble years, lots of CEOs and CFOs and accountants and investment bankers saw that the rewards for vice had sharply increased. We should not be too surprised—though we can still be outraged—that more than a few of them chose that path instead.

NOTE

Many of the pieces in this book tell stories that are still, in a sense, ongoing. In the months since these pieces were written, indictments have been handed down, companies have restated earnings and revenue, and former executives have been led away in handcuffs. Where it seemed useful, short follow-up notes have been appended to the stories that follow, recounting important developments since the pieces first appeared.

BEST BUSINESS CRIME WRITING OF THE YEAR

Part One

Visionaries, Hucksters, and Con Men: CEOs and the Games They Played

One of the striking things about this most recent wave of corporate fraud and deception is how much of it was not centered on Wall Street, the traditional home of financial scandal. Of course, all of the fraud was in one way or another connected to Wall Street, as CEOs misled investors and rigged financial results in an attempt to keep their stock price high. But whereas the Street was the site of the great scandals of the 1920s and the 1980s, this most recent wave swept up not merely investment bankers and stock analysts but CEOs, CFOs, and vice presidents. And the companies that made headlines were not fly-by-night operations, either. Enron was the seventh-biggest company in the *Fortune* 500. WorldCom was one of the world's biggest telecom companies. Tyco was routinely compared to GE. And Qwest, after merging with US West, had become one of the country's most important phone companies.

How did this happen? The pieces in this section, most of them compelling narratives about corporations sliding down the slippery slope toward fraud, go a long way toward answering that question. They give us CEOs, fed on a diet of hefty stock-option packages and hyped-up publicity, who came to drink their own Kool-Aid, imagining that they understood what no one else did, and that there were no obstacles to their visionary schemes. In many cases, it seems clear, executives did not start out intending to deceive. Instead, they made outrageous promises and then found themselves playing fast and loose with the rules in a desperate attempt to make those promises come true. Others, though, were more cynical about the process, using the hype machine to great effect and milking the system for all it was worth.

Peter Behr and April Witt, for instance, paint a vivid picture of the way Jeff Skilling's attempt to turn Enron from a stodgy old utility into a high-powered, "asset-light" New Economy firm led the company into ever riskier behavior. Similarly, both David Staples and the team of Peter S. Goodman and Renae Merle link WorldCom's collapse to Bernie Ebbers' strategy of growth-through-acquisition. Ebbers was so focused on buying new companies that he never really figured out how to run the one he had already assembled. At Qwest, meanwhile, Joe Nacchio did an excellent job of spinning elaborate scenarios of a digital future—which his company would control—but as three writers for the *Rocky Mountain News* show, those scenarios never came close to becoming reality. Dennis Kozlowski, meanwhile, told investors that he wanted to make Tyco the next GE. But as Mark Maremont and Jerry Markon show, what he really wanted to do was make Tyco his own personal bank. Money manager David Dreman sums up the feelings of more than a few investors when he tells Maremont and Markon, "I'm a little dazed about how much money they siphoned off."

What all of these pieces suggest is that at many companies, CEOs were simply convinced that the normal rules did not apply to them. David McClintick's narrative of Amyn Dahya's preposterous tenure as CEO of a small mining company called Casmyn Corp gives us a man who, as one board member put it, refused to take "any of the requirements of a public company seroiusly." Alex Prud'homme's profile of ImClone CEO Sam Waksal, who's been indicted for insider trading, reveals Waksal as a slick huckster more concerned with hype than reality. Marc Peyser's sharp analysis of the Martha Stewart–Waksal connection offers up a New York world in which personal connections and social networking count for too much. In "The Adelphia Story," Devin Leonard dissects the Rigas family, which came to regard Adelphia Communications, the cable company it ran, as its own private fiefdom. David

Streitfeld's portrait of Critical Path CEO David Thatcher, who ended up pleading guilty to securities fraud, is an overpowering picture of just how easy it was for executives to convince themselves that they were bending, and not breaking, the rules. And even when executives did break the rules, they weren't necessarily punished for it, as David Leonhardt shows in his investigation of CEO contracts. In the heyday of the bubble, even a felony conviction was sometimes not enough to shred an executive's golden parachute. Of course, as Almar Latour and Kevin Delaney remind us, self-dealing and corporate deception are not unique to the United States, but rather flourish across the globe. In fact, they suggest, safeguards to protect investors from fraud are actually stronger here than in places like Germany and Japan, a conclusion which, however true, comes as cold comfort to those who placed their faith in the Jeff Skillings and Bernie Ebberses of the world.

VISIONARY'S DREAM LED TO RISKY BUSINESS

Peter Behr and April Witt

The Washington Post, July 28, 2002

FOR VINCE KAMINSKI, the in-house risk-management genius, the fall of Enron Corp. began one day in June 1999. His boss told him that Enron president Jeffrey K. Skilling had an urgent task for Kaminski's team of financial analysts.

A few minutes later, Skilling surprised Kaminski by marching into his office to explain. Enron's investment in a risky Internet start-up called Rhythms NetConnections had jumped $300 million in value. Because of a securities restriction, Enron could not sell the stock immediately. But the company could and did count the paper gain as profit. Now Skilling had a way to hold on to that windfall if the tech boom collapsed and the stock dropped.

Much later, Kaminski would come to see Skilling's command as a turning point, a moment in which the course of modern American business was fundamentally altered. At the time Kaminski found Skilling's idea merely incoherent, the task patently absurd.

When Kaminski took the idea to his team—world-class mathematicians who used arcane statistical models to analyze risk—the room exploded in laughter.

The plan was to create a private partnership in the Cayman Islands that would protect—or hedge—the Rhythms investment, locking in the gain. Ordinarily, Wall Street firms would provide such insurance, for a fee. But Rhythms was such a risky stock that no company would have touched the deal for a reasonable price. And Enron needed Rhythms: The gain would amount to 30 percent of its profit for the year.

The whole thing was really just an accounting trick. The arrangement would pay Enron to cover any losses if the tech stock dropped. But Skilling proposed to bankroll the partnership with Enron stock. In essence, Enron was insuring itself. The risk was huge, Kaminski immediately realized.

If the stocks of Enron and the tech company fell precipitously at the same time, the hedge would fail and Enron would be left with heavy losses.

The deal was "so stupid that only Andrew Fastow could have come up with it," Kaminski would later say.

In fact, Fastow, Enron's chief financial officer, had come up with the maneuver, with Skilling and others. In an obvious conflict of interest, Fastow would run the partnership, sign up banks and others as investors, and invest in it himself. He stood to make millions quickly, in fees and profits, even if Enron lost money on the deal. He would call it LJM, after his wife and two children.

Stupid or not, Enron did it and kept doing more like it, making riskier and riskier bets. Enron's top executives, who fancied themselves the best of the brightest, the most sophisticated connoisseurs of business risk, finally took on more than they could handle.

Fastow's plan and Skilling's directive would sow seeds of destruction for the nation's largest energy-trading company, setting in motion one of the greatest business scandals in U.S. history.

On Oct. 16, 2001, Enron was forced to disclose $1 billion in losses, more than half from LJM deals gone bad. Thus began a chain of events that would drive Enron's stock price into the dirt and force the company into bankruptcy proceedings, wiping out thousands of jobs and tens of billions of dollars in savings.

Enron was the first of the recent business scandals that have devastated investor faith, contributed to a multitrillion-dollar market downturn and made corporate reform a political imperative.

The Washington Post examined Enron's epic collapse, focusing on the final five months, drawing on dozens of interviews with former Enron executives and employees and thousands of pages of Enron documents, records from an internal investigation, and sworn testimony from court cases and congressional hearings.

The company's story provides a powerful parable. Policymakers, investors and executives must grapple with its lessons today; business students and historians will study them for decades.

Enron was a fundamentally self-destructive institution, a house of cards where human error and a culture of ambition, secrecy and greed made collapse inevitable.

While Skilling has previously attributed Enron's demise to innocent misfortune—a "classic run on the bank"—the Houston firm was a victim of its own making, a virtual company with vastly overstated profits.

Skilling and Enron founder and chairman Kenneth L. Lay said they believe Enron remained profitable until its sudden collapse late last year. Skilling and Fastow declined to be interviewed for this article. Skilling has testified that he was unaware of any improper accounting or falsified financial statements. A spokeswoman for Lay said in a statement yesterday that Lay believes Enron's profits "were not inflated in any way."

Lay, who had turned day-to-day control over to Skilling in the late 1990s, was obliged as chairman of a company with 25,000 employees in 30 countries to "rely on talented people whose trustworthiness he had no reason to doubt," according to his spokeswoman, Kelly Kimberly.

Skilling, Lay's personally chosen successor as chief executive, was directly involved in the overstatement of profit, according to interviews and investigators' reports. He sponsored and approved accounting and tax gimmicks with private partnerships and funds that contributed billions in improper or questionable earnings. Those deals helped elevate Enron's stock price during the market's boom in the 1990s. Enron executives and directors sold $1 billion worth of shares in the three years before the company collapsed.

Enron hailed 2000 as a breakout year with $101 billion in revenue, more than double that of the year before, putting it at No. 7 on the list of largest U.S. corporations. Skilling, Lay and 17 other officers and directors signed the 2000 financial statements, declaring them to be a true picture on which investors could rely.

The numbers were shams and the portrait was a fake, the record shows.

In 2001, Enron spent money faster than it was coming in. Most of its huge revenue gains came from power sales on its highly touted Internet energy-trading site. But revenue was padded in various ways. Traders swapped power with each other, internal memos state. Billions in loans were counted as cash from operations. And Enron's accounting inflated revenue from long-term contracts, former executives say.

Enron's profits were a mirage.

The company claimed that it earned $979 million in 2000. But $630 million of that came from improper accounting involving LJM and other partnerships, investigators for the company's board concluded. Another $296 million in "profit" came from hidden tax-cutting transactions, not normal business operations.

Take away the accounting tricks and the company was making little profit, if any.

Enron used the bewildering complexity of its finances to hide its true nature. Some people had nagging suspicions. But like the cowed townspeople in the children's story, few questioned the emperor's new clothes.

"It's so complicated everybody is afraid to raise their hands and say, 'I don't understand it,'" Louis B. Gagliardi, an analyst with John S. Herold Inc. in Norwalk, Conn., said last year.

Enron's arc toward scandal and bankruptcy exposed the failure of watchdogs at every level. Its board defaulted on its oversight duties. Outside accountants ceded their independence and violated their profession's rules. Outside lawyers approved misleading deals and failed to vigorously pursue a crucial allegation of accounting misdeeds. Wall Street analysts led a cheering section while their firms collected enormous banking fees from the company. Regulators were overwhelmed by Enron's complexity. The media were blinded by its image of success.

Nobody looked inside the company and saw what wasn't there.

After Skilling gave Kaminski the assignment involving the LJM partnership in June 1999, the researcher and a member of his team worked through the weekend to check and recheck their analysis. On Monday morning, Kaminski was confident that it was a bad, even dangerous, deal for Enron. He told his immediate boss, Chief Risk Officer Richard Buy, that the Rhythms NetConnections–LJM partnerships venture should not go forward.

Kaminski described the deal as "heads the partnership wins, tails Enron loses."

Enron could not make the deal without the approval of its outside accounting firm, Arthur Andersen LLP. But accountants there had the same reaction as Kaminski. Andersen partner Benjamin Neuhausen e-mailed his colleague David B. Duncan, head of Andersen's Enron audit team, to complain about Fastow's proposed role in LJM:

"Setting aside the accounting, idea of a venture entity managed by CFO is terrible from a business point of view. Conflicts galore. Why would any director in his or her right mind ever approve such a scheme?"

Duncan responded: "I really couldn't agree more."

But Duncan did not try to oppose the deal. In his e-mail to Neuhausen, Duncan wrote that Andersen would go along if Lay and Enron's 18-member board of directors approved the arrangement.

In a one-hour teleconference on June 28, 1999, that included five other items of business, the board approved the LJM proposal presented by Lay, Skilling and Fastow. It also gave Fastow permission to work simultaneously for LJM and Enron, despite the conflict of interest.

"I couldn't stop it," Buy told Kaminski. Kaminski wondered how hard he had tried.

Paraphrasing Winston Churchill's rebuke of Neville Chamberlain's appeasement of Hitler, Kaminski told a colleague that Buy had chosen shame over confrontation. The confrontation would come, Kaminski predicted.

Several days later, Kaminski was sitting in his office when the phone rang, according to one executive's account. It was Skilling, saying Kaminski was being transferred out of Buy's risk-management division because he was acting like a cop, trying to kill deals. People did not like it.

To understand Enron's fate, it helps to start with its beginnings.

In June 1984, when Ken Lay became chairman and chief operating officer of Enron's precursor, Houston Natural Gas, the firm's finances were a lot simpler. It was just a pipeline company. Lay quickly doubled its size by acquiring a Florida pipeline company.

But Lay's dreams were bigger still. Pipelines were profitable, and Lay wanted to create the largest pipeline system in the nation. The next year,

Lay's firm merged with InterNorth Inc. Together, they owned about 40,000 miles of pipeline.

The company changed its name to Enron in 1986. It was just the beginning. Lay, its patriarchal visionary, was determined to create one of the biggest, most successful companies in the world.

With an ideological fervor for deregulation and a knack for winning influential friends, Lay campaigned for changes in federal energy rules that would allow natural gas to be sold on open markets like wheat or pork bellies. In doing so, he helped create an industry and made Enron a corporate political powerhouse.

In 1990, Lay hired the 36-year-old Skilling, a brilliant Harvard MBA who was a longtime Enron consultant, to pioneer the company's energy-trading operations. Skilling created the "gas bank," making Enron the first company to buy large volumes of gas from producers and resell it to industrial customers on long-term contracts. That stabilized the U.S. gas market, expanded gas production nationwide and fueled the phenomenal growth that Enron reported during the decade.

The synthesis of Lay and Skilling proved potent, putting Enron at a confluence of major political and financial currents. The deregulation of energy markets, spurred by the Reagan administration, created great opportunities. And Skilling's foray into energy trading came just as financial institutions were unleashing exotic investment tools—a flow of money looking for opportunities.

A guru-like pitchman with a disdain for traditional business practices, Skilling was perfectly placed to ride the new wave. He gave the impression that pipelines were hopelessly boring. As he rose at Enron, he retooled the company in his own image: smart and arrogant, confident and flashy. He assembled a fast-moving band of self-described pioneers who embraced risky new ideas as the route to profits.

"We like risk because you make money by taking risks," Skilling said in an interview with University of Virginia business school professors two years ago. "The key is to take on risk that you manage better than your competitors."

Skilling was proud of pushing boundaries. He persuaded federal regulators to let Enron use "mark-to-market" accounting, an approved mechanism used by brokerages for securities trading. Skilling applied it throughout Enron's operations, from the Rhythms NetConnections transaction to its commodities trading. It allowed Enron to calculate revenue from long-term contracts and count much of it as immediate profit, although the money would not come in for years, if ever. For example, the company booked a $65 million profit in 1999 based on its projection of natural-gas sales from a South American pipeline project. The pipeline had yet to be built.

In a bold stroke, Enron moved its gas and electricity trading on-line. Going far beyond energy, Skilling's young MBAs created unheard-of commodities markets—even offering weather derivatives, contracts that gave businesses financial protection against the costs of heat waves or blizzards.

"We made the gas market in the United States what it is today," said Robert Hermann, Enron's former chief tax counsel. "We decided we could do the same thing with electricity, and we were well on our way to doing it. Then we thought we could do it with anything. We had people who thought they could sell hairballs if they could find the buyers."

Wall Street and the business press were dazzled. For six years running, *Fortune* magazine ranked Enron as the most innovative company in the nation. At an exclusive conference of intellectuals and political leaders at Davos, Switzerland, in 2000, Lay declared Enron the prototype of the "new economy" corporation. Lay described Enron executives as guerrillas fashioning bullets out of ideas.

"Somewhere out there is a bullet with your company's name on it, a competitor . . . that will render your strategy obsolete," Lay said. "You've got to shoot first."

As the nation's tech sector boomed in the late 1990s, Skilling said the transformed energy firm, with its on-line trading arm, deserved the sky-high stock price of a dot-com company. The market bought it. From 1998 to 2000, Enron's stock tripled in value.

"We're the world's coolest company," Skilling told the University of Virginia professors.

Lay even considered the idea of draping a giant pair of sunglasses around Enron's headquarters tower in Houston, Skilling joked.

"It was an intoxicating atmosphere," said Jeff S. Blumenthal, an Enron tax lawyer. "If you loved business and loved being challenged and working with unique, novel situations . . . it was the most wonderful place."

It wasn't just the ideas. The place was giddy with money. Enron paid employees $750 million in cash bonuses in 2000, an amount approaching the company's reported profit that year.

The princes of Enron were its dealmakers or "developers," in-house entrepreneurs who launched businesses and structured deals so they could immediately claim huge profits for the company—and bonuses for themselves—while saving the problems for later.

From the company's earliest days, those princes flew around the world, overpaying for power plants in India, Poland and Spain, a water plant in Britain, a pipeline in Brazil, and thousands of miles of Internet cable. Enron accumulated 50 energy plants in 15 countries. Virtually none of them were profitable.

Lou L. Pai, a Skilling favorite, set up an Enron division that sold electricity to businesses. Pai received numerous stock options as compensation. He sold $270 million worth of Enron stock in the 16 months before he left the company last year.

"The culture at Enron is all about 'me first, I want to get paid,'" Hermann said. "I used to tell people if they don't know why people are acting a certain way, go look up their compensation deal and then you'll know. There were always people wanting to do deals that didn't make sense in order to get a bonus."

Porsches replaced pickup trucks in the company parking lot as even secretaries became paper millionaires. There were mansions in Houston's posh River Oaks neighborhood, vacation homes in Aspen. Everybody went along for the company's wild ride.

In June 1999, when Kaminski opposed the Rhythms deal that Skilling and Fastow were promoting, his boss's wry response was telling.

"Next time Fastow is going to run a racket, I want to be part of it," Kaminski recalled his boss, Buy, saying.

To much of the world, Jeff Skilling looked like a genius. Between January and May 2000, the stock price had risen nearly 80 percent, to $77 a share. Enron insiders—Lay and Skilling among them—had cashed out more than $475 million worth of stock. Everybody was getting rich.

But Enron had created only an illusion of ever-expanding revenue and profits.

The company still needed increasing amounts of cash for its profligate new ventures and expanding energy-trading operations. Its grab bag of pipelines and plants could not produce enough money to drive the growth that Lay and Skilling demanded.

As Fastow explained in a *CFO Magazine* article, Enron could not keep borrowing in traditional ways without scaring lenders away and damaging its credit rating. Enron's investment-grade credit was just high enough to ensure that it could get the cash it needed to settle its energy contracts when they came due.

So Enron turned itself into a factory for financial deals that would pump up profit, protect its credit rating and drive up its stock price.

In the 1990s, banks and law firms began aggressively peddling "structured finance," complex deals in which companies set up separate affiliates or partnerships to help generate tax deductions or move assets and debts off the books. With Skilling's ascension to the presidency in 1997, Enron became increasingly dependent upon such deals to hit its financial targets.

"Skilling's participation in the LJMs and the other vehicles was probably the most important part of his job," said John Ballentine, a former president of an Enron pipeline subsidiary and a corporate vice president.

The company teamed up with the brightest minds in banking, accounting and law to create scores of secretive deals with exotic code names such as Braveheart, Backbone, Rawhide, Raptor and Yosemite.

Enron used the deals for various purposes. The LJM partnerships hedged risky stock investments such as Rhythms. An affiliate named Whitewing took billions of dollars of debt off the company's books. In some cases, Enron "sold" money-losing foreign assets to the partnerships, added the proceeds to its quarterly financial statement and then bought the assets back in the next reporting period.

To entice banks and others to invest in the deals, Enron privately pledged millions of shares of its stock to guarantee against any losses. It was a risky gambit, exposing the company to losses if the price of its shares dropped and it could not cover its obligations.

It worked well for the short term, when Enron needed a quick boost for its quarterly earnings. But as Enron's trading expanded, its other businesses underperformed. Its debt and cash needs kept growing, so the company needed to make more and bigger "structured transactions" to keep the game going—pledging increasing amounts of stock. Enron's strategy began to resemble what members of Congress would later call a high-tech Ponzi scheme.

In May 2000, Alberto Gude, an Enron vice president, went to see Lay just before Gude retired. He had known Lay since 1977 and wanted to warn him about the "selfishness" and "arrogance" of the team that had transformed the company. Lay said through his spokeswoman that he does not recall this specific conversation.

"I really believe you are in trouble," Gude recalled telling Lay. "Jeff Skilling and his team are not the same kind of people we are used to managing Enron."

According to Gude, Lay responded, "They are okay guys."

One of Skilling's "okay guys" was Andrew S. Fastow, then 38, Enron's chief financial officer since 1998. Skilling hired him from a Chicago bank where he specialized in numbingly complex deals to raise money for clients.

As the top finance man at Enron, Fastow was responsible for Enron's overall financial stability.

He was known as an intimidating and single-minded self-promoter. He liked to say that capitalism was about survival of the fittest. He flogged his team so furiously to close deals that they often made business calls in the middle of the night. Executives who attended meetings with Fastow recall him freely putting down older colleagues or anybody he perceived as weak.

As unpopular as he was, Fastow was untouchable. Skilling was positively enamored of him. "Fastow was Skilling's favorite," Enron lawyer Jordan Mintz said later.

But even Skilling later conceded to investigators that Fastow could be a "prickly guy that would tell you everything wrong about others and everything right about himself."

Fastow was also something of a mystery. He rarely attended the quarterly briefings Enron staged for financial analysts, making him the butt of a Wall Street wisecrack: "Name Enron's CFO."

He spent much of his time as managing partner of the LJM partnerships. Although he later said he spent only three hours a week on the partnerships, colleagues complained that he was constantly working on his own deals. He jetted to New York, California, Florida and the Caribbean, hunting investors.

For Enron, Fastow's effort was time well spent. LJM1 had been a huge success.

The Rhythms stock was worth nearly $60 a share when the second quarter of 1999 ended, giving Enron a paper profit of about $300 million. That windfall exceeded Enron's net income for the quarter. By the end of the year, Rhythms stock had dropped to about $30 a share—but thanks to the hedge with LJM1, Enron avoided reporting any losses on the decline.

It was easy to see the deal as an act of financial wizardry.

So Skilling supported Fastow's drive to create a much bigger private equity fund, LJM2, capitalized with more than $300 million from outside investors—more than 20 times the size of LJM1. This time, the board required Fastow's colleague, Chief Accounting Officer Richard A. Causey, to monitor what Fastow was doing.

But nobody reined in Fastow.

In raising money for LJM2, he was both ruthless and charming, colleagues said.

Fastow strong-armed Enron's major Wall Street banking partners, threatening to take away Enron's banking business if they did not put money into his fund, former Enron treasurer Jeffrey McMahon said later.

The banks put up a "huge outcry," but many ultimately invested, including J.P. Morgan Chase & Co., Citigroup Inc. and Merrill Lynch & Co.

"The banks complained they were being told that investing in LJM2 was a quid pro quo for future Enron business," McMahon later told investigators.

Fastow used the soft touch with people like Joe Marsh. A wealthy Floridian, Marsh had been approached in 2000 by his Merrill Lynch stock adviser about investing $1 million in LJM2. Fastow's partnership would do deals with Enron, promising gaudy annual returns of 20 percent or more.

At first, Marsh was skeptical. "It sure sounded like a conflict of interest," he said. So his broker arranged for Marsh to do a conference call with other investors and Fastow.

Fastow was knowledgeable, at ease and persuasive, Marsh said. "He said he was putting in $5 million of his own. His wife was mad at him for doing it, but he really believed in it," Marsh said. Enron's lawyers and accountants, the board, Merrill Lynch, everyone had approved it. "It got flying colors." Marsh was convinced. He put in $1.6 million.

Fastow had married into a wealthy Houston family. He wanted wealth of his own, colleagues said.

At Enron, Fastow made about $2.4 million in salary, bonus and incentives. But he had long chafed at the huge bonuses that division chiefs were getting from big power plant and pipeline deals. He wanted a similarly lucrative payday for himself. He got one from LJM1 in the spring of 2000, when Enron and the partnership ended the Rhythms transaction.

Three London bankers who have been accused in criminal fraud complaints of joining with Fastow to cheat their bank in the Rhythms deal had a pithy take on what motivated him. "We should be able to appeal to his greed," one of the bankers e-mailed another in February 2000.

Fastow's dealings with the British bankers were not revealed until much later. Fastow's secret profit from LJM1 and the Rhythms deal was staggering: a $1 million investment turned into a $22 million profit in less than a year.

For a while, LJM2 looked like a great deal for everyone.

From 2000 on, the LJM deals provided most of Enron's profits, though they remained invisible to outside investors.

At the end of each financial quarter, whenever Enron needed to sell a pipeline or Internet cable, or execute a helpful commodities trade, it would turn to Fastow for almost instant results.

Even inside Enron, the exact details were a closely held secret. People gossiped that Fastow was getting rich, but nobody asked how rich.

Enron's board, which twice waived the company's code of ethics to allow Fastow's dual roles, could have asked, but it did not until too late. Board members later said they were misled by Enron executives. The board set up an elaborate system for monitoring Fastow, with three committees assigned to the task. But board members put little energy into it, repeatedly failing to ask pointed questions, a Senate subcommittee later concluded. As Enron's chief financial officer, Fastow was supposed to be the company's financial watchdog, even in the LJM transactions. But Fastow personally profited if LJM bested Enron in negotiations. Some

Enron colleagues say Fastow bullied subordinates to win an advantage for LJM. He pressured one, William Brown, to close a deal on terms unfair to Enron, Brown later told investigators.

As more colleagues came to believe that Fastow was enriching himself and a few close to him, the deals became a source of envy and suspicion.

In early 2000, McMahon complained to Skilling about Fastow's conflict of interest, McMahon later told investigators. Soon afterward Fastow confronted McMahon.

Fastow told McMahon that he "should have known everything said to Skilling would get back to him," McMahon recalled.

A week later, Skilling encouraged McMahon to take a job in another part of the company. Skilling replaced him with Ben F. Glisan, one of Fastow's closest aides.

The message flashed throughout Enron: Don't mess with Fastow.

When Mintz, a lawyer who worked under Fastow, later complained to Buy about the conflict, Mintz said Buy warned him not to "stick his neck out."

Enron had publicly identified Fastow as LJM's general manager in its proxy statements in 2000 and 2001. But in its quarterly and annual financial statements filed with the Securities and Exchange Commission, Enron had not named him. It merely referred in footnotes to "a senior officer of Enron," a vague description that troubled some Enron executives and left some investors in the dark.

But the word was getting out.

By spring 2001, Fastow's identity—and his LJM role—attracted attention from a few Wall Street analysts, financial speculators and journalists.

In May, a column on TheStreet.com cited a very critical analysis of Enron's finances by a private research firm, Off Wall Street, that alerts subscribers to high-priced stocks that are primed to fall. The analysis concluded that Enron's stock was worth only half of its $59 price.

"It probably should come as no surprise that Enron management appears to have resorted to a variety of transactions that are of questionable quality and sustainability to manage and to boost its earnings," the analysis said.

In the center of the TheStreet.com's column was Fastow's name as the head of one of the questionable Enron partnerships that "consistently bugs analysts."

Others questioned why so many top Enron executives were leaving—after cashing in stock. In June, *U.S. News & World Report* quoted skeptics asking whether Enron's financial reports masked an underachieving company. After starting 2001 in the $80 range, the stock had drifted downward. By July it was below $50.

Once investors and journalists started asking about LJM, Skilling "got concerned," Mintz and one of Enron's outside lawyers, Ronald T. Astin, later told investigators.

Some Enron lawyers had been saying all year that they wanted Fastow out of LJM. They were worried that the company would have to provide more details about Fastow's partnership to comply with SEC disclosure rules.

Mintz had written an internal memo stating there was "no possible legal argument" for not disclosing how much Fastow had profited personally from the LJM partnerships in the company's next proxy statement.

Enron was expecting a routine SEC review in the coming months, making it more urgent to get Fastow out of LJM.

But he was reluctant to walk away from the partnership. He tried at first to reduce his role, but the Andersen accountants said that Enron would have to disclose the relationship anyway.

Skilling sat down with Fastow and gave him a choice, Skilling later told investigators. He could be Enron's chief financial officer or run LJM, but he could not keep doing both.

Fastow wanted to think about it.

Ultimately, Fastow had what Mintz later described as a "melodramatic moment" and resolved to sell his interest to one of his closest associates, Michael J. Kopper, who left the company in order to take over LJM. Mintz did not know the terms.

Several Enron lawyers met to discuss whether Enron should know. A lawyer for Enron's main outside firm, Vinson & Elkins LLP, advised that Enron didn't have any obligation to know. So Enron didn't ask.

That summer, accounting professor Bala G. Dharan pointed out some opaque financial transactions in Enron's published financial statements to a class at Rice University in Houston. He flashed the cryptic reference to the "senior officer" on the screen. He wondered aloud about the executive's identity.

After class, a student—an Enron employee—approached. "Everybody knows that, Professor Dharan. It's Andy Fastow."

On July 12, 2001, in one of those routine rites of business, Skilling fielded questions from Wall Street analysts about the company's second-quarter financial results. Skilling batted away the analysts' mild queries. Enron had "outstanding" results, he said, a 40 percent increase in profit.

Finally, Skilling was asked an obscure-sounding question by Carol Coale, a securities analyst with Prudential Securities Inc. in Houston and a growing skeptic.

What about Enron's transactions with your "MLT affiliate" she asked, groping for the correct name, LJM.

Skilling mentioned there were "a couple of real minor things" with LJM, before dismissing the question: "There are no new transactions in LJM."

"He's lying to me," Coale thought. She, too, had been piecing together the sketchy clues from Enron's financial statements. She suspected that Enron was using LJM to hide big losses.

But she did not press him. People who dealt with Skilling knew not to do that. And despite her misgivings, Coale did not feel that she had enough information to advise investors to sell their Enron stock. By the end of July 2001, Lay and Skilling were on the road again, telling analysts that Enron had never been stronger.

The response was nearly unanimous: "Buy, buy, buy."

The full story of LJM remained hidden.

UPDATE

In August, Michael Kopper, a former assistant to Enron CFO Andrew Fastow, pled guilty to charges of wire fraud and money laundering, admitting that he, Fastow, and others used off-balance-sheet partnerships to misappropriate millions of dollars. Kopper agreed to pay $12 million in restitution, and still faces the possibility of up to 15 years in jail. In early October, Fastow was charged with securities fraud, wire fraud, mail fraud, and conspiracy in connection with the secret partnerships he set up and ran at Enron. Fastow faces up to 140 years in prison if convicted on all counts. At the time this book went to press, he had not yet entered a plea in the case. The SEC, meanwhile, filed civil charges against Fastow, seeking to bar him from ever acting as an officer or director of a public company again, and to have him give up all his "ill-gotten gains." As for Enron the company, it remains in business, operating under bankruptcy protection. A recent government report on the California energy crisis of 2000–2001 found evidence that Enron deceived regulators and manipulated prices in order to boost profits, and recommended further investigation into "possible misconduct" charges. —J.S.

A TELECOM PROPHET'S FALL FROM GRACE

David Staples

Edmonton Journal, July 28, 2002

IN EARLY JULY, a few days after the world's biggest corporate fraud scandal broke, Bernie Ebbers stood up in his church and tried to clear his name.

"I just want you to know you aren't going to church with a crook," he told the congregation at Easthaven Baptist in Brookhaven, a town of 10,000. "I don't know what all is going to happen or what mistakes have been made. No one will find me to have knowingly committed fraud."

At that point, Ebbers teared up. "More than anything else," he said, "I hope that my witness for Jesus Christ will not be jeopardized."

With that, the Easthaven congregation erupted in a standing ovation.

Ebbers is used to such adulation. Here in sweltering Mississippi, here in the land of believers, where the Bible Belt is cinched up tight, Edmonton boy Ebbers found his home, his faith and his WorldCom fortune.

In the 1990s, Ebbers turned WorldCom into the second-largest telecommunications company in America and became a Mississippi hero and icon. The entire state stood up and gave him a decade-long standing ovation.

Ebbers succeeded because he's a man of a certain faith. It's a modern Mississippi faith, a strange mix of differing creeds. It's made up of family values, state pride, American patriotism, God, Jesus, markets, mergers and money.

These elements all blurred together in the Mississippi of the 1990s, even if the values often contradicted one other, which is why Bernie Ebbers is also a man of contradiction and contrast.

He started out with nothing, but owned $1.4 billion in WorldCom stock at the height of his wealth in 1999. He's a small-town guy who came to rub shoulders with presidents, nobles and the sharpest minds of the corporate world. He's a church-going Christian whose Savior was hugely suspicious of greed and wealth, yet Ebbers came to dominate the Wall Street world of aggression, cunning and the thirst for profit.

These days, with WorldCom filing for the largest bankruptcy in history, with pundits labeling the company as WorldCon, with $120 billion of equity in the company obliterated in less than three years and, most of all, with Ebbers in the middle of a $4 billion fraud case that could lead to the U.S. government indicting and jailing him, the people of Mississippi are wondering what went wrong.

Any number of things are being blamed, most prominently Wall Street traders and WorldCom accountants, but there are also questions about Ebbers himself. For the first time, he is under scrutiny here, with at least six investigations being undertaken by Mississippi and Washington lawyers, forensic accountants and politicians. Journalists are also probing his life, right back to his time in Edmonton, Alberta, though they are having little luck in this regard.

Not much is known of Ebbers' Edmonton years. His family, which still lives in the city, refuses to talk about him. This silence is typical. To this day, most people close to Ebbers are close-mouthed when asked about him. For instance, the secretary at Ebbers' old church, First Baptist in Brookhaven, said that not only did no one at the church want to be quoted, they didn't want to be quoted as not wanting to be quoted.

His former business partners, his ex-wife, his family, his townspeople, almost all refuse to say a word, either good nor bad, about Bernard J. Ebbers. "It's just depressing," says one longtime Brookhaven business associate, Max Thornhill, of the investigation into Ebbers. "It's been going on so long, and I just don't want to talk about it."

"People in Mississippi are very proud and very loyal," says writer Lynne Jeter of the *Mississippi Business Journal.* "Bernie had his fingers in a lot of things behind the scenes, and that's one reason people won't talk. For one reason or another, people owe Bernie."

Still, through interviews and previous books and articles, his rise and fall can be traced.

Ebbers was born in Edmonton on Aug. 27, 1941, went to Grade One in the city, then moved to California for four years, then to a Najavo reservation outside of Gallup, New Mexico. His father, John, who most often worked in sales, was the business manager for the Christian mission there. "We didn't have much," Ebbers told writers Thomas Neff and James Citrin in their book, *Lessons from the Top*. "If my dad had a few dollars left in his pocket at the end of the month, we would go out and eat hamburgers as a family."

On his best Christmas ever, Ebbers got a deck of "Animal Rummy" cards.

While the family had little money, it had a strong work ethic and Christian values, Ebbers told Neff and Citrin. "We've all been very aggressive and worked hard at what we've done. . . . But I think more than anything, my father and mother taught us that the only real values are the eternal values."

In Edmonton, Ebbers went to high school at Victoria Composite, where his yearbook pictures show him to be a tall (6 feet, 4 inches), skinny, geeky-looking kid. A teammate on the basketball team, Irwin Strifler of Edmonton, says Ebbers wasn't a great player, not even a starter. He wasn't a great student, either, not overtly ambitious, not the kind you'd expect to make millions. "He never came across as a brilliant guy," Strifler says. "He was pretty average."

FROM MILKMAN AND BOUNCER TO COLLEGE BASKETBALL PLAYER

A friend from the basketball team, Brent Foster, recalls Ebbers as an honest young man, very bright but no scholar. Together, they'd zip out to the lake, just to hang out, not to chase girls, as both guys were too damn shy.

After graduating from Vic Comp in 1959, Ebbers studied at the University of Alberta to be a phys. ed. teacher, but flunked out, then flunked out of Calvin College in Grand Rapids, Mich.

Back in Edmonton, Ebbers worked as a bread and milk delivery man and as a bouncer. One day, he met up with his old Vic Comp basketball coach, who told him he was wasting his life. A basketball scholarship to Mississippi College, a small Baptist school in Clinton, Miss., was arranged. Ebbers decided to go, mainly because "delivering milk in 30 degrees below zero isn't a real interesting thing to do with the rest of your life," he once said.

Mississippi College was a deeply traditional school in the 1960s: no drinking, no black students allowed, mandatory chapel three times a week.

The place resonated with Ebbers, who became engrossed in religion and basketball. He found a mentor in his college coach, James Allen. Ebbers would later sum up the Allen philosophy: "With hard work, dedication, a commitment to principles, and a commitment to Jesus Christ, life can be worthwhile."

"My life changed at Mississippi College," Ebbers told the *Jackson Clarion-Ledger*. "My Christianity became not so much a theoretical thing, as a practical thing, a real part of my life."

He arrived with little to his name. "When I first met him and roomed with him, he had two pairs of blue jeans, two short sleeve shirts, one long sleeve shirt, a jacket and a '58 lime green Chevrolet," says William Lewis, Ebbers' best friend at college.

Neither Ebbers nor Lewis was a very good basketball player, but Lewis recalls that Ebbers was strong-willed, determined to get better. In his junior year, the two slender young men dove into a weight-training program in order to bulk up. "When he took on a task he was focused on getting maximum mileage out of it," says Lewis, who is now president of Pearl River Community College in Poplarville, Miss.

On his way back to school for his senior season, having spent the summer in Edmonton, Ebbers' car ran out of gas in a rough neighborhood in Michigan. He got in a scuffle. A bottle struck his leg, severing the Achilles tendon. The freak injury put him in a cast and ended his college basketball days.

Nonetheless, he was welcomed back at school. Students who didn't know him prayed for his recovery every day in the chapel. Mississippians take pride in their hospitality, and the warmth of the Deep South enveloped young Ebbers. He and a devout young woman, Linda Piggott of Magnolia, Miss., started to date. A year after Ebbers graduated in 1967, the two married, with Lewis acting as best man.

Ebbers went to work coaching and teaching in a small town, before getting out of teaching to work at a garment factory in Brookhaven, about 100 km south of the state capital, Jackson. He quickly worked his way up to be warehouse manager, but in 1974, again decided it was time to move on to a new vocation in another small Mississippi town. "I just bought a little motel in Columbia," Ebbers told his friend Lewis. "I always wanted to have my own business and this is my opportunity."

The Ebberses moved from a nice home in Brookhaven to live in a trailer on the motel lot. For a few years, they struggled, but things did pick up, partly because Ebbers was well-liked.

People saw him as a true Southerner, friendly, respectful, humble, the kind of fellow who will invite you to church and to a picnic afterwards. "He was more friendly than a normal recluse type of Yankee," says a Brookhaven businessman. "He was right friendly."

Ebbers convinced two friends, Max Thornhill and Carl Aycock, who would later sit on the WorldCom board, to help him out, borrowing against the equity in their homes to buy other small hotels in Mississippi. The two men trusted Ebbers as a fellow Christian, reports right-wing commentator George Gilder in his book, *Telecosm: How Infinite Bandwidth Will Revolutionize Our World.*

By the early 1980s, Ebbers had built the chain into nine hotels, a nice little business, but no *Fortune* 500 contender. Developments in the phone industry, though, would provide Ebbers with opportunity.

In the early 1980s, the U.S. government went to work breaking up the AT&T telephone monopoly. AT&T was forced to rent out long-distance phone lines at a 40–70 percent discount to small, regional companies, who would then resell the lines' data-carrying capacity, known as the bandwidth, to small businesses. In September 1983, Ebbers and several other businessmen started up a reselling company, Long Distance Discount Service.

Ebbers remortgaged his hotels to buy into LDDS. He knew nothing about engineering and little about accounting, but had a head for cost-cutting and deal-making. He quickly realized he could make more money by keeping a small staff while increasing sales, buying up more and more bandwidth and selling it at a greater discount than his competitors. He embarked on a path that would see him buy 75 companies in the next 15 years, first purchasing other long-distance resellers.

In 1989, LDDS became a public company, the shares selling for 84 cents. Ebbers now had another tool, Gilder writes: the ability to use LDDS stock to buy out other companies.

He found that shareholders in other companies were keen to get his stock, mainly because LDDS was doing so well. While other companies in the same industry grew at 5 percent a year, Ebbers could boast LDDS had never made less than 16 percent.

To encourage employees, Ebbers made sure they all had stock options. Around the office, signs were posted every day showing the employees how much their options were now worth.

His operation was sleek. He was a guy who came from nothing, no silver spoon, no Ivy League, no summers at the cottage, no winters at Aspen. He wasn't one to be lavish with employees. He'd buy a company, then tell his new execs they'd have to fly economy, to take cabs, not limousines, and go two-to-a-room in budget hotels.

"In this business we tend to talk a lot about technology and strategy. All that makes me sick," he told Internetweek.com. "The only statistic that matters—because everything else is derived from this one statistic—is how much new revenue your sales rep sells every month."

In the early 1990s, Ebbers realized there was only a limited amount of money to be made in reselling long-distance phone service. It's a low-end business, says telecom expert John C. Wohlstetter, a senior fellow at the Seattle-based Discovery Institute. It occurred to Ebbers that it would be best to own the actual lines, especially new fiber-optic lines, which had a tremendous capacity to move data. With fiber optics, LDDS wouldn't have to pay premium rates for another company's lines, and he could serve bigger businesses, where the real money was. "Ebbers decided he wanted to move up to the next level," Wohlstetter says. "He had bigger fish to fry."

This was Ebbers' one great idea, the one that made him a billionaire. His competitors were burdened with large staffs, old copper telephone wires and customers who didn't spend much—elderly clients who rarely used their long distance. He'd take on the telecom bigwigs through the Internet, Ebbers decided, moving data, voice and video on fiber-optic lines. The Internet, Ebbers proclaimed, was "a gorilla which is going to take over the entire industry."

LDDS started to gobble up companies that owned fiber-optic lines, its most dramatic move coming in August 1994, when for the first time it swallowed up a larger company, Wiltel, out of Tulsa, Okla., for $2.5 billion in stock. Wiltel owned the fourth-largest fiber network in the U.S.

Ebbers renamed the merged company, calling it WorldCom. Profit margins rose from 18 percent to the low 20s.

In the summer of 1995, two things happened that propelled World-Com forward, Wohlstetter says: the high-profile arrivals of Windows 95 and the Netscape browser. Suddenly, everyone wanted a piece of the Net.

By 1997, WorldCom owned 20 percent of the Internet backbone in the U.S. At the same time, the Internet was growing at 1,000 percent each year, leading to giddy optimism, which was captured in a 1997 speech by John Sidgmore, WorldCom's Internet boss. "No one has ever seen this kind of growth. In fact, my network engineers tell me, 'John, if you're not scared, you don't understand.' This is mind-boggling, explosive growth."

The market fell in love with WorldCom. The company's share price doubled each year. "A smart addition to any portfolio," said *Time* magazine.

Basketball star Michael Jordan was signed on as a company spokesman. In *BusinessWeek*, Oscar Castro, a longtime stockpicker based in San Francisco, said, "Talk to a lot of people and you'll find them crazy, fanatical about Bernie Ebbers. I'm no different."

The think tanks loved Ebbers as well. "He has shown the magic of entrepreneurial vision and temerity," wrote George Gilder of the Discovery Institute. "Ebbers' fiber and Internet empire stands ready to release many more trillions of dollars in wealth and Internet commerce and communications, and threaten monopolies around the globe."

On June 21, 1999, WorldCom stock reached its all-time high of $64.50 per share. *Forbes* magazine listed Ebbers as the 376th richest man in the world, with a fortune of $1.4 billion. He was on a first-name basis with President Bill Clinton, who gave a speech at WorldCom offices, telling Ebbers and his workers, "I came here today because you are the symbol of 21st-century America. You are the embodiment of what I want for the future."

While Wall Street saw WorldCom as a great investment vehicle, in Mississippi the company was seen as salvation.

Mississippi has long been one of the very poorest states in the union. Through the 1980s, Mississippi's biggest businesses were still cotton, soybeans and poultry.

At first, Mississippians doubted that this basketball coach from Brookhaven would succeed at telecommunications, but as LDDS, then WorldCom, ate up one big company after another, as WorldCom became the first *Fortune* 500 company in Mississippi, people in the state started to regard Ebbers as if he were a healer raising dead men from the grave. There was talk of widening roads, building bridges, increasing the size of the airport. Folks wanted him to run for governor.

"Parents hoped their kids would grow up to be like Bernie Ebbers," Jackson lawyer Lance Stevens says, "a likable, unpretentious fellow with a national reputation and a commitment to the community."

Down so long, Mississippians basked in WorldCom's achievements. "It shows everyone that we're not just nickel and dime stuff down here. We're real wheelers and dealers," said Frank Latham, the owner of Frank's Diner in Jackson, in 1997.

Mississippians are among the most Bible-reading, praying, preaching and giving of all Americans. The Bible had proved to be a lasting consolation during times of poverty. In the good times of the 1990s, the simple faith of many folk was extended to WorldCom.

It was not unheard of for Mississippians to put 80–100 percent of their retirement savings into one single stock, WorldCom, says Stevens. "I would laugh if it wasn't so sad."

Jean Sain, 72, a Jackson realtor, started to buy the stock after hearing about it from Bernie Ebbers' barber. In the end, 85 percent of her stock portfolio was in WorldCom. Its value rose to $450,000.

Three stockbrokers told her she had too much invested in one company, but she refused to listen. Instead she followed the advice of WorldCom boosters, such as Jack Grubman, of the Wall Street firm Salomon Smith Barney.

"I remember Grubman saying that it was going to go to $130. You don't forget that," Sain says. "We were all so sure we were going to make a fortune."

In Jackson's yuppie suburb, Clinton, where 17,000 people worked at WorldCom's headquarters, people had such faith in the company, they were hesitant to ever sell their stock. "Nobody ever touched them," says Jackson lawyer Dan Keefe. "They all just felt, 'I got a brother that works there, or a sister, a cousin.' So they didn't sell. And right to the end, Salomon Smith Barney was recommending they hold on to it."

IN MISSISSIPPI, DAMN YANKEES CAST IN A FAMILIAR ROLE

As in any Mississippi story of woe, Mississippians see evil Yankees lurking, these ones coming in the form of Salomon Smith Barney, which not only sold stock to investors, but handled the corporate mergers of WorldCom, mergers that were greatly facilitated by inflated stock prices. This amounted to a conflict of interest, alleges Lance Stevens, whose law firm voiced its complaints against Salomon Smith Barney in the Mississippi legislature and is planning to sue the company.

The need for a high-price stock led Salomon Smith Barney agents in Atlanta to push investors to hold far too much stock in one company, the law firm alleges. Instead of buying a house by cashing in stock, one of Stevens' clients was told to take out a loan against his stock portfolio, and buy his house that way.

Of course, the investors didn't have to listen to such advice. But many of them did.

When Mississippians bought the stock, they weren't just hoping to make a lot of money (although that was in the equation)—they were showing their support for the state and placing their faith in WorldCom bosses, such as Ebbers, who were thought to be good Christian men. In Mississippi, the Christian connection worked wonders for WorldCom's sales.

"In this part of the country, people would rather do business with a Christian person than somebody else. It's just a matter of trust," says Ronny "Worm" Smith, 55, a Brookhaven businessman.

Ebbers was regarded as the ultimate Christian businessman. At board and stockholder meetings, he started things off with a prayer. "The prayer always made a big impression on me," stockholder William T. Weathersby has said. "I thought with a person like that as CEO there would never be any wrongdoing taking place at WorldCom—everything would be run right.

"He seemed to be like the Rock of Gibraltar—solid and reliable."

Ebbers was a church deacon and a Bible study instructor, the best one Ronny "Worm" Smith says he's ever had. Smith, who drives a Harley and sells cars, partied like a madman in his youth before finding Jesus and becoming a student in Ebbers' weekly Sunday school class. He says Ebbers didn't just read scripture, he could talk about what it really meant. If anyone ever missed church, Ebbers was sure to be on the phone, seeing if they were OK. The local paper quoted Ebbers as saying that his Bible study class was his favorite 90 minutes of the week.

In Brookhaven, Ebbers not only mowed his own lawn, he'd sometimes cut his neighbors' as well. He was seen as easygoing, and often wore cowboy boots, jeans and a golf shirt to work. He didn't carry a cell phone or a beeper. He didn't have a computer in his office. His personal symbol was a well-chewed cigar. He showed up at one fancy New York meeting with no tie and an orange blazer. *BusinessWeek* dubbed him the "Telecom Cowboy." He was known for his charity work, supporting numerous groups with his time and money. He helped raise $1 million for the Easthaven Church, along with tens of millions for the building fund of his old school, Mississippi College.

He was sensitive to his leadership role. When a local TV personality criticized WWF wrestling telecasts, calling them "cultural sewage," Ebbers dropped WorldCom's advertising on the program.

In speeches, he attacked legalized gambling, talking about the suicides, bankruptcies and broken homes it caused.

When the Rev. Jesse Jackson visited Jackson, he complained that WorldCom never helped blacks, but was corrected by a local black businessman, LeRoy Walker Jr., who said that Ebbers had given greatly to a local black school, Tougaloo College.

Walker, who owns 16 McDonald's in the Jackson area, says Ebbers took time to mentor him, telling him how best to run his shop and how to borrow against his business in order to expand. Ebbers loved to help out, Walker Jr. says.

"His attitude was that if there is a need—and God has blessed me to get to the level I have—to whom much is given, much is expected. I think he cherished giving."

In interviews, Ebbers said he often sought the Lord's leadership in WorldCom affairs. "I look at my stewardship of this company as an opportunity that the Lord has given me," he told writers Neff and Citrin. "And that the fundamental principle in my life is to serve Him and to serve people through the opportunities He has given me."

The most happiness he ever got, Ebbers said, was from making others prosper.

"To be honest with you, this is the most satisfying part of my job. I could show you letter after letter from employees who write, 'If it had not been for the options, I never would have been able to send my child to college.' Or, 'I've never had the opportunity to own a home before, and now I can make a substantial down payment, thanks to what my options are worth.'"

Brookhaven is a community of believers, but it's not unusual for people to talk the Christian talk, but not walk the walk. It's a dry county, the majority Baptist population voting out liquor sales in a recent plebiscite, but that doesn't mean people don't drink, including the Baptists. A local joke pokes fun at religious hypocrisy: "If you go fishing with one Baptist, he'll drink all your beer. If you go fishing with two Baptists, you'll have all the beer to yourself."

In Brookhaven, Ebbers came across as a humble, unpretentious man of God, but on Wall Street he was seen as a butt-kicker. "When he was on his game, Ebbers had that special something that comes from the master blend of confidence, hubris, arrogance and testosterone," wrote business writer Dennis Mendyk in *Fortune*.

"He was just so pompous and arrogant," says Mississippi journalist Lynne Jeter. "It was just his way."

"Don't fall for that 'Aw shucks' stuff," his WorldCom associate John Sidgmore once said of him. "Ebbers is extremely street-smart. Most of all, he has a vision for the company. He is extremely aggressive and simply wants to build the biggest company in the industry."

Ebbers had an ostentatious side. He bought a huge yacht and called her *Aquasition*. He also paid $47 million to buy the Douglas Lake Ranch in B.C., the largest working ranch in Canada, which covers half a million acres, has 20,000 head of cattle, a luxury fishing village and a heavy equipment dealership.

In 1997, Ebbers and Linda, his wife of almost 30 years, divorced, citing irreconcilable differences. Ebbers married Kristie, a slender, 30-something blonde who worked for him at WorldCom. Ebbers could no longer be a deacon at his church, First Baptist. "When he got divorced, it made him stand back a bit because Baptists don't like divorce," says Ronny "Worm" Smith.

Ebbers once talked to Smith of the breakup. "Bernie just said they weren't sharing anything in common anymore.

"We all falter," Smith adds. "But we try not to do it."

As much as anything, the fall of Ebbers is related to two things: his $37 billion deal to buy the long-distance giant MCI in 1997, and his loose management style.

The MCI deal was WorldCom's boldest yet, the company swallowing a firm three times its size. As part of the takeover, WorldCom talked about cutting loose part of MCI's residential telephone business, which was becoming increasingly less profitable.

Federal regulators strongly objected to this plan. They also worried that WorldCom was trying to limit fiber-optic competition by buying up MCI's Internet division, which would have given Ebbers control of 60 percent of America's fiber-optic backbone. In the end, to please the regulators, WorldCom bought MCI's residential and long-distance service, but sold off the Internet network.

This was a fatal error, says the Discovery Institute's John C. Wohlstetter. Long distance had been profitable during the early '90s, when Sprint, MCI and AT&T controlled the market, Wohlstetter says. But with fiber-optic lines going in, prices had shot down, making a call across the country as cheap as a call across the street.

In the end, Ebbers betrayed his own vision, taking on a crushing debt to buy up the least profitable, most traditional part of MCI, while cutting loose the choice bit, the Internet, Wohlstetter says. Ebbers should have backed away from such a deal. "He threw 14 years of strategy out the window when he did it."

Ebbers gave credit for the MCI deal to his Chief Financial Officer, Scott Sullivan. Wall Street referred to WorldCom as the Scott and Bernie Show. "Scott knows his numbers like no one else," Ebbers told *The Wall Street Journal* in 1998. "I don't think WorldCom would be where it is today without him."

Ebbers wasn't a hands-on manager. He compared himself to a basketball coach who let his players take the shots and make the passes. "The way I see it, my function is not to be the most knowledgeable in any specific area," he told writers Neff and Citrin. "My challenge is to make sure that I have blue-chip players in each area—and we are fortunate that we have a lot of Michael Jordans—and then try to get them to play on the same team."

Ebbers wasn't an accountant or an engineer and didn't pretend to have expertise in those areas. He let Sullivan, his Michael Jordan of the ledger sheet, handle the WorldCom books, the same books that are now wrapped up in the fraud case.

After the MCI merger, Ebbers continued on with his deal-making, trying to merge with Sprint in a $129 billion deal in October 1999. This time, however, U.S. and European regulators blocked the move. At the same time, growth in the Internet dropped from 1,000 percent a year to 100 percent. WorldCom's profits leveled off and its stock shot down.

The drop in stock price was particularly hard on Ebbers. He'd had a million-dollar salary and multimillions of dollars in stock options, but he'd also borrowed hundreds of millions to buy high-priced WorldCom stock. His loans were called. On Oct. 5, 2000, he had to sell off three million shares to raise $84 million to pay off investment debts.

By January 2002, WorldCom stock had dropped to $9.80, from an all-time high of $64.50. Again, Ebbers went to sell shares. This time, the WorldCom board grew anxious. If Ebbers kept selling, the already fragile market for WorldCom would be flooded. To stave this off, the board lent Ebbers more than $400 million, giving him a 2.2 percent interest rate.

When word of this deal got out, many investors and analysts were outraged, wondering why Ebbers hadn't gone to the bank if he needed cash. Ebbers was forced to resign. He left the company on April 29, taking $1.5 million a year as a pension for life. He told reporters he had no plans to sell his remaining 27 million shares, that despite the company's falling stock and $40 billion debt, it was still a good buy, since World-Com still held important contracts and things would pick up when the economy did.

"People ask me how I am doing," he told the *Jackson Clarion-Ledger* after his resignation. "You know what, I am a child of the King, and the King is still King Jesus and I am absolutely content and happy.

"The good part about it is the good Lord has blessed me with assets that will more than pay back those loans. And now I certainly will have time to pursue liquidating those assets and the company will be paid back every dollar, plus interest, that is owed to them.

"This has been a phenomenal Mississippi story, not just a Bernie Ebbers story," he continued. "Just think, I am a guy from the other side of the tracks, who had trouble getting a college degree, who worked in very common businesses, and I had the opportunity to lead a company like this. Only by the grace of God. And I am very, very thankful for that."

And here the story of Bernie Ebbers might well have ended. This spring, however, a dogged internal auditor at WorldCom, Cynthia Cooper, started to poke around in WorldCom's books and found an odd thing.

Part of WorldCom's business was to lease fiber-optic lines, then sell the bandwidth to customers. In the late 1990s, WorldCom had leased a vast amount of this bandwidth, believing the Internet's rapid expansion was going to continue. When that failed to happen, WorldCom was stuck with billions of dollars of bandwidth it couldn't sell.

WorldCom had always listed the money used to lease bandwidth as a business expense. In 2001, however, much of this unused bandwidth, which was worthless, was suddenly deemed by WorldCom accountants to be an asset. More than $3.8 billion that had been spent to lease the lines was shifted over from the expense column in the financial statement to the asset column on the balance sheet.

WorldCom was able to state a profit, rather than a loss, which placated stockholders somewhat. But no explanation or rationalization of this shift was included in the company's annual report.

In a memo posted later on WorldCom's Web site, Sullivan provided a convoluted explanation for his actions, which most accounting experts dismissed as rubbish. *The Wall Street Journal* has reported that Sullivan will be indicted on fraud charges this coming week. What's not certain is whether Ebbers knew what was going on in WorldCom's books.

There's no doubt that he's a target. Both Republicans and Democrats, and other federal officials, seem eager to put some corporate executive or another in jail.

"There's a very tough cop on the beat here," said Harvey Pitt, chairman of the Securities and Exchange Commission, after the WorldCom fiasco came out. "I'm outraged. I think the American public is outraged. And in my view, criminal charges may be too good for the people who brought about this mess."

In early July, Ebbers was hauled before a U.S. congressional committee that was investigating corporate misdeeds. He refused to answer any questions, enraging politicians, both right and left.

"If you violate the public trust, if you flushed down the toilet the life savings of individuals, you should go and you will go to federal prison," Mike Ferguson, a New Jersey Republican, told him.

UPDATE

In late September, WorldCom controller David Myers pled guilty to one count each of conspiracy to commit securities fraud, securities fraud, and making false filings with the SEC. As part of his plea, he admitted that, at the direction of senior management, he had falsified WorldCom's financial statements beginning in October of 2000. A couple of weeks after Myers' plea, Buford Yates, WorldCom's former director of general accounting, pled guilty to one count of conspiracy to commit securities fraud and one count of securities fraud. Two lower-level accounting executives, Betty Vinson and Troy Normand, also pled guilty to conspiracy and securities fraud charges in October. WorldCom's former CFO, Scott Sullivan, who was the architect of the scheme to label operating expenses as capital expenditures, was indicted in August on charges of securities fraud and making false filings with the SEC. He has pled not guilty.

As for Bernie Ebbers, the House Financial Services Committee released documents that showed that he had been the beneficiary of special treatment by Salomon Smith Barney, which had given him the chance to purchase shares in a number of lucrative IPOs in the late 1990s. In late September, New York Attorney General Eliot Spitzer filed a civil suit against Ebbers, claiming that he had reaped millions in unjustified profits by selling cheap IPO shares that the investment bank Salomon Smith Barney had given him in order to win WorldCom's investment-banking business. Spitzer is seeking the disgorgement of the millions in IPO profits, as well as additional millions that Ebbers made by selling WorldCom shares, which Spitzer claims were artificially inflated by Salomon Smith Barney's pumping of WorldCom's stock. WorldCom itself, meanwhile, is trying to rescind Ebbers' severance package, which included $408 million in low-interest loans and a pension equal to $1.5 million a year for the rest of his life. Since WorldCom is in bankruptcy, it has an easier time getting out of unfavorable contracts, and it plans to argue that since its deal with Ebbers was made before the company's fraudulent accounting had been revealed, the contract should be declared null and void. The company is looking for a new CEO to replace interim head John Sidgmore. —J.S.

END OF ITS MERGER RUN
LED TO WORLDCOM'S FALL

Peter S. Goodman and Renae Merle

The Washington Post, June 30, 2002

OTHER PEOPLE COULD RUN companies. Bernard J. Ebbers liked to buy them—more than 60 by the time he was done. MCI, the Washington-based long-distance telephone company, already had a nice offer from British Telecommunications PLC when Ebbers and his company, WorldCom Inc., showed up out of nowhere in 1997 with a better one—$37 billion. MCI was worth three times more than WorldCom, but Ebbers made the purchase with stock. "No money is needed," he boasted, joking that maybe he would buy British Telecom next. "Not one red cent."

The MCI deal was the culmination of a relentless growth-through-acquisition strategy that finally hit a wall two years ago, when the government blocked Ebbers's boldest acquisition ever, WorldCom's $129 billion purchase of Sprint Corp. It forced him to do something he had never done before: make money by running what he already owned rather than buying something new.

It proved beyond him. And that is how WorldCom, a global company sprung from the unlikely soil of small-town Mississippi, apparently came face-to-face with an unpalatable choice: it could admit to Wall Street that it was losing money, staggering under the debts that came with its many purchases and its miscalculations about long-distance telephone service and the Internet. Or it could cook the books and keep showing profit.

The company's decision came into focus last week when WorldCom disclosed that it had misaccounted for $3.9 billion in costs on its balance sheet, turning what should have been a loss into profit. And as the Securities and Exchange Commission sued it, the Justice Department started to investigate it, and President Bush weighed in with a condemnation of its "outrageous" accounting methods, WorldCom completed its disintegration from an icon of the 1990s technology boom to purveyor of what may be the largest case of corporate fraud in U.S. history.

Enron Corp.'s demise had already proven that even a huge and admired company is not necessarily trustworthy. But WorldCom's unraveling was an even more significant indictment of corporate behavior. Only two years ago, its stock was among the most widely owned in the United States, held by more than 1,000 mutual funds. As it scrambles to survive as a going concern amid the seeming inevitability of bankruptcy and, perhaps, criminal prosecutions, its fate underscores how many of the fundamental notions that drove the technology boom now seem like fiction.

Ebbers's string of mergers was sold to Wall Street as a global construction project. He was not merely building a long-distance telephone business. He was laying the plumbing for the Internet, a force portrayed as so cosmically huge that one could never build enough pipes to accommodate it.

He was, of course, not alone in that endeavor. Cisco Systems Inc., Nortel Networks, Oracle Corp. and many others sold similar stories to an enthusiastic public that came to see Nasdaq as an acronym for wealth.

Stock analysts, in some cases working for the same Wall Street banks that were lending WorldCom money and brokering its deals, urged the public to get in on the action. WorldCom's stock soared higher, giving Ebbers even more currency to acquire the next pieces in his unceasing drive for global dominance. It was an upward spiral, one that investors rode skyward for a decade. Ebbers, whose cowboy boots and brash demeanor underlined his cherished maverick image, became a Wall Street folk hero.

But the story was built on a fallacy. The Internet was huge, but like everything else it had its limits. In the euphoria of investment that accompanied the spread of the World Wide Web, WorldCom and dozens of other companies buried more fiber-optic cable than their customers needed.

"There was only so much growth that could be gained in the communications industry," said John Sidgmore, who took over as World-Com chief executive after the board drove out Ebbers in April. "The rise of the dot-coms was misinterpreted to mean there would always be a never-ending series of growth curves. That turns out to be [expletive]. . . . There was this obvious overcapacity problem."

But some see WorldCom's spectacular rise and fall as a sign of something far worse than a grand miscalculation. They take the accounting scandal as an indication that bookkeeping gimmickry and the peddling of investment fantasies had more to do with the wave of wealth creation of the 1990s than any "New Economy" rules or innovation.

Scott Cleland, an analyst with the Precursor Group, a Washington-based research firm, has long been skeptical of WorldCom and its fast-growing, high-flying ilk. Mergers give such companies particularly useful opportunities to manipulate their earnings, he said, because they can pass off as one-time, deal-related expenses all sorts of real business costs.

Ebbers kept looking for the next deal, Cleland said, because it kept his balance sheet complicated enough to mask his real costs. "I believe they've been cooking their books for years," he said.

Born and raised in Edmonton, Alberta, Ebbers had hauled milk through frozen streets. He had been a barroom bouncer. He won a basketball scholarship at Mississippi College, a small Baptist school in Clinton, a town of 24,000 people about 10 miles from Jackson.

After graduating in 1967, he stayed in the area and landed in the motel business, amassing a chain of nine properties through the 1970s. One of his purchases brought with it a small sideline business, a discount long-distance telephone service. It bought telephone service wholesale from AT&T, then resold it retail.

Ebbers and three business partners sat in the coffee shop of a Day's Inn in Hattiesburg, Miss., in 1983 to talk about expanding that business. On the back of a napkin, they sketched out plans for what became Long Distance Discount Services (LDDS). They would take the model to the rest of southern Mississippi.

It was said at the time that Ebbers knew nothing more about his new business than how to make a telephone call. He portrayed that as a strength that would inoculate him against the foolishness that can accompany technological rapture. "The thing that has helped me personally is that I don't understand a lot of what goes on in this industry," he once told *Time* magazine.

He knew one thing, though: scale was his guiding light. His new company made no profit in its first year and he wanted to get bigger. Size meant spreading costs out over more customers by cutting overlapping departments. It meant more marketing power to take on Ma Bell. He went on a buying spree, mostly using stock as his purchasing currency. Each deal brought more customers and revenue.

"He wanted to be the biggest and just do whatever it took to get there," said Murray Waldron, one of Ebbers's original partners in LDDS. "Bernie was going to be the king of the mountain."

LDDS became a publicly traded business in 1989 when it merged with one, Advantage Companies Inc. By 1995, Ebbers had gobbled up more than 35 companies, mostly small, underfunded competitors of AT&T. Early that year, he added Williams Telecommunications Group LLC, securing its 11,000-mile fiber-optic network. He was no longer simply connecting voice telephone calls. Now he was moving "data," the electronic bits of commercial transactions and the Internet. The company changed its name to WorldCom.

WorldCom's $14 billion purchase of MFS Communications Co. in 1996 raised its profile considerably. The company brought a new fiber-optic network and was in the process of acquiring still another, UUNet, Sidgmore's company. But it was the MCI Communications Corp. deal the following year that really catapulted WorldCom and made Ebbers a legend.

Despite the global scale of the enterprise, Ebbers kept the company headquartered in Clinton, the only *Fortune* 500 company in the state. He mowed his own lawn and attended basketball games at his alma mater. He taught Sunday school at Easthaven Baptist Church and dropped in at a nearby restaurant known for its home-style cooking.

"He don't come on to me like a snob," said the owner of the place, Sam Hudgins. "He has been quite wealthy; he could fly to New York to dine. But after church he's at Hudgey's Family Restaurant."

The MCI deal swelled WorldCom's annual revenue to $32 billion from $5.6 billion and was enthusiastically applauded at the time. "This company remains the must-own large-cap growth stock for anyone's portfolio," wrote Jack Grubman, a telecom analyst for Salomon Smith Barney Inc., which helped broker the purchase and, over the span of its merger run, earned more than $100 million in fees from WorldCom. Grubman would remain WorldCom's most ardent cheerleader right until the fraud charge, a role that last week brought him a subpoena from Congress.

"It's all over," wrote George Gilder, whose *Gilder Technology Report* was an emblem of the boom. "Welcome to the reign of King Bernie."

But as the kingdom has crumbled, the MCI merger has come to be seen by many as a critical misstep. New entrants were coming into the market and dropping prices lower. The Baby Bell companies, the local telephone monopolies carved from the breakup of AT&T, won the right to enter the long-distance business, posing an enormous threat.

As AT&T's long-distance revenue plummeted, it spun off its residential business as a separate stock. Last summer, WorldCom followed suit, making the old MCI long-distance business a tracking stock. Analysts took it as an acknowledgment that the MCI merger had failed.

Even in the high-growth realm of the Internet, there was trouble. So many networks were being built that there were whispers of a "bandwidth glut": too many cables and not enough electronic bits for them to carry. It would push the price of service below what was needed to recover costs.

Sidgmore, now charged with saving WorldCom, dismissed such talk. At a 1999 conference in Washington, he chided a questioner who asked him if he feared such a glut. He put a PowerPoint slide on the wall showing explosive demand for Internet transmission. Was the questioner saying the Internet wasn't a huge deal?

"That was three years ago," Sidgmore said last week. "I bought into the same elixir that everyone else did. There is no way that anyone predicted all this. You look at [Intel founder] Andy Grove's speeches, [Cisco Systems chief executive] John Chambers's speeches and they're all [expletive]. Same as mine."

The glut was indeed real and its consequences would only get worse. Large companies with huge capacities stumbled and failed—PSINet

Inc., Global Crossing Holdings LLC, XO Communications. Each bankruptcy raised the prospect of some new company taking over networks free of debt, dropping the cost of service even lower and making it harder for those left in the game to survive.

Faced with that nasty reality, some Internet companies engaged in creative—and potentially illegal—means of manufacturing revenue. They swapped transmission capacity with one another in cashless transactions, but logged the increased use of their networks as revenue. Federal authorities are now investigating that practice.

WorldCom said it did not use those "bandwidth swaps" to create the illusion of revenue, but it did engage in another bogus practice: It counted the costs of maintaining its networks and the payments it makes to local telephone companies that complete its calls as "capital expenses," meaning one-time investments in the future. That inflated its earnings for 2001 and the first quarter of this year, turning what the SEC now says were really $1.2 billion in losses into $1.6 billion in profits.

How that happened and who was responsible are at the center of the WorldCom scandal. The company last week fired its chief financial officer, Scott Sullivan, blaming him for the practice. Sidgmore said he knew nothing about it until internal auditors spotted it last week. "This accounting scandal shocked the hell out of the management team," he said.

Did Ebbers know what Sullivan was doing? He has yet to speak publicly. Sidgmore said he doesn't know, but he did say that Ebbers, famously disengaged from operations, became more and more removed as WorldCom's fortunes diminished.

"I thought for many years that Bernie was the best CEO in the industry," Sidgmore said. "In the last few years, Bernie just flat out didn't pay attention."

Ebbers was focused on fixing WorldCom's predicament using the same strategy as ever: doing the next deal. In the spring of 1999, Sidgmore negotiated an agreement to buy Nextel Communications Inc., the Reston-based mobile-phone company. As he tells it, he shook hands with Nextel chief executive Duane Akerson and the deep pockets behind the company, Craig O. McCaw. But by the next morning, Ebbers had changed his mind. Sullivan had talked Ebbers out of buying Nextel, arguing that it would add too much debt.

The episode left a deep rift between Ebbers and Sidgmore, who thereafter played little role in running the company, though he continued to sit on its board.

The most aggressive move was still to come. In October 1999, World-Com stunned Wall Street with its bold plan to buy Sprint. It was, at the time, the largest corporate purchase of all time. The trouble was, it was a virtually impossible deal.

After the MCI merger, Ebbers had been told by both the Federal Communications Commission and the Justice Department not to bring them another huge telecom deal or they would challenge it, according to sources with knowledge of the discussions. The Sprint deal would combine the nation's second- and third-largest long-distance companies. "How can this be good for consumers?" FCC Chairman William E. Kennard said on the morning it was announced.

But WorldCom's lawyers said the deal could be done. Grubman and the other analysts in New York told Ebbers to ignore the nonsense coming out of Washington; the deal was doable and it made great strategic sense.

According to that argument, long distance essentially no longer existed as a distinct market. WorldCom and Sprint were merely two medium-size players in a crowded field of all-service communications companies. The real threat to competition was the local Bell companies that still had a near-monopolistic grip on their local markets. If World-Com and Sprint combined, they could make inroads into those markets and expand consumer choice.

But WorldCom and its boosters failed to appreciate the bad taste left in Washington and at European Union headquarters in Brussels from the MCI deal. To win approval for that merger, WorldCom had been forced to sell MCI's Internet network to assuage concerns that too much of the global computer network would fall into one set of hands. Now, the buyer in that spin-off, Cable & Wireless, was crying foul, arguing that WorldCom had sabotaged the sale.

To have any chance of winning approval for the Sprint deal, World-Com would have to persuade the regulators to accept a similar spin-off, because Sprint also had a huge Internet network. But both the Justice Department and European Union antitrust authorities were wary of giving WorldCom another try, particularly after WorldCom agreed to give Cable & Wireless $200 million for its past claims. The agreement seemed a tacit admission of wrongdoing.

Justice sued to block the deal in July 2000, and that was pretty much the end of WorldCom's blaze of growth.

"Bernie Ebbers's company was a momentum stock that ran out of propulsion," Cleland said. "His rocket fuel was acquisitions, but when Justice blocked Sprint he ran out of gas."

Sidgmore said WorldCom could have ridden out the industry meltdown had the company simply disclosed its losses instead of papering them over with false accounting. Now, it must persuade frightened bankers to continue to advance the company credit despite the scandal.

"We still have 25 million customers and $30 billion in revenue," Sidgmore said. "It's so disconcerting to think that a company like ours could be pulled down by this."

Even after the Sprint merger died, Ebbers was still grasping for deals. In September 2000, WorldCom bought Intermedia Communications Inc., a struggling local telephone and Internet network, for $6 billion. Intermedia had a controlling interest in Digex Inc., which ran Web sites for businesses. To Sidgmore, it clearly signaled that Ebbers had lost his way.

"That is the stupidest deal of all time," he said. "We paid over $6 billion for a company that's worth maybe $50 million."

According to Sidgmore, WorldCom was well into discussions to launch a joint venture that would have combined similar resources. Then, Gary Winnick, chief executive of Global Crossing, called Ebbers to report that his company was going to buy Digex.

"Bernie said '[expletive],'" Sidgmore said. " 'We're going to get hold of it ourselves.' He was afraid he was going to look bad from a testosterone point of view."

WorldCom's stock was plummeting and its debt was about $30 billion. Its debt ratings were slashed to near junk status. The old path to growth through merger was essentially foreclosed. With no other moves left, Ebbers turned to cost-cutting.

At a board meeting in April, with WorldCom's senior leadership gathered in Clinton to hear their boss outline his vision to rescue the company, Ebbers sermonized on the need to conserve coffee in the employee break room, turn the lights off at the end of the day and limit use of air-conditioning.

"Bernie is running a $40 billion company as if it were still his own mom-and-pop business," a WorldCom executive told *BusinessWeek* magazine. "He doesn't know how to grow the company, just shave pennies."

Ebbers was using up his own money to find cash to pay off $400 million in loans to his company. They had been tendered to prevent him from having to sell company stock to cover personal losses. He sold his 60-foot yacht, *Aquasition*.

By the end of April, the only chief executive WorldCom had ever known was gone. At the entrance to the pine-tree lined driveway to Ebbers's 1,500 acre farm in Brookhaven, Miss., a barricade went up.

"We were so proud," said Nancy Anderson, a longtime Clinton resident. "And the thing that we were so proud of is a little bit embarrassing right now. It just feels bad that now we're going to be known as the place where they had the biggest fraud in stock market history."

INVESTIGATING IMCLONE

Alex Prud'homme

Vanity Fair, June 2002

ON THE EVENING OF December 6 last year, Sam Waksal's spacious duplex loft in SoHo was packed with a rollicking, eclectic crowd for his annual Christmas party. Martha Stewart held court on a couch near the door, while the celebrity photographer Patrick McMullan snapped recognizable faces such as Mick Jagger, Patricia Duff, Lally Weymouth, Mort Zuckerman, Marvin Traub, Andrew Stein, and Andrew Cuomo mingling with less recognizable scientists, lawyers, and bankers associated with their host's biotech firm, ImClone Systems. This year's party, one reveler noted, featured more Wall Street analysts and fewer long-legged women with impressive cleavage in tiny black dresses than in the past. And there, in the midst of the swirl, was smiling Sam Waksal—a reedy, charming bachelor biotech entrepreneur—dazzling guests with his quick mind, fabulous art collection, and self-deprecating jokes. That night, Waksal had particular reason to celebrate: not only was the party a perfect amalgam of all that he had aspired to—big money and serious science spiced with celebrity and society—but 2001 had been the defining year for his long-struggling business.

SINCE FOUNDING IMCLONE WITH his brother, Harlan, in 1984, Waksal had toiled in the fickle biotech industry with mixed success. In 1992, Waksal bet the company on a potentially revolutionary cancer treatment called Erbitux, and then spent the next decade convincing others that it was destined to become a blockbuster.

"Erbitux is going to be huge," he had promised me many times in his

Tribeca offices last winter. "It's going to be one of the biggest drugs in the history of oncology—a drug that is going to alter the way cancer therapy is done."

Back then, his dream seemed to be taking shape. In February 2001, Erbitux was granted fast-track status by the Food and Drug Administration (FDA). In July the drug landed on the cover of *BusinessWeek*. In September the pharmaceutical giant Bristol-Myers Squibb bought a 20 percent stake in ImClone for $1 billion, and pledged another $1 billion for the rights to market Erbitux in North America and Japan—the largest single-product deal between a biotech firm and a pharmaceutical giant. In October, Sam and Harlan sold some of their stock for $57 million and $54 million, respectively. They were rich, even by their ambitious standards. And on December 6, the day of Sam Waksal's Christmas party, ImClone shares reached an all-time high of $75.45. That day Harlan sold another chunk of stock for a further $50 million. The only piece missing from the puzzle was the FDA's stamp of approval, which would allow the Waksals to start manufacturing and selling the drug.

That *ought* to have been no problem. According to Sam Waksal, Erbitux is a leading monoclonal antibody, part of a new class of "targeted therapies"—drugs such as Gleevec and Herceptin—that doctors hope will revolutionize cancer treatment. In the 22 years since its discovery by Dr. John Mendelsohn, now president of the University of Texas M. D. Anderson Cancer Center in Houston, it has been in development, at a cost of well over $100 million. Once it reaches the marketplace, analysts have predicted, it could generate up to $1 billion in annual sales. (Each year about a million Americans are diagnosed with cancer, and it will kill some 550,000 of them.)

No one could have promoted the drug better than the ubiquitous Waksal. Flitting from oncology conferences to government hearings to investor meetings, networking on tennis courts in the Hamptons and in the Grill Room at the Four Seasons restaurant, he has won over pillars of the scientific and financial communities. The ImClone board is stocked with respected names, including Dr. Mendelsohn; Dr. Vincent DeVita Jr., the former head of the National Cancer Institute and now executive director of the Yale Cancer Center; Robert Goldhammer, the former vice-chairman of the investment-banking firm Kidder Peabody;

and attorney David Kies, a partner at Sullivan & Cromwell. Last November, Blackstone Group chief and former secretary of commerce Peter G. Peterson joined their ranks.

"SAM WAKSAL SINGLE-HANDEDLY made biotech sexy," says Ian Alterman, a onetime ImClone employee, "which, for a fairly conservative stock, is amazing. He was a pioneer of bringing biotech to New York City. It's hard to forget someone like him."

On Friday, December 28, 2001, three weeks after his party, Waksal paced his office as he waited to hear from the FDA. Despite misgivings by some analysts, he was confident that the agency would green-light his drug and that Erbitux would be on the market by this spring. He glanced out the window. As dusk settled over Lower Manhattan, the hole in the skyline where the World Trade Center towers once had stood began to fill with a harsh white glow from the giant work lights at Ground Zero. At 7:14 P.M., after the market closed for the weekend, the fax machine buzzed and began churning out a nine-page letter informing him that the FDA had made a highly unusual decision: ImClone's application for Erbitux was so badly flawed, the letter said, that the agency refused even to consider it.

"I was in shock," Waksal told me a few days later. He was dressed in a dark-blue suit, his face looked drawn, and his slender frame was folded into a chair. We were sitting in an ImClone conference room, where a cabinet holds some of his collectibles—ancient Jewish coins, Roman oil lamps, baseballs signed by Willie Mays and Ted Williams, and a crystal pyramid inscribed "Who Dares Wins," the motto of the British Special Air Service. "I was very disappointed," he said.

Waksal scrambled to control the damage. In a conference call with investors and journalists early on Monday, December 31, he downplayed the FDA's response, insisting that there is no question that Erbitux is safe and effective. He said that the agency's concerns were mostly about ImClone's "train of documentation." He said he could supply the missing information, and predicted that Erbitux would be approved by the third quarter of this year. At one point he explained it to me by using a typically homespun analogy: "It was a question of showing the work. We were like the kid who writes down the answers to his math equations but doesn't show how he got them. The FDA wants to see the work. So now we're working with Bristol to fix it." But that morning the market was not reassured, and when it opened, ImClone's stock fell 19 percent.

Four days later the news grew dramatically worse when *The Cancer Letter*, an industry newsletter, leaked excerpts from the FDA's confidential refusal-to-file letter, indicating that ImClone's problems were far more serious than Waksal had acknowledged. Not only was ImClone's application "scientifically incomplete" and filled with "deficiencies," but the pivotal clinical drug trial was not "adequate and well controlled"—something, the letter revealed, that the FDA had repeatedly warned ImClone about in a series of meetings, letters, and phone calls since August 2000. In January, after serving for only two months, Pete Peterson resigned from the board.

THE RASH OF NEWSPAPER reports that appeared did not neglect to mention the very timely sale the Waksal brothers had made of their shares. Last July, Sam borrowed $18.2 million and Harlan borrowed $15.7 million from ImClone in order to acquire 4.2 million more shares of the company's stock. Shares in ImClone were trading at about $45 at the time, but the Waksals, along with other insiders, bought their shares from the company at a steep discount for about $8. After the Bristol-Myers deal, ImClone executives sold their shares to Bristol-Myers for $70, a sharp premium; the Waksal brothers' net totaled some $111 million. Had the shares been sold after the FDA's rejection, they would have been worth far less. Did the Waksals know something that their shareholders and Bristol-Myers did not? "The timing [of the FDA's rejection] is unfortunate but not something I could foresee," Harlan told *The Wall Street Journal*.

In February, Peter R. Dolan, the 46-year-old CEO of Bristol-Myers—which had already paid ImClone a nonrefundable $1.2 billion—threatened to cancel the deal and withhold the remaining $800 million stop payment. Most extraordinarily, Dolan demanded that the Waksal brothers step down from ImClone until Erbitux received the FDA's marketing approval, and that they allow Bristol-Myers to take control of the development of Erbitux. The ImClone board rebuffed Dolan's demands, and a standoff ensued.

Then, also in February, it was discovered in a document released by the Securities and Exchange Commission (SEC) that Sam Waksal's youngest daughter, Aliza, a 28-year-old actress, sold nearly 40,000 shares of ImClone—worth almost $2.5 million—on December 27, the day before the FDA's rejection of the Erbitux application. Angered by Waksal's refusal to voluntarily supply financial records, investigators have demanded that he appear before Congress to detail his family's ImClone stock transactions.

Today three federal bodies—the House Committee on Energy and Commerce (which is also investigating Enron), the SEC, and the Department of Justice—are investigating ImClone's business practices. It is an ominous development at a time when the nation is wary of Enronesque malfeasance. The government is pursuing two central lines of questioning: Did ImClone officials defraud their investors and Bristol-Myers? Did they engage in insider trading?

Enraged shareholders filed two dozen class-action lawsuits seeking hundreds of millions in damages from ImClone and its officers. They alleged that the Waksal brothers gave "false and misleading" statements about the drug's prospects for FDA approval. More recently investors have filed a lawsuit accusing Bristol-Myers Squibb of allowing ImClone to mislead them about Erbitux's status.

At an important industry conference in San Francisco in early January, Waksal struggled through his presentation and, in a hoarse voice, admitted, "We screwed up." That accurately summarizes the view of cancer patients who have been waiting to receive the drug.

"It was a huge blow," says Addison Woods, a 50-year-old software salesman from Houston who has colon cancer. "Our expectations had been built up that Erbitux would be available early this year. I thought of it as my magic bullet, and had gotten physically and mentally prepared to take this drug. Now I have to find another treatment to save my life."

Vee Kumar, a 47-year-old school psychologist from Kirkland, Washington, who also has colon cancer, says, "There is no excuse for raising patients' hopes and then not delivering. There's been a lot of talk about ImClone's monetary rewards from Erbitux, but not enough about getting it to the patients who need it. They really ought to have done their homework better."

Oncology-industry insiders were also mystified by ImClone's blunder. "Sam Waksal says, 'We screwed up.' But the shareholders' suits paint the ImClone guys as 'the Producers,'" says Paul Goldberg, editor of *The Cancer Letter.* "Where's the truth here? That's the $2 billion question."

IN A RUSH OF contrition Waksal has hired a crisis-management firm, Abernathy MacGregor; he has reimbursed ImClone $486,051 he made on sales of company stock last year, and has engaged in vigorous dialogues with the FDA and his irate partners at Bristol-Myers Squibb.

As for the criticism about the timing of his financial transactions last July, Sam, like his brother, maintains that no one at ImClone had any foreknowledge of the FDA's decision.

He says he plans to donate to charity and invest in biotech and health-care start-ups. "Has anybody ever said to Bill Gates, 'Gee, you've made a lot of money on the company you built—that's really terrible!'?"

By March, ImClone had reached an understanding with its partner: the Waksals would keep their jobs; Bristol-Myers would reduce its payments by $100 million and gain more control of the drug's development. And the share price was starting to rise again. Still, the cloud of the lawsuits and investigations hovers on the horizon and the repercussions are potentially far-reaching. As a result of Bristol-Myers's botched handling of Erbitux and an experimental hypertension drug, Vanlev, the company's stock price has hit a five-year low and CEO Dolan is on the hot seat.

Those who know Sam Waksal well are sympathetic to him following his sudden fall from grace, if not entirely surprised. "Sam is brilliant, relentless, and charming. He sweeps you up into his dream," observes Elena Castaneda, a friend and former girlfriend. "But he never thinks about the downside—which is his flaw, but also his asset. Without that, he wouldn't have gotten this far. He built ImClone from nothing! But he can't say 'No.' He wants to please everyone, and by doing that he hurts many people."

As I spoke to those who have known Waksal over the years—a wide range of people from very different walks of life—the stories began to show a pattern: he launches into an endeavor with great hope, but then something goes wrong; the project often ends in confusion, bruised feelings, or acrimonious lawsuits. Indeed, the corporate ethos of ImClone seems to have been determined to an unusual degree by the supremely optimistic, risk-taking personality of its CEO.

Sam Waksal put Erbitux on the map. The question now is whether his impatient ambition has put a potentially revolutionary drug in jeopardy. "Who fucked up? That's what you want to know," Waksal asked rhetorically last January, when he was still talking to me—before his advisers muzzled him. After a long critique of the Independent Response Assessment Committee (IRAC), which reviewed the Erbitux data, and a lecture on the workings of the FDA bureaucracy, he answered his own question: "It was our fault."

LAST WINTER I SPOKE to Waksal more than half a dozen times: I interviewed him in his large, disheveled corner office; I watched him charm a roomful of biotech analysts at New York's Plaza hotel; I ran into him at one of the heavy-duty A-list Upper East Side parties he attends each week; I also had numerous phone conversations with him. A lean, balding man with roaming eyes and a quick smile he uses to great effect, he was gracious and entertaining. Unusually, he can quote Davy Crockett, Camus, and his mother all in the same conversation. And though he's not an oncologist (or even a medical doctor, for that matter; he's got a Ph.D. in immunology), Waksal speaks with fluid enthusiasm about the world of cancer research, translating complex scientific language into layman's terms and dramatic visualizations.

"Look," he once exclaimed, jumping up from his chair to flick off the lights. "That's pretty much how Erbitux turns off the EGF [epidermal growth factor] receptor."

Then he led me on a whirlwind tour of the ImClone office and lab, located on two floors of a former shoe factory in New York's Tribeca. (The company has a manufacturing facility in New Jersey.) Striding down hallways and through laboratories, introducing me to scientists, lawyers, and secretaries as he went, he suddenly pulled open a door and led me into an antiseptic air-conditioned room filled with cages. "This is where we keep the lab mice," he said conspiratorially. "We're not supposed to be in here without protective footwear, but c'mon, take a peek. Pretty neat, huh?" Later, he regaled me with stories—about the night Sean Connery, Dustin Hoffman, and Matthew Broderick had been here shooting the movie *Family Business* with his friend the director Sidney Lumet; about buying a meal for Joe DiMaggio in return for his signature; about watching the World Trade Center towers collapse from his office.

After moving to Manhattan from Boston in 1982, Waksal, now 54 (publicly, he maintains he is 52) and the divorced father of two grown daughters (Elana, 29, a former New York City Council candidate, and Aliza), set out to create a name for himself in the world of biotech. "I'm not your run-of-the-mill scientist," he concedes with a grin. "My interests are eclectic. I think about doing lots of different things—creative, important things."

FOR YEARS HE DETERMINEDLY put the pieces together, one by one—parlaying one connection into another in the intertwined scientific, financial, and social circles that count. He dated high-profile women such as Martha Stewart's daughter, Alexis (Martha too, according to the *New York Post*, although both the Stewarts and Waksal deny it), and the socialite Patricia Duff. Alexis Stewart, 36, says, "I learned a lot about science from Sam. He's a great teacher." She laughs when recalling the time the Waksal brothers took her and Harlan's wife, Carol, on a rented sailboat in the Bahamas, "cockroaches and all." She is scared of the water, she says, "and they didn't make me feel that comfortable. They *say* they can sail, but . . . luckily we didn't hit any storms. We had a good time. . . . My favorite thing about Sam is you can ask him anything, and even if he doesn't know the answer, he'll give you a great answer and make you feel really comfortable. For a long time you'll be totally thrilled. I don't think he's usually wrong."

Waksal's interests range from reading philosophy and attending the ballet to playing poker with men such as Triarc CEO Nelson Peltz, newspaper publisher James Finkelstein, and financier Carl Icahn. In the summer he shuttles in fancy cars (he's a notoriously absentminded driver) between his 7,000-square-foot SoHo loft and his house in the Hamptons. His friends, he'll tell you, range from the British actor Terence Stamp to U.S. Supreme Court justice Antonin Scalia.

Raised in Toledo, Ohio, the son of Holocaust survivors from Poland, Waksal invariably cites his background as the reason for his driving ambition "to do positive things for mankind." Indeed, in discussing his parents' struggles he paints a picture of tragedy and heroism. His mother, Sabina, he says, watched her mother being dragged away to the gas chambers at Auschwitz. His father, Jack Vaksal, witnessed the Germans shooting his three-year-old sister through the head and fought in the Polish Resistance; during the day Vaksal would hide next to a corpse in a crypt, Sam tells me, and at night he would sneak out of the cemetery to steal food and fight the Nazis. In Ohio, Jack ran a scrap-metal business.

"My father was an incredible hero," Waksal says. "I feel there is nothing I could ever do that could match the things he did. . . . The way my parents survived affects every day of my life."

WHEN YOU ASK PEOPLE about Waksal, virtually everyone cites his intelligence and charisma. Friends insist that any doubts about his integrity are simply the result of the fact that Waksal is a loud, flamboyant personality making waves in the conservative and competitive world of medicine.

"I've invested in ImClone since the beginning," says Martha Stewart. "I was almost Sam's mother-in-law! He dated my daughter, Alexis, for a very long time—until my daughter threw him away. . . . Even though people complain that Sam's wacko, and that he runs around, his attention to the real fundamentals of research and science are there. We've always kept our ImClone stock and profited handsomely from it. . . . My driver bought a house in Connecticut on ImClone."

At the same time, others say that Waksal habitually overextends himself. "Sam is not a bad person," says Elena Castaneda. "He never intentionally goes into something trying to burn or hurt someone. He believes what he tells you, and in his head it's done already. But getting it executed—that doesn't always happen."

Sometimes he simply stretches himself too thin: in 1993, Waksal's friend the venture capitalist Charles Antell sued him in order to recoup a $100,000 loan. An $85,000 check Waksal wrote to partially repay the debt bounced. With the check, Waksal had sent a personal note to Antell, saying, "Thanks for being such a good friend. I do not deserve it I know." Antell eventually recouped most of the loan.

"Sam is a very clever guy, but he's a nebbish—a nerd—whose desperation to be part of the fast crowd is so obvious that people joke about it," notes an old friend. "He is prepared to do whatever it takes, at whatever cost, to become 'a player.' From the moment I met him I felt he was going to trip himself up by trying to be something he isn't."

At times, Waksal's extra-scientific business ventures have turned into costly distractions. He has invested in movies such as *The Last Party* (starring Robert Downey Jr.); restaurants such as the ill-fated Sam's in Midtown Manhattan (with Stephen Crisman, Mariel Hemingway's husband); Manhattan real estate; the downtown style magazine *Nylon*; and a dot-com venture, ibeauty.com (an on-line beauty-products site).

Last August, just days before the Bristol-Myers deal was signed, Waksal was sued again—to the tune of $57.4 million this time, for fraud and "extreme emotional distress"—by Gabriella Forte, the notoriously energetic former top executive at Giorgio Armani and Calvin Klein, Inc., now the president of Dolce & Gabbana USA. According to the suit, Waksal recruited her as CEO of ibeauty.com, where he was chairman and chief stockholder. Forte claims that he lied to her about ibeauty's financial state and didn't pay her at a time when her husband was suffering from cancer and heart disease. "Gabriella quit ibeauty. She wasn't fired," Waksal says. And in March, James Neal Jr., the former CFO of Scientia Health Group, a small biotech company that operates from ImClone's offices, sued Waksal for fraud, charging him with "illegal and unethical conduct."

WAKSAL'S OVERREACHING STARTED EARLY—in his 20s, when he was at Stanford University School of Medicine, working in the lab of Dr. Leonard Herzenberg, a noted genetics expert.

"Waksal was a very bright guy, a charmer, but not completely straightforward," recalls Herzenberg. In 1974, Waksal claimed to be in possession of some rare antibodies. Herzenberg didn't believe him. "[Waksal] became a 'big man' in the laboratory by saying he had these antibodies that we weren't able to get. But when a postdoc [postdoctoral fellow] used them in an experiment, the results weren't right. Then one day we found his test tubes—and his only—spilled in the bottom of the lab fridge," which destroyed the evidence. "So I called the supposed source of the antibodies at Sloan-Kettering, and he had not given them to Sam. . . . I don't know what he had in those test tubes. When I confronted him, Sam insisted they were real. A few years later he called my wife, admitted he hadn't told the truth, and apologized," Herzenberg says. He remains nonplussed. "Why would someone so brilliant lie?" (Waksal declined requests for comment.)

From 1977 to 1982, while Waksal was assistant professor of pathology at the Tufts Cancer Center in Boston, the eccentric behavior reportedly continued. Former colleagues recall Waksal as an "unusual" character. Odd people, they say, would call Waksal's extension at all hours—they included bill collectors, Waksal's irate ex-wife, Cindy, and "slimy characters"—until coworkers disconnected his line. He surrounded himself with a coterie of attractive lab technicians—"The profile was tall, legs-legs-legs, dark hair," says a former colleague—known around the Center as the Disco Techs. His lab appeared dark and unused much of the time, and people who were clearly not scientists dropped by late at night. "It was kind of scary," says a source. A rumor sprang up that Waksal was somehow involved with cocaine, although no one ever saw him with the drug. "The joke was that the only piece of equipment used in his lab was the balance," says a person who worked nearby.

THE JOKE SUDDENLY GAINED credence on February 14, 1981. At nine o'clock that evening two undercover sheriff's deputies noticed Harlan Waksal, then a 27-year-old Tufts medical student, in the Delta ticket area of Fort Lauderdale International Airport. Harlan—who today is 49, looks like a more robust version of Sam, and lives in a genteel New Jersey suburb with his wife and children—appeared nervous. He had used cash to purchase a one-way ticket to Boston and did not check any luggage. The police felt that he fit a "drug-courier profile," took him to a storage room, and searched him. Stashed in Harlan's underwear, bag, and coat pocket was a kilo of cocaine.

When I asked Sam about this incident his face turned red and he replied, "This is a very difficult subject, one that I prefer not talking about. It's a matter of public record. Harlan was never finally convicted of anything. He had an unfortunate incident when he was very, very young."

After being sentenced to nine years in prison for possession of cocaine with intent to distribute, Harlan appealed; in 1983 his conviction was overturned on the grounds that "the search resulted from an illegal seizure without a valid consent."

The case was never retried, and Harlan served no time. He wasn't compelled by the SEC to disclose the incident when ImClone went public in 1991. Nevertheless, the episode has shadowed the brothers ever since. A 1993 article in *Barron's* reports that at least two potential institutional investors shied away from ImClone because of the incident. And a surprising number of people mentioned it to me, unbidden.

There is a postscript to the story: after hearing of his brother's arrest, Sam allegedly put on Harlan's lab coat and did his brother's medical rounds at Tufts. "It's a great story, but silly," Sam says, a vein in his forehead throbbing. "I have my own coat, thank you. I did not leave [Tufts] because I did rounds for my brother. It would've been a nice thing for me to do, but I didn't. He's my brother and a jewel of a human being. It's not something I think should be brought up 21-plus years later."

Speaking to *Barron's*, however, he answered the same question differently. When asked about impersonating Harlan, he said, "There was a patient of Harlan's who . . . only spoke Yiddish. And Harlan, when he wasn't in town at one point, wanted me to go talk to her. . . . So I went and talked to her. That was the scope of it." When I asked about the discrepancy, he looked away and said, "Umm, I might've gone to visit an older Jewish woman. But not as Harlan. As Sam." In an icy voice he added, "I think she would've known the difference if she was his patient."

I was never able to speak to Harlan Waksal. He canceled three interviews and refused to return my phone calls. When *Barron's* asked Harlan about the drug bust, he maintained that he hadn't used drugs then or since, and that that was the only time he'd ever transported drugs: "It was a dramatic mistake in judgment. I did it as a favor for someone, and it's a favor I have obviously regretted."

SAM WAKSAL BELIEVES his detractors bring up the story out of envy; he's successful, so they want to knock him down. This rationale has popped up before. In 1982, in his last job before starting ImClone, Waksal was named associate professor of pathology and director of the immunology division in the department of pathology at New York's Mount Sinai School of Medicine. This was a prestigious post, but Waksal left after only three years. Again there are many rumors about why—

one being that he misrepresented data—and again he denies there was a problem.

"There were people at Mount Sinai that I had some big fights with. [They] hate me. I, at times, am arrogant and abrasive," he told *Barron's*.

"I don't think anybody *hated* him," says Dr. Stave Kohtz, who worked as Waksal's graduate assistant at Mount Sinai in the early 1980s and is now an associate professor in the department of pathology. "I just think he was not appropriate for the position. There were certainly a lot of heated arguments, but that wasn't unusual. . . . Sam is very smart, but he didn't fit the stereotype of a rigorous, conservative 'bench' scientist. . . . At the time, Sam told me that Dr. [Jerome] Kleinerman [who headed the department and is now deceased] called him into his office and said he loved Sam like a son, but couldn't keep him there. Sam was very upset. I think it was a bad fit, rather than bad faith."

"It wasn't a bad fit," Waksal snaps. "When I left Mount Sinai I was going on sabbatical. I was founding ImClone at the time." When I ask him to explain the pattern of his career, he shrugs and says, "I do lots of things in ways that academic centers don't always love to do. . . . Life has ups and downs."

Dr. Kohtz hasn't seen Waksal in years, but he says, "I've spent many hours thinking about Sam. . . . He affects everybody he comes in contact with. Some people just disapprove of him. I admire him, in a sense, although I couldn't be him. Most people facing what he's faced would have a huge therapy bill, but Sam comes out of it with the biggest biotech deal in history. . . . He's certainly unique. He's got something that you can learn from him—I'm just not sure what it is."

"I've never been driven to therapy by issues—that's a great luxury that most people outside of New York's Upper East Side don't have," Waksal says defiantly. "When one hits a roadblock, one's job is to correct things and succeed."

How did Waksal continue to fail upward all these years? Waksal-ologists point to the series of influential mentors he has cultivated. A partial list of these father figures includes, along with Herzenberg and Kleinerman: Dr. Michael Feldman at the Weizmann Institute of Science in Israel; Dr. Robert Schwartz, formerly of the Tufts Cancer Center; and Dr. Zvi Fuks at Memorial Sloan-Kettering Cancer Center. At

ImClone, Waksal's intellectual mentor has been Dr. Mendelsohn and his protector has been the chairman of the board, Robert Goldhammer. But perhaps Waksal's most significant backer has been his longtime poker companion and tennis partner Carl Icahn.

When things have turned sour for Waksal, some of these men have staunchly defended him. But one of his early champions says, "A number of us recognized that Sam was very smart and articulate. We said, 'If there's any way we can help, you let us know.' We pushed hard to get him into [prestigious positions]. But then we did site visits later; his work never seemed to pan out. I felt betrayed."

SAM AND HARLAN STARTED ImClone Systems in 1984 with $4 million in venture capital. Ian Alterman, who worked at ImClone as a legal assistant from 1987 to 1992, recalls it as "a professional, but collegial, place to work." He didn't have to wear a tie, and the atmosphere was familial—employees were encouraged to wear costumes on Halloween, and Sam would dress as Santa at Christmas. The Waksals, he says, "have great integrity. They truly cared about the work their company was doing."

The company, named for the three fields it hoped to enter— immunology, DNA cloning, and medical-information systems—initially focused on products such as diagnostic kits, gonorrhea vaccines, and AIDS drugs. Despite a few successes, ImClone never turned a profit. In 1987 the company's planned IPO was a victim of the stock-market crash, and it was only because Waksal was able to persuade friends and investors to keep the company afloat that ImClone could finally launch its IPO, in 1991.

In April 1992, Dr. Zvi Fuks introduced Waksal to Dr. John Mendelsohn over breakfast. Waksal could scarcely believe his good luck when Mendelsohn told him about a drug—C225, now know as Erbitux—he had developed while researching cancer at U.C. San Diego. Essentially, Mendelsohn explained, that drug "put chewing gum in the lock" to stop tumor growth.

"It was an 'Aha' moment—I got the drug's potential immediately," says Waksal. "We bet the house. But the biologics made such sense [that] it was not a blind bet. It was an intelligent bet. We simply understand the biology better than other people do."

Cancer is so difficult to treat because it is not just one disease: it's an umbrella term for hundreds of similar diseases, each of which is driven by a different set of factors and behaves in different ways in different patients.

The most promising cancer therapies today are so-called targeted treatments, which are based on our increasingly sophisticated understanding of diseased cells. Small numbers of EGF receptors exist on the surface of normal cells, but cancerous cells can have a million or more receptors. EGF binds to its receptors on the surface of a cell and then sets off a chain reaction of enzymes inside the cell that keeps the tumor nourished: the cell "auto-stimulates" and grows rapidly. In the early '80s, Mendelsohn knew that EGF receptors are found in a third of all solid tumors; he surmised that blocking the EGF receptor would stop the tumor from growing. He spent a decade developing C225, which blocked tumor growth in cells.

His work had generated excitement in the scientific community, but the financial community was another matter. Despite grants from the National Cancer Institute and the National Institutes of Health, funding was scarce. By 1984, Mendelsohn had used C225 to stop the growth of human tumors transplanted into mice. In the mid-1980s he was working at Sloan-Kettering and looking for funding in order to turn the mouse antibody into one with human protein. U.C. San Diego owned the license to C225, but did nothing to attract a licensee, and Mendelsohn says he "wanted to do the research and let someone else raise the money."

Enter Sam Waksal.

ALTHOUGH THE WAKSAL BROTHERS had no clinical experience, no manufacturing capability, and very little money, they decided to aim for the skies with C225. For a nominal processing fee, UCSD gave ImClone permission to convert the mouse antibody into a mostly human antibody in the lab. Then the Waksals bought a bankrupt computer-chip manufacturing plant in Somerville, New Jersey, and turned it into a biologic-drug production facility. But in the early '90s the biotech market collapsed: ImClone pink-slipped a third of its workforce, and others left; a skeleton crew of 50 kept the place going. "We were completely out of money," Waksal recalls. To avoid bankruptcy

ImClone sold its stake in the Cadus Pharmaceutical Corporation to Carl Icahn for $6 million. They poured the money into full-scale development of Erbitux.

To help finance the costly process of bringing a drug to market—it often takes a decade and anywhere from a $300 million to an $800 million investment to prove a drug's effectiveness—many fledgling biotech companies partner with a larger pharmaceutical company. This helps them to survive, but also limits the profits the principals can bank. The Waksal brothers, however, made the unusual decision to go it alone, claiming ImClone would be one of the first biotechs in history to take a product from the laboratory to commercial launch without teaming up with a partner. It was an audacious move, and it meant that ImClone would have to shepherd Erbitux through the exacting FDA approval process on its own—something the company had never done with any other drug. (Waksal says Bristol signed the deal too late to be involved in ImClone's application to the FDA.)

May 19, 1995, was the turning point for ImClone. On that day Dr. Mendelsohn presented his C225 data to the annual meeting of the American Society of Clinical Oncology, the world's largest gathering of cancer researchers. "Our stock started going up the next day," Waksal says. "The oncologists started buying it." Major pharmaceutical companies began sniffing around for a deal.

IMCLONE DIDN'T REALLY HIT it big, however, until Shannon Kellum's survival story made headlines.

In April 1998, Kellum, a fresh-faced 28-year-old Florida state tax auditor, was diagnosed with colon cancer. Her colon was surgically resected, but over the next year her condition worsened. "I tried every kind of chemotherapy available," she recalls, "but nothing even fazed the tumor." Twelve months after her initial diagnosis, the tumors had spread to her abdomen and had grown "as big as grapefruits," she says— too big to be removed surgically. She was "out of options" and facing death.

Then her oncologist, Dr. Mark Rubin, suggested that Kellum might be eligible to try an experimental treatment known as C225. (Rubin had once worked with Dr. Mendelsohn at Sloan-Kettering.) Rubin explained that C225 had been tested only on patients with head and neck cancer; if Kellum was granted special "compassionate use" permission by ImClone and the FDA, she would become the first to use the drug for colon cancer. Was she willing to try it?

"I really didn't have any choice," recalls Kellum. "If the tumors got any bigger they were going to take over my liver. At that point I was willing to eat or drink anything to [save myself]. So I became the guinea pig."

Unlike chemotherapy's shotgun blast, which kills both healthy and cancerous cells and causes terrible nausea, Erbitux acts like a sniper shot aimed precisely at the growth signal in malignant tumors; one of its few side effects is a mild skin rash. Erbitux is not a cure: it stops tumors from spreading, which is significant because it is a tumor's ability to reproduce and metastasize throughout the body that kills. By stopping cancer growth, Erbitux allows other kinds of therapy to shrink or destroy the tumors. Used in conjunction with chemotherapy, it may prove to be highly effective against colon cancer, the nation's second most deadly form of cancer.

"When you are [facing death], even a few more months, or even days, of life makes a huge difference," Kellum says.

Granted permission to take Erbitux, Kellum became the first person with metastatic (spreading) colon cancer to use the drug. Beginning in April of 1999, it was administered intravenously once a week along with irinotecan, the chemotherapy that had previously failed to help her. The results were astounding: within a month Kellum's tumors had shrunk by 50 percent; by September the tumors had shrunk 80 percent. In December, surgeons were able to remove two tumors completely.

"I call Erbitux my 'miracle drug.'" Kellum says. "It has given me a lot more years of life than I expected. I am very, very fortunate. If Dr. Rubin hadn't [had the foresight to use Erbitux], you wouldn't be talking to me right now."

Because of her remarkable response to the drug, Erbitux suddenly caught the attention of the legions of colon-cancer patients who have few therapy options. In May 2000 her story was featured in USA Today and on Good Morning America. Within hours of these reports, ImClone employees and even friends of friends of the Waksals found themselves bombarded with requests from cancer patients around the country desperate to try the "miraculous" but still experimental drug. Between May

2000 and February 2001, Waksal says, ImClone received more than 10,000 requests for "compassionate use" of C225. President Clinton reportedly intervened on behalf of a patient, who got the drug. Many others, however, did not.

In May 2001, CBS's *60 Minutes* aired a story on the debate. The show featured two women, 51-year-old Ruth-Ann Santino and 36-year-old Amy Cohen, both of whom were mothers with colon cancer, "begging for their lives." Despite months of effort, Santino was unable to get the drug and died. Cohen, however, managed to reach Sam Waksal on the phone very early one morning, persuaded him to give her C225 on a compassionate-use basis, and survived. She credits the phone call with causing him to see her as "a real live person" and not "just a patient."

OVERWHELMED WITH REQUESTS FOR the drug, ImClone no longer gives out Erbitux on a compassionate-use basis—a decision that worries and angers patients. Last June, at a congressional hearing chaired by U.S. Representative Dan Burton (Republican, Indiana), Kellum testified in favor of allowing more cancer patients access to Erbitux. She recalls, "One person recently lost his wife. Another lost his daughter. A gentleman spoke of his 16-year-old son who was dying. It was very, very emotional. I didn't cry, but I felt a little guilty. They all lost someone and I was still alive." Yet she remains frustrated: "I made a big effort. I got up there and testified for four hours, but nothing's changed. I'm spinning my wheels."

Kellum, now 32 and married, has had part of her liver and both ovaries removed in cancer surgeries. Recently, Dr. Rubin told her he'd found a new tumor on her spine. She is one of the lucky ones; she continues to use Erbitux and tries to remain upbeat, but says she feels "very, very nervous." The drug, she says, "is keeping me alive. I need it. And there are a lot of other very sick people out there waiting for it, too. Some of them have died waiting. This is their last hope. Now their hope is going to fly out the window. It's very disheartening. I don't know who to blame: The FDA? ImClone? We've got Erbitux sitting right in front of us, but if we can't use it, what good can it do?"

On the morning of September 11, 2001, the Waksals gathered their top executives to announce a $2 billion deal with Bristol-Myers Squibb, once the world's leading maker of oncology drugs. But just before nine that morning terrorists attacked the World Trade Center, and the announcement was canceled. "People were dying just a few blocks away. I couldn't focus on this," Waksal recalls. "But the next day we decided that it was important to continue our work. We're supposed to make the world better. To not come in to work allows evil to win. I'm a child of survivors. What did people do as they walked out of a concentration camp? I'm watching people jumping out of the World Trade Center. Sartre said, 'Life begins on the other side of despair.' I have always believed that. Our job is to move forward."

The deal was theoretically great for both partners. Bristol-Myers no longer controlled the patent for its key oncology drug, Taxol, and its own drug pipeline was running dry; the deal with ImClone allows it to receive 39 percent of the profits on Erbitux sales in North America and to stay ahead of the competition. ImClone benefits from Bristol-Myers's financial muscle and its enormous sales force. The pharmaceutical company paid $1.2 billion for 19.9 percent of ImClone and for the right to sell Erbitux. Had the FDA accepted the drug's application, ImClone would have received another $300 million, and full FDA approval would have brought a further $500 million.

On September 19, the agreement with Bristol was finally signed. "When you spend so long working against the established paradigm, then the vindication feels good," Waksal told me. But the elation would prove short-lived.

"After the Bristol-Myers deal, Sam was God for a while," says Elena Castaneda. "We all felt happy for him—he'd finally made it. But when you're at the top, there's only one place to go: down."

AT THE CORE OF the FDA's rejection of the Erbitux application is the fact that the clinical trials were not constructed in a way that shows the drug is an effective weapon against cancer on its own. In other words, no one really knows if Erbitux works.

In February, *The Cancer Letter* obtained a copy of the confidential protocol on which the Erbitux clinical trials were based, and which was written by someone at ImClone, and had three prominent, independent cancer-trial experts review it. The experts agreed that it was vague and slipshod. It "generates far more questions than it could ever answer," one wrote.

"You couldn't design a worse protocol if you tried," says Paul Gold-berg, *The Cancer Letter*'s puckish editor. "You don't know who's in the trial, and you don't know which drug does what."

Critics such as shareholder Ira Gaines, who filed a lawsuit claiming Bristol-Myers "knew all along" that ImClone's application to the FDA was flawed, have charged that Bristol-Myers failed to exercise due diligence with regard to ImClone, the Waksals, and Erbitux before signing the landmark $2 billion deal last fall. In January, Richard J. Lane, the president of Bristol's worldwide medicines group, told *BusinessWeek*, "The company remains confident about the future of Erbitux. There is no doubt it works." Nonetheless, Bristol was forced to take a $735 million write-down of its ImClone investment in January, and in April, Lane was forced out of the company.

LAST DECEMBER, WHEN I asked Brian Markison, Bristol's president of oncology and virology, about the company's due diligence, he replied, "We approached [ImClone] two years ago, looked through the information, and decided to let it wait. As the data matured, we went back to them at the beginning of summer. We [did an] extraordinarily rigorous review of every piece of information: lab data, X-ray scans, the toxicity—every single thing." Bristol officials have not returned subsequent calls.

On February 15, Waksal's old backstop, the corporate raider Carl Icahn, announced his intention to buy up to $500 million in ImClone stock—nearly 40 percent of the company. For ImClone it was a welcome endorsement, yet the company quickly installed a "poison pill" antitakeover defense. The move, which would dilute the company's outstanding shares if any investor were to buy more than a 15 percent stake, may have been aimed at Icahn, or at Bristol-Myers. Since his announcement, however, Icahn has not actually purchased a large stake in the company. While he has reportedly had a change of heart about ImClone, Icahn's true intentions are a mystery. Some speculate that he is sending mixed messages as part of an elaborate arbitrage.

At the end of February—after a meeting in Washington, D.C., among ImClone, Bristol-Myers, and the FDA—investors sent ImClone shares shooting up 32 percent on hopes that the FDA might accept a new Erbitux application this year. A new application would have to contain more data from ImClone's completed clinical trial, plus data from a 225-patient clinical trial being performed by Merck KGaA, ImClone's European partner (no relation to the American Merck). If the FDA were to accept the new application, which is far from certain, Erbitux could reach the market sometime in the next 18 months—later than Waksal had initially promised, but a lot earlier than if a new round of clinical trails is required.

Robert L. Erwin, a patient advocate for the Marti Nelson Cancer Research Foundation (he is also CEO of a biotech company), attended the meeting and says, "Both the FDA and ImClone seemed to be working together in a constructive, not hostile, way to move Erbitux along. The Waksals admitted that mistakes had been made, but they committed to correct them. When the FDA saw that attitude, they got specific about what needs to be done. The encouraging news is that it looks as if the drug will be available sooner than I [previously] thought."

Finally, in early March, ImClone and Bristol-Myers announced a thaw in their Cold War. Andrew Bodnar—a Bristol-Myers senior VP who is on ImClone's board—would lead the effort to shepherd Erbitux through the FDA's approval process. Further, the new agreement caps royalty payments at 39 percent, delays Bristol's milestone payments to ImClone, and cuts them by $100 million. Wall Street generally viewed the announcement as a compromise that would benefit both sides and a sign that the partnership is on the mend. But the damage may have already been done. In April, Bristol chairman and CEO. Peter Dolan shocked Wall Street when he acknowledged that the company's sales and earnings were dramatically off track. In addition to the ImClone debacle, he is facing an empty pipeline for new products, a clogged inventory of existing treatments, and increased competition from generic-drug makers. Bristol's earnings for the year are expected to fall as much as 30 percent, a development analysts call an utter disaster. Indeed, some predict that Bristol, the world's fifth-largest drugmaker, is ripe for a takeover.

THE IMPORTANCE OF TARGETED treatments such as Erbitux is that they may render cancer a chronic, treatable disease like diabetes. The hope is that one day an oncologist will be able to look at a tumor and choose a drug specifically designed to shut it down; the patient would take intravenous doses of the drug once a month, perhaps for years.

As with other existing targeted treatments, such as Gleevec (for leukemia) and Herceptin (for breast cancer), Erbitux (for colon, pancreatic, head and neck, and lung cancer) doesn't work for everyone. At a recent health-care conference Harlan Waksal reported that in a 57-patient "single-agent" clinical trial, the response rate for patients using Erbitux without chemotherapy was only 10.5 percent. One participant in a similar trial says that "Erbitux stopped my tumor growth for seven months—and it was really easy to take, with no side effects. But then my tumor started growing again."

Important voices in the medical community believe that Erbitux is an important step forward, and have urged its prompt release. Dr. Leonard Saltz of Sloan-Kettering, who was the lead investigator on the drug's clinical trials, showed that 22.5 percent of his colon-cancer patients—27 people—responded positively to a combination of Erbitux and irinotecan, meaning that their tumors shrank by more than 50 percent. The others died. Nevertheless, this was still the best response rate ever achieved in patients who previously had no hope of survival. "In this setting, [such results] were unheard of," he says. "I'm very positive about the drug. It's not a home run. I look at it as a single, but in an area—colorectal cancer—where we are desperately in need."

Dr. Larry Norton, head of the Division of Solid Tumor Oncology at Sloan-Kettering, and president of the American Society of Clinical Oncology, is also a believer. "Once Erbitux is used in a frontline setting it's going to show much more pronounced activity. That will reassure all the critics. I'd like to see Erbitux's approval as rapidly as possible so that patients will benefit."

WHILE SAM WAKSAL HAS sharply curtailed his public pronouncements on ImClone, he has not skipped a beat in his high-profile socializing. "I just saw him the other night," reports a friend. "If I were in his shoes I'd be moving to Minnesota, but he seemed fine." Waksal can be spotted on a regular basis at hip New York restaurants such as Da Silvano, and he continues to host monthly salons at his SoHo loft.

Recently, the author Francine du Plessix Gray, whose book *At Home with the Marquis de Sade: A Life* was nominated for a Pulitzer Prize, gave a talk about the genre of biography to a literary group in Waksal's living room. Waksal introduced her and handled the Q&A with aplomb. "I [didn't] know him at all, but he was extremely pleasant," she reports. Noting his art collection, especially "extraordinary [Cy] Twomblys and an extraordinary Richard Serra painting," she adds, "He has impeccable taste." Another guest that evening, *Vanity Fair* contributing editor David Margolick, says, "He was obviously feeling the pressure of his situation. He brought it up and even cracked several jokes about it—saying how, because of the torture he was going through, he could relate to the Marquis de Sade. He was funny and charming. He's sardonic."

SOME PREDICT WAKSAL WILL be vindicated. "Sam's at his best in this kind of [adverse] situation. He'll bounce back," says his friend Elena Castaneda. "He's pulled the rabbit out of the hat before." Bob Erwin, the cancer-patient advocate, says, "The Waksals have devoted so much time and money to this effort that if they were just motivated to get rich, well, there's a lot of faster ways of doing it." And the Waksals' sister, Patti, a Maryland antiques dealer, says, "Whatever [negative] spin people want to put on it, my brothers have been doing this for all the right reasons. ImClone has tried very hard to help people."

While that may be true, the ImClone case has been viewed in the dark light of the Enron scandal. The press has made much of the fact that Dr. Mendelsohn—a renowned oncologist with a squeaky-clean reputation—is on the board not only of ImClone (he sold $6 million worth of stock last October) but also of Enron. "It's a coincidence," he says. Another person caught in the tangle is Charlotte Beers, the former head of Ogilvy & Mather, who is now undersecretary of state for public diplomacy. In 1999 she and Waksal paid $37.5 million for ibeauty; she has held stock in ImClone, Enron, and Martha Stewart Living Omnimedia Inc. (The last two have been audited by Arthur Andersen.) In a further odd twist, Arnold J. Levine—an award-winning biologist who is an ImClone board member and also sits on the company's scientific advisory board—abruptly resigned as president of Rockefeller University last February. Levine, 62, says he resigned for health reasons, but his departure was reportedly triggered by a drunken fling with a twentysomething grad student in a campus lounge in January.

A friend worries about how investigations will affect the Waksal brothers. "Either Harlan will take the fall," she predicts, "or the government will try to turn Harlan and Sam against each other, which could bring the whole company down."

"I don't think the Waksals will be around by the middle of 2003," Morningstar analyst Todd Lebor has said. "Their credibility is shot. When you are dealing with a drug company, trust in management is very important. ImClone is lacking that."

ON THE EVENING OF January 15, a highly agitated Sam Waksal called me on his cell phone. It was the last time we spoke; indeed, it was one of the last times the usually press-friendly Waksal spoke one-on-one to any journalist.

The day before, the *New York Post* had run a gleeful story about ImClone's predicament—deeming it the "newest scandal to sweep Wall Street" and saying that "Sam has been loitering at the fringes of the New York society crowd for two decades, leaving an oil slick behind him that has been colorful, to say the least." Waksal hotly disputed some of the facts in that story, and complained that he was becoming the target of unfair "slam pieces." His mood swinging from combative to self-pitying, he gave me his version of events.

"Two thousand two was going to be a big year—and it still will be a big year. It just didn't begin the way I thought it would," he said. "The truth is Erbitux works. Yes, there are regulatory hurdles, but there have been for tons of drugs. This will go away. And ImClone will be a very successful company."

With a snort, Waksal dismissed the myriad class-action lawsuits he's facing: "Every time a stock drops in price [the lawyers charge in]—you know that. We have to deal with those. And when our stock goes back up, that will change."

In an earlier conversation Waksal said, "To run a biotech firm you have to be real quick. I liken it to being a scrambling quarterback on a football team. Pharmaceutical companies [can have] a big fullback: you give him the ball, and he'll just keep running. In biotech, if you see you're not going anywhere, you'd better be quick enough to run in the other direction—otherwise you're gone."

UPDATE

In October, Sam Waksal pled guilty to six counts—including securities fraud, bank fraud, perjury, and conspiracy to obstruct justice—in connection with insider trading at ImClone. Waksal admitted that before the news broke that the FDA would not be approving the drug Erbitux, he had tipped his daughter, Aliza, to dump her ImClone stock. The counts carry a maximum sentence of 65 years in prison. Waksal's plea was not part of any deal with prosecutors, and at press time seven counts related to insider trading were still pending against the former CEO. In addition, the government's investigation into ImClone is still continuing, and prosecutors have said that additional charges against Waksal and others may still be forthcoming. Waksal's brother, Harlan, is now CEO of the company. Erbitux has still not been approved by the FDA.

—J.S.

THE INSIDERS

Marc Peyser with Keith Naughton, Peg Tyre,

Tamara Lipper, T. Trent Gegax, and Lisa Bergtraum

Newsweek, July 1, 2002

IT WAS TWO DAYS after Christmas, and Martha Stewart—magazine editor, TV host, syndicated columnist and high priestess of domesticity—wanted to get away from it all. She was flying with two friends from Connecticut to Mexico's ultratony Las Ventanas resort (a junior suite starts at $585) when her private jet stopped in San Antonio, Texas, to refuel. Just like the rest of us hardworking folks, she called her office to check her messages. The most important one was from her broker, Peter Bacanovic, and Stewart had her assistant patch him into her cell. Bacanovic's news: one of her stocks, a high-flying biotech company called ImClone, had dropped below $60, the price at which she says they had previously agreed to sell. Stewart told Bacanovic to dump her 3,928 shares. Then she did something that only the Martha Stewarts of this world can do. She dialed Sam Waksal, who just happened to be the CEO of ImClone, not to mention one of Martha's closest friends. "Something's going on with ImClone," Martha said in her message, "and I want to know what it is."

And thus sprouted a very big weed in Martha Stewart's well-manicured life. In the past few weeks, Stewart has found herself drawn deeper and deeper into another one of those Wall Street scandals that turn the rich and powerful into losers. Martha isn't accused of setting up phony off-balance-sheet companies like the Enron boys, or of borrowing an obscene amount of money from her own corporation like the guy at WorldCom. Nor did she pretend to ship artworks out of state to avoid sales taxes, as Tyco's CEO allegedly did. She's being questioned on the more mundane issue of insider trading, for selling her ImClone shares (and banking $228,000) just a day before the FDA announced it wouldn't review the company's cancer drug called Erbitux. (If she'd sold after the FDA announcement, it would have cost her $43,000.)

Stewart denies any wrongdoing, but the heat keeps rising. Just days after the congressional committee investigating ImClone seemed to be backing away from Martha, Merrill Lynch last week abruptly put her broker on leave. Investigators, who hope to interview Bacanovic on Thursday or Friday, now say they are specifically targeting the nature of his conversation with Martha on Dec. 27 for evidence that she knew more about ImClone's fate than she's saying. For politicians eager to make a show of frying high-profile CEOs, they may be closer to reeling in a very big fish.

But *l'affaire* Martha isn't just about ImClone. It has also pulled back the crushed-velvet curtain on the clubby world of New York's social elite, a place where the rich and powerful pass around insider business gossip as readily as the help passes out smoked-salmon canapés. With post-Enron investors already questioning the fairness of the marketplace, Stewart's case is the most visible reminder yet that folks on the inside get richer while the rest of us watch our 401(k)s shrivel. And that's put Martha smack in the middle of the one thing in the world she hates the most—a mess.

The irony is that, for a brief, shining moment, it seemed like people were getting tired of bashing Martha Stewart. The latest tell-all book, *Martha, Inc.*, got lousy reviews and faded after a few weeks. *Saturday Night Live* parodied her only twice this season. One skit made her look downright heroic, with the *SNL* Martha stitching a needlepoint napkin that read SUCK IT, OSAMA. Even the bankruptcy of Kmart, where Stewart has been selling her housewares since 1997, didn't bruise her for long. We'd finally come to accept her. She was tough. She was a survivor. Time and time again, Martha had been given lemons, and she'd always found a way to make sparkling ginger-plum lemonade.

This time, she may need a heavy-duty juicer. The case against Martha will come down to what she knew about ImClone, when she knew it and, most important, how she got the information. Just before Stewart dumped her stock in December, ImClone was a very hot company. Erbitux, a miracle cancer drug that was its primary product, had already appeared on the cover of *BusinessWeek*, and the FDA had accelerated its process for approving it. But suddenly, something went wrong. On Dec. 26, Waksal learned that the government found the Erbitux clinical trials to be inadequate, and it wouldn't be approved after all. According to congressional investigators, the next day Waksal attempted to sell 72,000 shares before news of the FDA's decision broke. When ImClone's lawyers stopped him, he allegedly attempted to give his shares to his daughter Aliza, but was again blocked. (Aliza has refused to comment.) Nonetheless, she unloaded her own 39,472 shares on the morning of Dec. 27 for $2.5 million. Not coincidentally, Aliza's broker was also Bacanovic. Just hours after he is believed to have executed her sales, he spoke to Stewart. If the daughter of the CEO was bailing out, surely Bacanovic knew there was trouble, right? And wouldn't he have wanted to pass along that information to Stewart? "He's the one that's either going to blow this thing wide open or put it to bed in terms of Martha Stewart," says Ken Johnson, a spokesman for the House committee. Bacanovic could not be reached, and Merrill Lynch has refused to comment.

It's often said that New York is actually a very small town, and nowhere is that more true than at the tippy-top of the social ladder. In the world of black-tie parties and nonstop charity events, executive musings are what make for idle cocktail chatter, at least after the guests finish gossiping about who just had another face-lift. "A lot of information is being passed amongst each other just for reasons of talking," says David Patrick Columbia, editor in chief of NewYorkSocialDiary.com. "They don't even think of it as insider information." In fact, while stockbrokers usually require the little people to fill out a written order to automatically sell a stock when it reaches a predetermined price, that's not always the case with the Park Avenue crowd. "Sometimes verbally he would say, 'We should sell this when it gets to a certain point,' and I don't remember any paperwork," says Patrick McMullan, who is something of the official photographer to New York society, as well as a client of Bacanovic's. "Sometimes there would be an order written, but sometimes he'd say, 'Look, I'll call.'"

And Stewart, Waksal and Bacanovic travel in an especially small social circle. Waksal actually came to know Martha through her daughter, Alexis, whom he once dated, even though Alexis is now 36 and Waksal is 54. Martha and Waksal often talk on the phone as early as 6 A.M.

She designed the kitchen in his palatial Manhattan loft. He treats her like the royalty she sometimes appears to think she is. Two years ago Waksal asked Martha to be the guest of honor at the annual gala at the New York Council for the Humanities, which he chairs. The guest of honor traditionally has made a significant contribution to the humanities, which, despite her tireless efforts to promote the importance of handmade paper, does not really apply to Martha. "The response by people invited to the benefit," says someone affiliated with the organization, "was close to incredulity."

Then again, Waksal is famous for over-the-top gestures. His 5,000-square-foot apartment is littered with paintings by Picasso, de Kooning, Rothko and Bacon—$20 million in art. He hosts a monthly salon, inviting dozens of people to hear an artist or writer discuss his work. And his Christmas parties are lavish and legendary. The guests (Mick Jagger showed up last year) are always A-list. So A-list that two years ago, some high-priced call girls managed to slip through the front door. This year Waksal had someone checking names, though, presumably, they didn't bother with Martha. When she breezed through the door, the buzz from the roomful of politicos and power brokers grew noticeably quieter. Waksal abruptly stopped his conversation and walked over to her. For a brief moment, his head touched Martha's softly.

Even though he is more of an employee than a peer, Bacanovic, 40, was a full-fledged member of the Waksal-Stewart universe. He's accompanied Martha on photo shoots for her magazine (though it's Waksal whose picture turned up in a spread last year about her backyard birthday party). Bacanovic has been friends with Alexis Stewart for more than 20 years and was the person who helped introduce her to Waksal, when Bacanovic was the director of business development at ImClone in the early '90s. Perhaps just as important, he shares with Stewart (born Martha Kostyra, to a working-class Polish family in New Jersey) and Waksal (the child of two Holocaust survivors who got a Ph.D. in immunology from Ohio State) the tireless desire to climb the social ladder. Bacanovic delights in telling people that he lives in the town house used to shoot the exteriors for *Breakfast at Tiffany's*. Bacanovic has also made a name for himself as a "walker," a single man who often escorts well-heeled older women to social functions. Even rarer in that rare breed, he actually insists on paying his own way. "Peter Bacanovic is one of my dearest friends," says Nan Kempner, widely considered to be the grande dame of New York high society. "He is probably the most honest, conscientious, generous, kind, sweet, wonderful, intelligent person I know. I just can't believe that he has done anything scandalous." Though he can be a tad shallow. When he was interviewed for an interior-design book called *Bright Young Things*, he was asked, "What to your mind would be the greatest of misfortunes?" His answer: "For one's child to predecease you and male-pattern baldness."

For Martha, the greatest misfortune may be that the scandal comes when her own company is thriving. Martha Stewart Living Omnimedia is performing so well, Martha's just brought out her own line of linoleum. (Who knew Martha even approved of linoleum?) The question is whether Stewart's company can keep up that steam in the middle of a PR storm. The stock is down 16 percent since news broke of her involvement with ImClone (Martha's personal hit on her 31 million shares: $94 million). More than most corporations, Stewart's is unusually sensitive to criticism because her image and the business are so closely entwined. But not everyone thinks that bad Martha publicity will hurt—after all, it's hardly new. "There's a love-hate thing with Martha. You always hear negative stories," says Laura Richardson, an analyst for Adams, Harkness Hill. In Bedford, N.Y., where Stewart is building yet another home, folks are still talking about how she brought homemade chocolate-chip cookies to win over the zoning board, only to insult her neighbors by saying she wanted to enlarge her barn to block the view of the ugly property across the street. Still, says Richardson, "most readers don't care about that. They accept her for what she is." What about stockholders? "If this turns out to be a temporary problem, the stock will weather it," she says. "If it means Martha can't be on TV anymore— well, that would be a crippling blow."

At the moment, the chances of Martha's going to prison are unlikely, though cartoonists are already having a field day imaging how she'd spruce up her jail cell. To be convicted of insider trading, Stewart would have to know both that she was acting on insider information when she sold the ImClone stock and that the person who gave her the information was trying to illegally tip her off. Considering that Waksal said he didn't talk to her on Dec. 27, he's probably not a source of trouble. It's more likely that Bacanovic deduced that ImClone was sinking and acted accordingly. "If Martha Stewart was tipped off, we always thought it was from her broker," says a congressional investigator. "If Bacanovic was tipped by Aliza, he probably called his A-list clients. That's the way this jet-set crowd works." But Martha—who worked as a stockbroker in the '70s—would still have had to know she was acting on insider information, and no one has asserted that she did. "I haven't heard anything more than fairly weak, circumstantial evidence against Martha Stewart," says Jack Coffee, a professor at Columbia Law School.

But this is Martha Stewart, the woman who insists that visitors outside her house walk in a prescribed direction so the grass will wear evenly. She is not leaving anything to chance. Last week, just as the Energy and Commerce Committee was poring over her records, *Martha Stewart Living* broadcast an episode featuring Billy Tauzin, the congressman leading the ImClone investigation. Talk about amazing timing—or was it? In fact, the Tauzin segment, in which the congressman cooks gumbo with Martha, first ran a year ago. Oh, and by the way, Tauzin's segment also featured him promoting his own book. Its title: *Cook and Tell*.

UPDATE

In October, Douglas Faneuil, Peter Bacanovic's assistant, pled guilty to a misdemeanor charge of receiving money and other valuables as a consideration for "not informing." Court papers said that Faneuil had been given a week's extra vacation, a free airline ticket, and an increase in his commission rate for deceiving investigators. Although the court papers did not name Martha Stewart, referring only to a "tippee" who sold ImClone stock after being tipped off that Sam Waksal was trying to dump his stock, the details of the sale—the "tippee" sold 3,928 shares on December 27, just as Stewart did—left no doubt that Faneuil was implicating her. Just after the plea was entered, Merrill Lynch announced it had fired Faneuil and Bacanovic. Stewart has not been charged with any crime, but the stock price of her company has been severely punished because of the fallout from the scandal, and in July the company's CFO said that the ImClone imbroglio was having a material effect on the company's actual business, hurting advertising sales in particular. In October, Stewart resigned from the New York Stock Exchange's board of directors, citing "the media attention currently surrounding me." —J.S.

QWEST'S RISE AND FALL

Lou Kilzer, David Milstead, and Jeff Smith

Rocky Mountain News, August 3, 2002

JOE NACCHIO WAS BARGAIN shopping on that Tuesday in January 2001.

At $45 a share, Qwest's stock was undervalued, making it a great deal for the company's stockholders, said Qwest's chief executive officer. So he was buying back 22 million shares for the company, spending nearly $1 billion.

Was it a manifestation of Nacchio's unflagging enthusiasm about Qwest's future, his absolute certainty that Qwest would be the one telco to prevail in a marketplace littered with obstacles? Or an attempt to prop up the stock's price?

Whichever it was—and Qwest now concedes that accounting errors were helping to bolster the Denver company's bottom line, and by extension its stock price, during this period—Nacchio wasn't adding Qwest stock to his own portfolio at that bargain-basement price.

He was selling.

During January, both before and after his buy-back announcement on Jan. 16, Nacchio sold 799,467 shares, raking in $32 million.

It was a pattern repeated by Nacchio and some of his key lieutenants time and again during the three-year period from 1999 through 2001.

Nacchio publicly touted Qwest's impressive growth projections while he and others sold hundreds of thousands of shares of Qwest stock, records show. They sold stock worth nearly a half-billion dollars during that period; Nacchio alone sold about $250 million.

Now, Nacchio is gone, ousted by Qwest's board on June 16. His replacement, Richard Notebaert, is trying to negotiate a settlement with the Securities and Exchange Commission, which is investigating the company's accounting practices. And an avalanche of accusations by Wall Street analysts, government regulators and furious investors swirls around Qwest.

The *Rocky Mountain News*, using documents and records as well as public comments made by Qwest to shareholders, reporters and analysts, has assembled a timeline that traces the public and private events during a period that is now the subject of such hot dispute.

INTENSE, DRIVEN NACCHIO PUSHED QWEST TO NEXT LEVEL

Salomon Smith Barney's Jack Grubman, an influential telecom analyst and deal-broker during the industry's go-go years, was riding high in 1996 when he told Denver tycoon Philip Anschutz: "I bet I could get you Joe Nacchio."

Anschutz was looking for the spark that could get Qwest, his fledgling fiber-optic communication company, to the next level.

He would find that entrepreneurial spark in Nacchio.

The grandson of Italian immigrants and son of a bartender, Nacchio had worked for 26 years at the stately old-economy firm of AT&T.

But Nacchio, who had just lost his chance to head Ma Bell, was not the laid-back corporate insider that his background suggested. At 47 years old, he had the intense drive and confidence—some would later call it arrogance—that Anschutz sought.

Anschutz had spent about $1 billion to build Qwest. But he knew he needed to take his company public to finance the next big push, building out its nationwide fiber-optic network.

When that happened in June 1997, Nacchio was at the helm.

Five years later, Anschutz would stand as Qwest's biggest winner and arguably its biggest loser. Over that time, he reaped a billion-dollar profit. But he sat still while his remaining 300 million shares lost more than $18 billion in value from Qwest's peak of $64 a share on March 3, 2000. Qwest's stock sold for $1.58 a share on Friday.

The actions of Qwest insiders during the company's wild ride have caught the interest of investors and investigators.

At the head of the list is the brassy New Yorker who ran the show—Joe Nacchio.

AFTER TWO STOCK SPLITS, NACCHIO AMASSED 12 MILLION STOCK OPTIONS

Qwest was hot.

When its stock debuted on June 24, 1997, it jumped from $22 to $28 the first day.

The 27 percent gain was just the beginning, Nacchio promised.

"We see almost an unlimited future," he told reporters. "The network we're building is state-of-the-art."

Little-noted at the time were the 3 million stock options Anschutz had granted Nacchio—a number that would quadruple, to 12 million, as Qwest's shares skyrocketed and the stock split twice.

Each year, 20 percent of Nacchio's options "vested"—or became available for sale. So on every Dec. 31, starting in 1997, Nacchio had 2.4 million stock options to exercise. And from the beginning, he used the options—immediately selling the Qwest stock he received.

In 1998, he sold 1,131,098 shares—nearly half his available options—netting $15.6 million. In each of the following two years, he exercised slightly more than half the options available to him.

By the time he stopped selling in May 2001, Nacchio had cashed in 7.36 million options, earning pretax profits of $248 million. He kept roughly 500,000 of those shares, choosing to sell the other 6.8 million shares of stock on the open market.

"I don't know if it's a fast clip or not a fast clip," Nacchio's lawyer, Charles Stillman, said of the stock sales. "But the fact of the matter is any sales of the stock that he made were done appropriately, were done after consultation with appropriate counsel. He did it right.

"He had the legal right to sell his stock. He did it carefully, he did it thoughtfully and he did what any rational person would do whose assets were so tied up in one place. He lightened his position."

SPECULATIVE SALES RECORDED ON BOOKS, INVESTORS ALLEGE

By December 1999, Nacchio was overseeing Qwest's furious growth curve. The stock, which had already split twice, was trading in the $40 range. (For comparison, the splits made the IPO price of $22 equal to $5.50—the exercise price on Nacchio's options.)

Six months earlier, Qwest had announced its intent to acquire US West, the Denver Baby Bell that Nacchio called stodgy and in need of new blood. Qwest also announced it was hiring a new auditor—Arthur Andersen.

In November, the fast-moving Qwest announced an initial public offering of its European fiber-optic network partner, KPNQwest.

Nacchio was winning praise from all corners. Lew Wilks, a Qwest executive, said his boss was a cross between Gen. George Patton and India's Mahatma Gandhi.

Nacchio did his best to downplay the accolades.

"This isn't my company," he said in an interview. "This is a public company owned by public shareowners. I am the steward for their fiduciary rights."

But according to an investor lawsuit filed in 2001, his stewardship was already slipping. Investors charge that Qwest's "flashing" of projected revenue had begun in 1999 to distort the company's books. Rather than wait for invoices to be sent and products shipped—the standard criteria for recognizing sales as revenue—Qwest was recording unconfirmed or speculative "flash" sales in its financial statements, the plaintiffs allege.

What is certain is that Nacchio was accelerating his sales of Qwest stock.

In 1999, Nacchio gained more than $64 million from stock options. He earned $2.65 million in other compensation.

No one seemed to mind. These were the halcyon days and Joe Nacchio was leading the way.

Qwest was predicting revenue growth of 37 percent to 42 percent and said EBITDA (earnings before interest, taxes, depreciation and amortization) would leap by up to 75 percent.

CONTROVERSIAL KMC TELECOM DEAL WASN'T DISCLOSED FOR A YEAR

It was a new millennium. And in February 2000, Nacchio declared Qwest to be "the new Internet communications company of the next decade."

Nacchio sold 100,000 shares on Valentine's Day for $4,874,690. Four days later, he sold another 100,000 shares, for $5,005,940.

Barely a month later, the stock market began its long painful rupture.

March was also the month that Qwest entered into a controversial deal with a company called KMC Telecom Holdings Inc. Qwest sold $134 million of telecom equipment to KMC. In return, KMC would provide communications services to Qwest through 2004. The revenue from the sale was booked up front and the Internet services being provided were those that Qwest is in the business of providing itself. Qwest didn't disclose the deal until 2001.

At the end of June, the merger with US West was finalized, creating a company with a market capitalization of $85 billion. Qwest said it expected uninterrupted growth of 15 percent to 17 percent a year through 2005.

Two trading days later, Qwest stock hit $59.88—up from the $42.19 it traded at on June 1.

On July 17, there was still more good news. Qwest had beaten analysts' expectations for the second quarter.

Nacchio's stock sales immediately increased, measuring $5,500,000, $1,850,000 and $4,975,000 before the end of the month.

In August, the pace quickened again. Nacchio sold $28 million in stock during the first eight days of the month, while the stock was trading in the $50 range.

In September, Qwest announced that it had beat the Street for both revenue and EBITDA. Unfortunately, not everyone would share in the company's progress. About 4,500 employees would be laid off.

"We are relentlessly pursuing growth," said Nacchio.

A few days later, Qwest again said it would beat Wall Street estimates for the third quarter.

The investors' lawsuit charges that some of that apparent growth came through a third-quarter "capacity swap" of some $230 million.

The swaps were one of two controversial ways Qwest accounted for capacity sales.

In the swaps—which Qwest now calls "contemporaneous capacity transactions"—the company sold rights to capacity on its network to another telco while buying capacity from the same company at about the same time. The companies exchanged some cash with each swap.

With the cash exchange, and for other technical reasons, Qwest argues that it didn't violate a prohibition on swapping assets and booking revenue and profits from the deals. The Securities and Exchange Commission is not so sure.

Qwest also was booking revenue up front from long-term capacity leases on its network, a practice in contrast with nearly every other company in the telecom industry. Most other companies spread out the revenue over the life of the multiyear deals. In a 20-year deal, this technique allowed Qwest to show 80 times the revenue in one quarter that a competitor with a similar deal would have booked.

The effect of these two accounting practices—approved by the Andersen auditors—was to goose Qwest's revenue growth rate every quarter. But investors from Wall Street to Main Street were largely unaware of the extent of Qwest's capacity sales and the way it accounted for them.

By the end of October, Qwest announced that it would meet or exceed estimates for revenue and EBITDA through 2005 and said its KPNQwest investment was "succeeding in Europe as it was taking market share from existing players that were having financial problems."

In a meeting before analysts at Manhattan's Waldorf Astoria, a Qwest executive said, according to the investor lawsuit, that even as other telecom companies had problems and reported disappointing results, Qwest would report continued growth and would survive the downturn.

Qwest still was trading in the high $40 range.

During the next 17 days, Nacchio sold 425,000 shares for $19.2 million.

But trouble was on the horizon by December.

On Dec. 20, 2000, Qwest stock was down to $32.12. The next day, Nacchio came out slugging. Insisting that Qwest would meet or beat projections, he said his company was different from the others.

"Qwest believes it is not having the same problems announced by several competitors because Qwest has newer assets, a lower cost position and a product line targeted to capitalize on the high-growth sectors of the industry," Nacchio said.

Investors claim that part of Qwest's bottom line was improved by another $250 million swap booked in the fourth quarter.

NACCHIO SAYS HE SHOULD MAKE MORE THAN "SECOND BASEMAN"

By January 2001, Qwest's stock had staged a small rally, climbing back to the mid-$40s. Even then, Nacchio said it was undervalued, announcing the 22 million–share repurchase from Bell South.

The company repeatedly assured Wall Street that it was on track to make projections.

In an April 24 press release, Qwest emphasized pro forma profits of $218 million for its first quarter 2001, and $2 billion in earnings before interest, taxes, depreciation and amortization.

It was only in a line item in an attachment that Qwest disclosed that it had lost $46 million under generally accepted accounting principles, known as GAAP.

The shareholder lawsuit says that the loss came despite $425 million in what it alleges were improper swaps.

By late April, Qwest's stock was heading down, never again to see the salad days of $40-plus per share.

And Nacchio continued to sell. In April, he sold $43 million worth of stock, followed by $21 million in May.

On May 1, Nacchio faced stockholders, some of whom were wary of his compensation. Nacchio had sold $93,454,000 worth of stock in 2000. He'd made $4,222,000 in other compensation.

He wasn't blushing.

"I know these are big numbers," he told reporters in a press briefing before the meeting. "I'm neither apologizing for it nor embarrassed by it. I should be allowed to make more than a second baseman. I create more economic value than they do."

Nacchio announced that he was going to sell 675,000 shares, beginning in June. But that didn't happen. In fact, May 31, 2001, was the last known date that Nacchio traded Qwest stock.

Company insiders speculate that Nacchio thought he could get a better price in the future.

But Nacchio was still upbeat in public. He said the overcapacity that was tripping up other telcos wouldn't hurt his company.

"I continue to be amazed that people don't get the fact that there are radical differences between our product lines as compared to some of the start-ups who came into business with imperfect business models and who are now failing," he said on June 19, 2001.

The next day, a team of Morgan Stanley analysts dropped a bombshell.

They said Qwest had boosted income after its merger with US West by "quietly" writing down $2.1 billion of assets, calculating a higher pension fund investment return and spreading hundreds of millions of dollars of software costs over a number of years. Morgan Stanley also said Qwest was likely to write down the value of its investment in KPN-Qwest.

Nacchio was furious. He took the unusual step of publicly attacking a major Wall Street investment bank. He called the report "hogwash" and said "innuendos on our integrity are not going to be tolerated."

But in July, Qwest wrote down $3.1 billion in its KPNQwest investment, giving Qwest a record second-quarter loss of $3.3 billion. Qwest said it had planned the write-down before the Morgan Stanley report.

And in August, as Qwest shares settled into the mid-$20 range, Qwest filed an amended annual report, noting that its 2000 earnings benefited from a pension credit of $299 million. Qwest, in response to the investor lawsuit, maintained that it had made timely disclosure.

Meanwhile, Nacchio was continuing the fight. On Aug. 8, he spoke at a Piper Jaffray investment conference. An outline of his presentation was sent to the SEC.

There is little doubt that Nacchio was effusive. These are some of the speech notes contained in the outline:

"Highest growth rate of any large cap telecom."

"DSL growth 100%."

"Qwest revenue growth continues to lead the industry."

"Total revenue growth more than 2x closest competitor."

But once-hidden troubles began bubbling to the surface.

Nacchio was now publicly addressing the swaps, which he placed under the heading of "nonrecurring revenue."

The outline said these are "not news to industry," and "always will be part of all companies' revenue."

What was news, though, was the disclosure in the company's second-quarter report to the SEC on Aug. 15 that fiber-optic capacity sales accounted for $430 million in the quarter. These deals—hated by Wall Street because they're one-time sales, not recurring revenue—made the difference between industry-leading double-digit growth and far more modest single-rate growth.

Morgan Stanley pounced again, with a follow-up report that said they had serious doubts—based on this new information—that Qwest could sustain the high-flying revenue growth it was promising. Two other analysts, both from smaller firms, backed Morgan Stanley; one, Drake Johnstone of Virginia's Davenport & Co., cut Qwest stock three notches to "sell."

Salomon Smith Barney's Jack Grubman, who had hooked up Anschutz and Nacchio, maintained his "buy" rating until March 2002.

On Sept. 10, 2001, Qwest warned Wall Street that it was lowering revenue projections for 2001 and had suspended projections for 2002. Five thousand more jobs were cut.

The company cited "deteriorating economic conditions, a decrease in consumer confidence, the rate of growth in access lines, and changes in the terms and conditions of optical capacity sales."

Qwest stock traded as low as $16.28, but managed to close the day at $19.90.

A relentless decline had set in.

At the end of September—on the last day of the quarter—Qwest and Enron entered into a $500 million swap agreement.

Qwest signed a deal to pay Enron $308 million for assets that included dark fiber, or not-yet-activated capacity, on a secondary route from Salt Lake City to New Orleans. Qwest already was showing the route as part of its nationwide network.

In exchange, Enron agreed to pay Qwest $195.5 million for optical wavelength services over a 25-year period.

Qwest and Enron exchanged checks for about $112 million, and Qwest immediately booked revenue of $86 million for its third quarter.

The transaction came at a time of an industry glut, when such capacity could be bought cheaply on the spot market.

And the questionable deal still wasn't enough to keep Qwest out of the red.

On Oct. 31, Qwest reported flat revenues and an unexpected $142 million quarterly loss.

Even so, Nacchio said in a press release "we continue to be the model to which the industry will eventually evolve."

He was still steaming about the Morgan Stanley report.

He told the *News* in November that "Morgan Stanley analysts aren't the sharpest knives in the drawer, either. That's their problem."

Asked if analysts were right when they said Qwest was boosting revenue through aggressive accounting, Nacchio snapped: "Well, analysts who believe that need to go back to school and learn accounting. This is the craziest thing I've heard."

By the end of the year, Qwest said it would not book "nonrecurring revenue" in 2002. It also said it was freezing salaries.

In 2001, Qwest had booked fiber-optic capacity sales and swaps totaling approximately $1.1 billion.

CASH CRUNCH IN 2002 SENDS QWEST SCRAMBLING FOR CASH

This year, the cash crunch came. In February, Qwest was shut out of the commercial paper, or short-term loan, markets and in March had to scramble to renegotiate its $4 billion line of credit to avoid a possible bank default.

A lawsuit against Global Crossing revealed another swap transaction with Qwest and criticized the way Qwest represented it on its balance sheet.

Qwest announced in March that it was under SEC investigation for its fiber-optic capacity sales, equipment sales and its Dex directory publishing accounting. It also announced a new agreement with banks that could keep the company afloat.

At the end of April, Qwest announced a quarterly loss of $698 million, up from a loss of $46 million the previous year.

And on June 16, 2002, Joe Nacchio was fired. During his 5½ years in Denver, he'd made more than $300 million in option profits and compensation including a $10.5 million severance payment.

UPDATE

On July 28 Qwest announced it had improperly accounted for up to $1.16 billion in optical sales revenue over three years, the same years during which Joseph Nacchio was selling tens of millions of dollars in Qwest stock. The company also said it would restate its financial results, but said the improper accounting was the result of a mistake, and not fraud. In September, worries over its accounting forced the company to withdraw its FCC application to reenter the long-distance market in nine states. Qwest is now under investigation by the Justice Department, the SEC, and the House Energy and Commerce Committee, which said the company was dragging its feet on producing documents the committee had requested.

In late September, New York Attorney General Eliot Spitzer filed a civil suit against both Nacchio and Qwest's former chairman, Philip Anschutz. Spitzer claims that Nacchio made a million dollars and Anschutz five million dollars selling cheap IPO shares that the investment bank Salomon Smith Barney had given them in order to convince them to give Salomon Smith Barney Qwest's investment-banking business. Spitzer is seeking the disgorgement of the millions in IPO profits, as well as additional millions that Anschutz and Nacchio made by selling Qwest shares, which Spitzer claims were artificially inflated by Salomon Smith Barney's pumping of the company's stock. Nacchio's attorney denied that the IPO allocations had anything to do with any decision to employ Salomon as an investment banker for Qwest.   —J.S.

FORMER TYCO EXECUTIVES ARE CHARGED

Mark Maremont and Jerry Markon

The Wall Street Journal, September 13, 2002

NEW YORK PROSECUTORS CHARGED Tyco International Ltd.'s former chief executive, L. Dennis Kozlowski, and its former chief financial officer, Mark H. Swartz, with stealing more than $170 million from the company, and accused them of running a "criminal enterprise" aimed at defrauding investors.

Manhattan District Attorney Robert M. Morgenthau charged the two executives with numerous counts of grand larceny, enterprise corruption and falsifying business records. Mr. Morgenthau also charged Messrs. Kozlowski and Swartz with illegally obtaining a total of more than $400 million by selling Tyco shares while concealing information from investors about executive compensation and loans. They could each face a maximum of 30 years in jail.

Mark A. Belnick, the company's former general counsel, was separately charged with six counts of falsifying business records, and faces as many as four years in prison.

The indictment, and a related civil complaint filed by the Securities and Exchange Commission, allege that Mr. Kozlowski siphoned money from the company for personal uses, including to buy yachts and fine art, to build a mansion for himself in Florida, and to buy a $5 million estate on the Massachusetts island of Nantucket. Mr. Swartz similarly used company funds improperly to buy a yacht and invest in real estate, among other things, the SEC said. A front-page article by *The Wall*

Street Journal last month detailed a pattern of unauthorized use of Tyco funds by Mr. Kozlowski dating back to 1997.

The Manhattan district attorney obtained a restraining order from a state judge, unsealed Thursday, temporarily freezing $600 million in assets owned by Messrs. Kozlowski and Swartz. A hearing will be held on that proceeding on September 24.

The indictment represents a marked escalation in the Tyco scandal that began in June with the indictment of Mr. Kozlowski on charges of conspiring to evade $1 million in sales tax on art purchases. Mr. Kozlowski resigned from Tyco the day before that indictment, and Mr. Belnick was fired in June. Mr. Swartz left the company in August.

Mr. Kozlowski "looted the company by granting himself and others excessive compensation, including bonuses, without regard for restrictions put on compensation by the board of directors," prosecutors said. At a news conference, Mr. Morgenthau said it was unfortunate the defendants weren't caught sooner, but expressed confidence that the severity of the charges would deter others. "I hope that a number of corporate officers aren't going to sleep well tonight," he said.

All three defendants pleaded not guilty in State Supreme Court in Manhattan. "These charges are exactly that—they're accusations, and they are unproven," Mr. Kozlowski's lawyer, Stephen Kaufman, said. "When they are aired in their entirety, they will prove to be unfounded." Charles Stillman, a lawyer for Mr. Swartz, said his client "is going to answer these charges, and I tell you he is going to be acquitted at the end of the day." An attorney for Mr. Belnick, Robert Katzberg, declined to comment after the hearing. The three men were released, but were ordered to post bonds by Thursday. Mr. Kozlowski is required to post $100 million, Mr. Swartz $50 million, and Mr. Belnick $1 million.

Although some Tyco shareholders were glad that charges were confined to former executives, others said the apparent extent of the chicanery raised new questions about the reliability of Tyco's accounting under Messrs. Kozlowski and Swartz. "In all my years of following companies, when executives are stealing money they're also cooking the books," said Marc Cohodes of Rocker Partners LLC, a hedge fund that is shorting Tyco's stock, or betting on its decline. Mr. Kozlowski served as CEO from 1992 until he resigned in June.

Tyco, which has been seeking to distance itself from Mr. Kozlowski, on Thursday filed a civil lawsuit against him seeking to recover more than $100 million it claims he misappropriated. The company also announced the nomination of five new directors to its 11-person board, and said its board had voted not to support the re-election of any of the nine Kozlowski-era directors at its annual meeting in March. Tyco, which is registered in Bermuda, is an industrial conglomerate with roughly $35 billion in annual revenue.

In a sign of a boardroom rift, three Tyco directors dissented from the 8-3 board vote and said they have hired an attorney to explore whether the wholesale replacement of the board is in accord with proper corporate-governance procedures. The three—Wendy Lane, Stephen Foss and Richard Bodman—believe directors did nothing wrong, and were duped by Mr. Kozlowski and other executives.

"It looks like the directors were asleep, but we were not," said Ms. Lane, adding that she knows of no board—including Enron Corp.'s—that has been totally replaced. She argues that it isn't good for such a complex company as Tyco for the entire board and top management team to be replaced within a few months.

A person close to the directors who voted for the majority plan called that argument "ridiculous," and pointed out that Mr. Foss was head of Tyco's compensation committee, while Mr. Bodman was a member of its audit committee. "Look what happened to the company while they were in charge," this person said.

Tyco said it doesn't believe at this point that any material adjustments to its prior financial statements will be required. Still, a Tyco spokesman said that to reassure shareholders, newly appointed CEO Edward Breen recently ordered an in-depth review of the company's past accounting practices, which is scheduled to be finished in "late fall."

The complaints by New York prosecutors and the SEC focus on compensation and loans granted to Messrs. Kozlowski and Swartz without board approval. From 1997 to 2002, the SEC said Mr. Kozlowski improperly borrowed $242 million from a Tyco program intended to help executives pay taxes on restricted-stock grants. Instead of using the funds for that purpose, Mr. Kozlowski spent the money on yachts, fine art, estate jewelry and luxury apartments. Mr. Swartz similarly used $72 million in loans from the program for personal investments and business ventures, the SEC said.

Messrs. Kozlowski and Swartz also borrowed a total of $78 million from Tyco for real-estate "relocation" loans that weren't in accord with Tyco policies, the SEC said. Mr. Kozlowski used the money to build a mansion in Florida and to buy a $5 million estate in Nantucket for himself, and to buy a $7 million New York apartment for his first wife, whom he since has divorced. Mr. Swartz used some of the funds to buy a yacht and invest in real estate, the SEC said.

Rather than repay all of these borrowings, the Tyco executives allegedly found various ways to get Tyco to forgive huge sums, without board approval or disclosure to shareholders. In 1999, for example, the two executives simply wiped clean $25 million in loans to Mr. Kozlowski and $12.5 million in loans to Mr. Swartz, the SEC claimed. The SEC also alleges that Tyco purchased one of Mr. Kozlowski's New Hampshire houses for $4.5 million, or three times its market value, without disclosure to shareholders.

The SEC also charged that Messrs. Kozlowski and Swartz covered up some of their unauthorized compensation by directing subordinates at Tyco "to bury" the amounts in unrelated accounts, in one case by offsetting them against gains from the sale of a unit. In addition, New York prosecutors said Mr. Kozlowski had the company's internal auditors report to the board through himself, and "ensured they would not audit" a Tyco unit through which the loans and other payments were made.

Tyco's civil suit against Mr. Kozlowski also details an array of questionable conduct. Mr. Kozlowski, the company alleges, spent $700,000 of company funds for a personal investment in a movie, titled *Endurance*, and billed Tyco for $1.1 million for personal expenses including jewelry, clothing, wine and flowers.

The company also says the former chief executive spent $43 million of its money on charitable donations made in Mr. Kozlowski's name or to benefit him. One donation, of $1.3 million, went to a Nantucket conservation group to purchase land adjacent to Mr. Kozlowski's property to prevent development.

David Dreman of Dreman Value Management, which owns seven million Tyco shares, said of Mr. Kozlowski and other executives: "I'm a little dazed about how much money they siphoned off." But Mr. Dreman praised Tyco for taking steps to rid the company of directors tied to

Mr. Kozlowski and to try to recover money they believe he was improperly paid. "It seems to me to be almost a clean sweep," Mr. Dreman said.

UPDATE

Just days after prosecutors indicted the former Tyco executives, the company released a report showing just how adept Dennis Kozlowski and his cronies had been at lining their own pockets at shareholders' expense. Among the items for which Kozlowski had the company pick up the tab were a $6,000 shower curtain, a $2,200 wastebasket, and a $17,100 traveling toilette box. In 2000, Kozlowski had Tyco give out $96 million in unapproved bonuses to select employees, with Kozlowski and former CFO Mark Swartz allegedly taking home $50 million. Kozlowski also had Tyco shell out $1 million to pay for his wife's birthday party in Sardinia. At press time, Kozlowski and Swartz were out on bail, awaiting trial.   —J.S.

HARDBALL

David McClintick

Forbes, March 4, 2002

HOW DO RESPECTABLE NAMES like Deloitte & Touche and Arthur Laffer get tangled up with a seedy outfit like Casmyn Corp?

Dazed after a 28-hour plane trip from Cape Town, South Africa to New York, Amyn Dahya looked forward to a comfortable limousine ride into Manhattan and a night's rest in the Park Central hotel before the next morning's board meeting of Casmyn Corp. Publicly held Casmyn was a money-losing gold-mining outfit Dahya had formerly headed and for which he now served as a director.

Dahya was met at Kennedy Airport that subfreezing afternoon in December 1999 by a short, bald man with a cell phone. The man escorted him to a limousine, where the driver secured Dahya's luggage in the trunk. But the driver, who was later dubbed with the unsettling nickname of "Benny the Enforcer," said they had to go to another terminal and "wait for another passenger."

The wait was nearly two hours, during which "Benny" allowed Dahya out of the car only once, to use a restroom. When he finally showed up, the other passenger turned out to be Richard Jacobson, then a partner in the renowned law firm of Fulbright & Jaworski, whose late leader, Leon Jaworski, had been Watergate special counsel in the Nixon impeachment investigation in the early 1970s.

Jacobson, who denies Dahya was held in the car against his will, got into the limo and announced that he had been retained as a special counsel for Casmyn. When they reached Manhattan, the bald man served Dahya with a subpoena and a package of legal papers, including a copy of a lawsuit about to be filed by Casmyn in U.S. Bankruptcy Court in Los Angeles accusing Dahya of fraud.

Jacobson instructed the nonplussed Dahya to report to Fulbright & Jaworski's New York office at 666 Fifth Avenue the next morning to be deposed. There would be no board meeting. Casmyn says a meeting had been scheduled but canceled for lack of a quorum. Dahya claims the board meeting was merely a ruse to lure him back to New York.

Born in Tanzania, Amyn Dahya, 44, is a Canadian citizen now living in Spain. Trained as a chemical engineer, he worked in the U.K. and Toronto for a British engineering firm for seven years before becoming a mining consultant and stock promoter. Along the way he also became a self-proclaimed "New Age prophet" and the author of two books on "self-awareness." An affable and charming huckster, Dahya is the kind of person who could sell shoes to snakes. During the ride in from the airport, even Jacobson was momentarily tempted to back a new oil-spill cleanup technology Dahya was flogging.

Probably a good thing he didn't. According to the lawsuit, since transferred to U.S. District Court in Los Angeles, Dahya has had a history of milking public companies through questionable stock promotion activities, including orchestrating a "pump and dump" scheme to swindle Casmyn and its shareholders. "You're a f—— thief and a mastermind criminal!" Casmyn's new chief executive Mark Zucker barked at Dahya during the deposition. The comment is contained in a private memorandum prepared by Dahya and obtained by *Forbes*. Zucker doesn't remember using those exact words, but the suit's harsh allegations are certainly consistent with the characterization.

In recent weeks, after nearly two years of nasty legal tussling, lawyers for Dahya and Casmyn have reached a tentative settlement. It calls for Casmyn's auditors, Deloitte & Touche, the U.S. arm of Deloitte Touche Tohmatsu, to pay Casmyn $2.3 million, and its law firm, Los Angeles–based Loeb & Loeb, to pay $900,000. The liability of the former management group, including Amyn Dahya, was set at $3.5 million, to be paid by a directors-and-officers-insurance carrier.

These are modest penalties in a world of billion-dollar debacles like Enron. But this is a tale of true corporate blood sport that has just about everything—and virtually no heroes. The story begins in March 1994, when Dahya acquired 2.4 million shares, or 74%, of Casmyn, with a $100,000 note. While he was acquiring Casmyn, Dahya was busily touting Auromar, a Canadian company he controlled, with interests in South African gold mines.

Auromar had been under investigation by the Royal Canadian Mounted Police and the Vancouver Stock Exchange on suspicion of failing to disclose material information and making misleading statements. Over a period of 22 months Auromar stock rose from 23 cents to $7, then fell to $4.60 just before the exchange halted trading on Dec. 1, 1994. Auromar was delisted Mar. 13, 1995.

Though Casmyn was based in Sparks, Nev., Dahya worked in a plush corner-office suite on the 18th floor of a Vancouver skyscraper overlooking the mountains. Under a giant painting of a dove, Dahya gave interviews not only about his businesses but also about his latest self-published book, *Reflections from the Origin*.

Dahya, who has referred to himself as a "humble servant, a speck of dust," once told a reporter he didn't so much "write" *Reflections* as "take dictation" from God. But Dahya's lifestyle was anything but humble. While drawing salary and bonuses totaling $2.2 million between 1994 and 1998 from Casmyn and related companies, Dahya ran up more than $1 million in questionable advances and expenses, the suit says.

These included ski vacations, first-class air tickets to luxury resorts for himself and various relatives, personal flying lessons and hundreds of thousands of dollars of cash advances never accounted for. Dahya concedes he sometimes put personal charges on a Casmyn credit card but says he always reimbursed the company.

Dahya packed the company and board with cronies, including his brother Hanif (Wally) Dahya, a Harvard M.B.A. who had been a partner at money manager Sandler O'Neill in Manhattan. Wally, also a defendant in the suit, was a director and a member of the audit committee. In a court filing, he denies any wrongdoing.

Another director, at least for nine months, was Arthur Laffer, the economic guru of the early Reagan Administration, who signed on in January 1997. In his resignation letter to Dahya, Laffer wrote: "I reluctantly have to conclude you're not taking any of the requirements of a public company and an outside board seriously."

At the time Laffer was a partner of Alexander Cappello, chief executive of the Cappello Group, a Los Angeles-based merchant bank that invested—and lost—$33 million in Casmyn preferred stock on behalf of investors, including most of the nation's leading gold funds.

"Arthur went on the board at my request," Cappello says. "This is the worst deal we've ever been involved with." Says Laffer: "The whole thing was terrible."

Part of what alarmed Laffer and Cappello was how Dahya had touted gold interests in Zimbabwe. In August 1996 Dahya pushed through a stock-swap merger with Auromar, whose shareholders received 1 share of Casmyn for every 2.6 shares of Auromar. This transaction secretly brought Dahya and his nominees holding Auromar shares up to $24 million in paper profits, the suit says. Dahya says that figure is inflated but won't say what his stake was.

The suit also claims part of the motivation for the merger was to remove Auromar from Canadian jurisdiction and thus stop a potential criminal investigation. And by having the merger authorized by a Canadian court, Dahya was able to legally sidestep filing a registration statement with the Securities and Exchange Commission, a process that presumably would have exposed Casmyn to inquiries relating to Auromar's regulatory troubles. Dahya says he wasn't trying to hide anything. Just following his lawyer's advice.

A year before, Dahya had entered into a personal transaction to buy gold at below-market prices from individuals in Ghana "of questionable reputation," according to the suit. The deal was a scam. Only a small amount of gold was ever delivered. The first shipment turned out to be a crate of yams; the second, a box of blue jeans. Dahya was on the hook.

In a second deal he arranged for Casmyn to advance, in multiple installments, "sometimes in cash in paper bags," the suit says, nearly $700,000 to the Ghanaian sellers. Casmyn had to write the expense off the next year as a special charge. The files relating to the Ghana contracts are missing, the company says. Dahya concedes he was duped, and that there was a write-off, but insists no money ever changed hands in paper bags.

How much gold did Casmyn really have after the Auromar merger? That depends on what you were reading. A Dec. 23, 1997 10-K filing with the SEC listed the firm's reserves at 500,000 ounces. The company's Web site cited 4.6 million ounces.

Why the discrepancy? "Geological models always change," says Dahya, who adds that he was getting conflicting information from his managers. Production costs for the first three months of 1997 were over $400 an ounce, but Dahya said they averaged below $190 in an Apr. 8, 1997 report to Manhattan-based Elliott Associates and five other firms that participated in a $20 million private placement of preferred stock. The money was supposed to be used solely for mining and exploration costs. Within a month of the offering Casmyn was using $5 million of the proceeds to buy up its stock.

Why? By May 1997 Casmyn stock was already down to $7 a share from its peak of $26 in November 1995. By February of 1998 it was down to 25 cents. No wonder. If there was lots of gold in Zimbabwe, Casmyn certainly wasn't mining or selling much of it profitably. After having earned a meager $47,000 in 1994, Casmyn lost $52 million over the next four years.

During this period Dahya used his offshore Bahamian accounts to sell off $1 million of Casmyn stock, buying a $60,000 Mercedes for himself and a $500,000 home in Reno, according to the suit; the Bahamian accounts allowed Dahya to dump his stock at a profit without creating an audit trail that would normally accompany significant insider stock sales. Dahya denies using offshore accounts for such purposes.

As Casmyn was cratering, the board increased his annual salary to $249,600 from $150,000 in January of 1998. His final act was to remove corporate files, furniture and art from the company's offices before fleeing to Spain in September 1998, the suit says. Dahya resigned as chief executive Oct. 1, 1998, but before leaving negotiated a one-year $100,000 "services agreement."

In 1999 a group of Los Angeles businessmen led by Zucker, a tough-talking bond trader who had run his own hedge fund, took over the management of Casmyn at the behest of creditors. Shortly after the services agreement ended, the company asked Dahya to New York for the "board meeting." Casmyn filed for bankruptcy Dec. 7, 1999. It emerged from bankruptcy on Apr. 11, 2000, and now trades over-the-counter as Aries Ventures.

During the deposition in Fulbright & Jaworski's offices on Dec. 10 and 11, 1999, Casmyn's new management wasn't exactly friendly. According to Dahya's written memorandum, Zucker told Dahya's brother: "What happens in this room will decide whether you and your family can go on with life or be crushed." Zucker flatly denies threatening Dahya in any way.

According to Dahya's version of events, Casmyn wanted to implicate the firm's former auditors and law firm in the alleged fraud. "We are interested in going after the deep pockets of Deloitte & Touche and Loeb & Loeb," his memo quotes Zucker as saying. Zucker refuses to comment on this.

But Dahya claims Zucker and Jacobson repeatedly stopped the deposition and demanded that he amend his answers to bolster the new management's interpretation of what happened. In Dahya's written account the deposition is characterized as "extortion, blackmail and mental and emotional abuse." The deposition is under court-ordered seal. The transcript, obtained by *Forbes*, shows 80 interruptions.

Dahya says he's now developing a consultancy to work on the oil-spill cleanup technology he tempted Jacobson with. Dahya says he is "ruined" and "must start over." But with Casmyn now behind him, he says "I have my wings, and I am soaring in the skies, like the eagle!"

UPDATE

Aries Ventures is still in business, trying to mine precious metals in Zimbabwe, Zambia, and South Africa. Amyn Dahya's whereabouts are unknown, but you can still purchase his book *Reflections from the Origin* at Amazon.com.   —J.S.

WATCH IT: IF YOU CHEAT, THEY'LL THROW MONEY!

David Leonhardt

The New York Times, June 9, 2002

THERE MAY BE ONLY one type of job in which somebody can commit a felony and, after being fired as a result, still receive a severance package worth many years of salary. The job is chief executive of a large corporation.

Over the last decade, many top executives have quietly persuaded their boards of directors to insert a remarkable set of protections into the executives' employment contracts. The contracts have made the executives nearly immune from dismissal, ensuring that they will receive millions of dollars when they leave their posts, under almost any circumstances.

In effect, the protections have reduced the risk in a job that the executives themselves describe as high-risk, high-reward.

Some contracts have gone so far as to restrict the kind of felony convictions that permit companies to deny executives a severance payment. At Fortune Brands, the maker of Jim Beam bourbon, Master Lock and other consumer products, for example, a felony must result in personal enrichment for Norman H. Wesley, the chief executive, at the expense of the company.

At J. C. Penney, a felony conviction would cost Allen I. Questrom his severance only if it involved "theft or moral turpitude." And before LG&E Energy, based in Louisville, Ky., was acquired by a British power company in 2000, it exempted its chief from good-cause dismissal for any felonies "arising from an environmental violation."

More broadly, executives have asked companies to remove contract clauses that could deny them severance payments, also known as golden parachutes, if they fail to perform their duties. In a sign of how much influence executives have gained over their own compensation, many companies have complied, inserting clauses that restrict dismissible offenses to deliberate misbehavior. "The scope of what constitutes cause has gotten narrower over the last 10 years," said Robert J. Stucker, a lawyer in Chicago who has represented Leo F. Mullin of Delta Air Lines, Robert L. Nardelli of Home Depot and other chief executives during contract negotiations.

"There is an understanding on both sides of the equation that you have to do something pretty bad for it to be constituted as cause," Mr. Stucker said.

CVS, Kellogg, Honeywell International and many other companies cite "willful gross misconduct," along with a conviction, as one of the only reasons they can fire an executive for good cause.

Executive employment contracts came to the fore last week after L. Dennis Kozlowski was indicted on charges that he failed to pay more than $1 million of New York sales taxes on paintings he had bought. At the board's request, Mr. Kozlowski resigned as chief of Tyco International, a conglomerate, forfeiting his contractual right to a severance payment that would have exceeded $120 million.

Had he chosen to fight the board, however, Mr. Kozlowski's contract might have given him room for an argument. The contract states that he could be fired for cause only if he were convicted of a felony that was "materially and demonstrably injurious to the company" and if three-quarters of the Tyco board then voted to oust him.

The board and Mr. Kozlowski will negotiate a new severance package after Tyco finishes its investigation into whether he used company money for personal expenses, a person close to the directors said.

Stephen E. Kaufman, Mr. Kozlowski's lawyer, declined to comment. Since 1999, Mr. Kozlowski has made more than $300 million in salary, bonus and sales of Tyco stock.

A growing number of investors, angered over the ways executives have protected themselves, have tried to restrain the size of golden parachutes, by introducing and voting for shareholder resolutions. But the effort is unlikely to have a big impact in the near future, analysts say.

Outside the executive suite, most employees work at the will of their employers and can lose their jobs for almost any reason. Many companies have a code of conduct mentioning broad ideals like integrity and responsibility, and violations of the code can result in termination.

"Generally, employees can be fired for anything—whim, the color of their shirt—other than discrimination," said Michael C. Harper, a professor of employment law at Boston University.

Even those workers covered by a collective bargaining agreement or a company policy that says they can lose their jobs only for a specific reason—the failure to do their job or a conviction, for instance—usually receive just a fraction of their annual pay as severance, if they get anything, lawyers said.

Top executives, by contrast, have increasingly received golden parachutes that pay a few times their highest annual compensation, including their bonus and sometimes even their proceeds from stock sales. Many packages also award large chunks of company stock. Jacques A. Nasser of Ford Motor, Jill E. Barad of Mattel and Durk I. Jager of Procter & Gamble are among the chief executives who have received millions of dollars in severance despite tenures widely considered to be failures.

The payouts typically produce a chorus of criticism from investors, but boards often had no choice at the time. Having agreed years earlier to narrow contract language, many boards locked themselves into giving these large severance packages to their chief executives.

Many analysts see the shifts in language as further evidence that the market for executive pay is largely devoid of the tension inherent in most negotiations. Corporate directors, whether out of desperation to hire someone they want or out of sympathy for someone with whom they have worked closely, often agree to executives' wishes. Many boards may give raises even in bad years and allow the executives to control much of their contract language.

As a result, not only has executive pay grown much more rapidly than other workers' salaries, but rules covering executive benefits like pensions and severance have also become more generous—even as they have become stricter for other employees.

For executives, "it is not unusual to see that 'for cause' equals felony, which is, of course, absurd," said Nell Minow, a co-founder of the Corporate Library, a research group in Washington that studies executive contracts. "There is just not another job in the world in which 'for cause' would not include not actually doing your job, or otherwise embarrassing the organization."

Ms. Minow added: "The reason we pay these people so much money is that it's a high-risk job. And in a high-risk job, if you don't perform, you should be out," without a large severance payment.

Albert J. Dunlap, the notorious former chief executive of the Sunbeam Corporation, is one of the few executives to be denied a severance payment by his board of directors. The board fired Mr. Dunlap in 1998, when a series of accounting scandals nearly caused the company's collapse.

Earlier this year, Mr. Dunlap and other former Sunbeam executives agreed to pay $15 million to settle a shareholder lawsuit accusing them of releasing misleading information. Mr. Dunlap is still in a legal fight with the company over millions of dollars in severance pay he is seeking.

Many compensation consultants and executives' lawyers contend that only an extreme case like Mr. Dunlap's should result in no golden parachute. They say that chief executives are recruited away from very appealing jobs and that they need to have some job security in their new positions.

"These contracts are negotiated on the way in, when everyone thinks the person is going to do a good job," said Jannice L. Koors, a vice president at Pearl Meyer & Partners, a compensation consulting firm in New York. "That's why they're hiring him."

Mr. Stucker said that broadly worded clauses about performance could allow a board to fire an executive arbitrarily and face little consequence. More specific contracts ensure that executives can be denied severance only if they clearly violate business norms, like not coming to work, abusing drugs or committing a crime directly related to the job.

"To say that all felonies are reason to terminate, I'm not sure about that," Mr. Stucker said. "You could say it reflects badly on the company. Well, yeah, so does divorce."

Clarkson Hine, a spokesman for Fortune Brands, said the language about felonies in Mr. Wesley's contract was also in previous chief executives' contracts at the company.

A spokeswoman for Jane C. Pfeiffer, an independent consultant who is the head of J. C. Penney's compensation committee, declined to comment on its chief executive's contract, as did a spokesman for LG&E Energy.

The contract of the current LG&E chief, Victor A. Staffieri, does not make an exception for environmental felonies, as the previous contract did. Instead, it makes almost the opposite exception.

Mr. Staffieri can be fired without severance only if he commits "repeated willful misconduct" or a felony in the course of his duties. The contract does not say if other felonies would be considered cause for dismissal without severance.

In the months since Enron's collapse, shareholders have tried to restrain the size of golden parachutes in ways they did not during the long bull market of the 90's. At more than 20 companies, including Boeing, Citigroup, General Electric, PepsiCo and Verizon Communications, investors have introduced resolutions this year to reduce future severance payments, according to the Investor Responsibility Research Center in Washington. Investors submitted 13 of these proposals last year.

In the balloting so far this year, the resolutions have received an average of 41 percent of shareholder votes, up from 32 percent last year.

For a simple reason, however, the votes are unlikely to make severance payments less common or contract language less narrow. Under current law, boards can ignore even most of the resolutions that pass.

Left to their own devices, directors seem more willing to listen to their executives' ideas than to their shareholders'.

THE ADELPHIA STORY

Devin Leonard

Fortune, August 12, 2002

DALE COWBURN WAS ALLERGIC to bee stings. He carried medication at all times in case he encountered an angry swarm. Last summer, however, while he was working in his barn, Cowburn was stung twice on the head. He had a heart attack and died on the spot.

The news traveled quickly through Coudersport, Pa., the town of 2,600 near the New York border where Cowburn had lived. One of the locals moved by his death was John Rigas, chairman and CEO of Adelphia Communications, the nation's sixth-largest cable television provider, a company with $3.6 billion in annual revenues and headquarters in—of all places—this rural town. Rigas knows about bees. He owns a farm outside town that sells Christmas trees, maple syrup, and honey. Soon after Cowburn's death, there was a knock on the door at his house. It was Rigas' beekeeper. He'd been sent to destroy the offending insects.

More than just the town's richest man, Rigas was a 76-year-old worth billions. He owned the Buffalo Sabres hockey team. He hobnobbed with Ted Turner. But the silver-haired cable mogul told people in a humble whisper that he was just a small-town guy who loved helping his neighbors. He sent busloads of children to Sabres games. He used Adelphia's corporate jet to fly ailing people to faith healers and cancer treatment centers.

Townspeople flocked to the Masonic temple every year for Adelphia's Christmas party. At last year's celebration there were two towering

Christmas trees, each decorated with 16,000 lights at the direction of John's wife, Doris. The Buffalo Philharmonic Orchestra played the Nutcracker Suite and Vaughan Williams' "Fantasia on 'Greensleeves.'" That was really something for a town like Coudersport. "Each December the Rigas family brings their world to us, and I am grateful," wrote a columnist in the local paper. "How many would have the opportunity to hear a symphony orchestra, were it not for their generosity?"

John Rigas was also revered in the cable business. He was one of the pioneers who had started stringing wires and urging customers to throw away their rabbit ears in the early 1950s. He was inducted into the Cable Television Hall of Fame last year. Colleagues praised him not just for his business accomplishments but for his good works in Coudersport. In a celebratory video, Decker Anstrom, CEO of the Weather Channel, said, "If there's one person I'd like my son to grow up to be, it would be John Rigas."

Then, in the blink of an eye, John Rigas lost everything—his company, his reputation, even the affection of his beloved Coudersport. Last March, Adelphia disclosed it was on the hook for $2.3 billion in off-balance-sheet loans the Rigas family had used mostly to buy company stock. Rigas resigned, as did his three sons—Michael, Tim, and James—who held top executive positions and sat on the board with their father. The independent directors now running the company say they discovered that under the Rigases, nothing was as it seemed. They say Adelphia inflated subscriber numbers. Routine expenses like service calls had been booked as capital items, inflating Adelphia's reported cash flow. But what was perhaps most unsettling was the unabashed manner in which the Rigases had helped themselves to shareholder dollars.

Adelphia financed the family's $150 million purchase of the Sabres. It paid $12.8 million in 2001 for office furniture and design services provided by Doris Rigas. Even John Rigas' good works were tainted. Adelphia paid a Rigas family partnership that owns the Sabres $744,000 for "luxury-box rentals, hockey tickets, and other entertainment costs." That means shareholders probably picked up the tab for all those children who went to games. The same goes for the beekeeper's visit to Cowburn's house. It turns out the primary source of income at Rigas' farm wasn't honey sales; it was providing landscaping, snow removal, and other maintenance duties for Adelphia.

As Adelphia slid toward bankruptcy—it filed for Chapter 11 protection in June—the entire cable industry was affected. The stock of competitors like Comcast and Charter fell because Wall Street feared they might have similar secrets. Investors dumped shares of entertainment companies like Disney, afraid that Adelphia wouldn't pay its programming bills. Two federal grand juries are sorting through the wreckage, and indictments are expected soon. The Securities and Exchange Commission has set up an office in Coudersport and is preparing a civil suit.

The Rigases have spent the past several months sequestered in their family compound outside Coudersport. They refused to talk to *Fortune*, referring all questions to criminal attorney Paul Grand, who denies they did anything wrong.

Citizens of Coudersport no longer speak so worshipfully about John Rigas. But even now there are people who praise him as a principled man who refused, for instance, to allow porn channels on his cable systems. The John Rigas they describe believed in small-town values: strong families, hard work, church on Sunday. That's why, they say, he remained true to Coudersport all those years. But surely there was another reason. There were things John Rigas and his sons got away with in Coudersport that would never have been tolerated anywhere else.

John Rigas didn't impress anybody much when he first arrived in Coudersport in 1951. The son of a Greek immigrant who ran a hot dog restaurant in nearby Wellsville, N.Y., Rigas was a character. He was 5 feet 5 inches tall. He had a gap-toothed smile, a wandering left eye, and a lot of energy. His father had tried to entice him to work at the restaurant when he came home with an engineering degree from Rensselaer Polytechnic Institute in 1950. But after a few months at the grill, John thought better of it. He borrowed money from his dad and several other Greek businessmen and bought the Coudersport movie theater for $72,000. He sold tickets, made popcorn, and sometimes slept on a cot in the theater when he was too tired to drive home to Wellsville.

Back then Coudersport didn't seem like a place anybody would go to make a fortune. It was a one-stoplight town in the Allegheny Mountains, far from any major highway. Main Street was four blocks of low-slung brick buildings dominated by the Potter County courthouse. It wasn't quaint; there was a hard edge, even a sense of desperation in the air. Coudersport had missed nearly every economic boom in rural Pennsyl-

FAMILY ASSETS, SORT OF

Some of the notable ways the Rigas family used Adelphia shareholder dollars

On the receiving end . . .	Who's behind the entity	How much
Dobaire Designs	Adelphia paid this company, owned by Doris Rigas, for design services.	$371,000
Wending Creek Farms	Adelphia paid John Rigas' farm for lawn care and snowplowing.	$2 million
SongCatcher Films	Adelphia financed the production of a movie by Ellen Rigas.	$3 million
Eleni Interiors	The company made payments to a furniture store run by Doris Rigas and owned by John.	$12 million
The Golf Club at Wending Creek Farms	Adelphia began developing a ritzy golf club.	$13 million
Wending Creek 3656	The company bought timber rights that would eventually revert to a Rigas family partnership.	$26 million
Praxis Capital Ventures	Adelphia funded a venture capital firm run by Ellen Rigas' husband.	$65 million
Niagara Frontier Hockey LP	Adelphia underwrote the Rigases' purchase of the Buffalo Sabres hockey team.	$150 million
Highland 2000	Adelphia guaranteed loans to a Rigas family partnership, which used the funds to buy stock.	$1 billion
Total		**$1,271,371,000**

vania. There was no coal to mine, no oil beneath the surface. The hills around town had been logged bare. By the 1950s the joke was that the town hadn't felt the Great Depression because it hadn't known prosperity. Each spring when diplomas were passed out, the locals muttered, "Say good-bye to another graduating class at Coudersport High."

People who stayed behind weren't sure what to think about a man like John Rigas, who wore his ambition on his sleeve. "It's the same plague you see in other small communities," says Bruce Cahilly, a local attorney who befriended Rigas early on. "People who have more talent and expertise are perceived as threats." So John was snubbed when he moved to town with Doris, a former high school English teacher from a poor family in the Finger Lakes area. John was wounded. "I've never been accepted in this town," he complained to a friend later on. "I couldn't even get elected to the school board."

But he seemed determined to win everybody over. He stayed until midnight talking to moviegoers after the lights went up. He stopped people on Main Street to ask about their children. He began attending the Episcopal church preferred by the town's business leaders, even though he'd been raised in the Greek Orthodox faith.

With Doris' prodding, John also pursued other business opportunities. In 1952 he overdrew his bank account to buy the town cable franchise for $300 from a local hardware store owner who'd erected an antenna on Dutch Hill. A doctor and a state senator agreed to put up $40,000, and John was in the cable business. He wired up Coudersport. Four years later he and his brother Gus did the same in Wellsville.

By the mid-1960s Rigas could afford to build a house just outside town with a pool for his four children. He was invited to sit on the board of the local bank. For a man who wanted to be accepted, the offer meant a great deal. Besides, he could always use a loan.

John Rigas and his sons would become famous in the cable industry for taking huge risks and leveraging Adelphia to the hilt. That would not have surprised anybody in Coudersport. After wiring the town John acquired more rural cable systems in New York and Pennsylvania, and he bragged to friends about how much debt he was taking on to finance the deals. "Hey, I just borrowed $10 million," John blithely told Henry Lush, a local furniture store owner. His secretary was forever going to the bank and moving funds from account to account so that her boss could stay ahead of creditors. People who tried to collect debts discovered it was no simple matter. Bruce Cahilly once drove out to John's house to seek payment for some legal work. When all else failed, he grabbed two five-gallon cans of blue pool paint from the garage. "That's just as well," John shrugged. "Doris doesn't like blue. She wanted green."

John wasn't always so sanguine. There were times when he lay awake worrying. "Well, Angie," he told his secretary, "I'm either going to become a millionaire or I'm going to go bankrupt."

A lot of people in Coudersport would have been satisfied with a house, a pool, and a seat on the bank board. But John kept pushing himself. He and Doris drove their children just as hard. They raised Michael, Tim, James, and Ellen, their youngest, to be model students. No smoking, no drinking, no hitchhiking across the country like their cousins in Wellsville. Doris, locals say, seemed to feel that the family was too good for Coudersport and drove her children to outshine their classmates. John didn't cut them any slack either. Says Bob Currin, a retired social studies teacher who taught the Rigas children: "John always let them know they had it and they could do it—and they'd better do it." Michael, James, and Ellen were class valedictorians. Tim was on track for the same honor when a boy with a better academic record moved to town senior year and edged him out.

One by one the Rigas children went off to elite colleges. Michael, the oldest, went to Harvard and then on to Harvard Law. Friends recall that he was smart and ambitious but monkish, usually spending Saturday nights studying.

Tim, the second child, was equally bright. He got a bachelor's degree in economics from Wharton, and he had a social life too. He played intramural volleyball and belonged to a singing group called the Penny Loafers.

James, the youngest of the boys, went to Harvard and then to Stanford Law School. He drank beer and played pinball, but he impressed everybody as a straight arrow. "He was the last person you would have thought would have gotten into trouble," says Steven Durlauf, a Harvard classmate.

For all their winning qualities, there was something odd about the Rigas boys. Unlike their father, they were awkward socially. When they attended their cousins' weddings in Wellsville, they stood in their tuxedos against the wall, arms crossed. "They didn't mingle," a Rigas family member says sadly. "They just stood there. Somebody said, 'They must be the bouncers.'"

The boys clearly preferred being with their immediate family in Coudersport. Not long after getting their degrees, Michael and Tim moved back in with their parents. Neither married. James spent a year and a half in San Francisco after Stanford, working at Bain & Co., but then he too returned to Coudersport, where he married and got a place of his own in town. "John just controlled everything with those boys," laments a relative. "He wouldn't give them any rope." (Ellen, the youngest child, went to Harvard and then pursued a career in music and film production in New York.)

All three sons went to work for their father. John couldn't have been happier. He now had three highly qualified young men to help run his cable company.

Adelphia was still a shoestring operation: John ran the company out of an office over a hardware store with three secretaries and a lineman. Once his sons joined the business, things changed rapidly. In 1981, Adelphia moved into an old church around the corner. People wondered what John was going to do with all that extra space. In 1985, Adelphia went from 53,538 subscribers to 122,500 after it acquired a cable system in Ocean County, N.J. When the Rigases took Adelphia public the next year, it had 370 full-time employees and deals on the table that would increase its subscribers to 253,767. By the mid-1990s Adelphia had moved into the old Coudersport High School building on Main Street, where the boys had gone to school. It was an odd place, perhaps, for what was now one of the nation's ten largest cable companies, managing 1.2 million subscribers. But the Rigas systems were the envy of their peers. They were clustered together in six areas—western New York, Virginia, Pennsylvania, New England, Ohio, and coastal New Jersey—making it easier for Adelphia to control costs. That allowed Adelphia to enjoy 56% operating cash margins, the highest in the cable industry.

John and the boys came to be considered savvy businessmen. John was the resident wise man, but he was also obsessed with details. He knew every inch of his cable systems; he looked at every résumé that came in. Michael was responsible for the daily operations of the cable systems. Tim was CFO. James supervised Adelphia's push into new technologies, including telephone service.

Yet as the cable industry grew up, the Rigases operated as if they were a million miles away from prying investors. Says Tom Cady, a former Adelphia sales and marketing executive: "Decisions were made at the dinner table rather than in a boardroom or somebody's office." John and his sons showed up late for meetings so often that people joked that the family operated "on Rigas time." They were famous for not returning calls from analysts. Occasionally, when they spotted a cable acquisition they really liked, they simply kept it for themselves.

What's more, the Rigases structured Adelphia so that there were no checks and balances at the top. Adelphia issued class A shares with one vote each to the public, but the Rigases retained all the class B stock with ten votes per share. Therefore they got to pick the board of directors. John, the three boys, and Ellen's husband, Peter Venetis, held five of the nine board seats. They filled the other four with John's friends and business associates. Who else would want to travel to Coudersport for meetings anyway?

By all accounts Tim Rigas ran the financial side of the business like a Saudi prince. He was CFO, and he was also the chairman of the board's audit committee, which oversaw the CFO's work. So how effective was the audit committee? That's hard to say. Sources say attorneys for the company haven't been able to find minutes of any meeting that Tim ran. (A Rigas family spokesman says minutes do exist and were kept by an outside law firm.)

To anybody who'd followed John Rigas' career, what happened with Adelphia's financing was predictable. The small-town businessman who had boasted about his stomach for leverage now saddled Adelphia with outlandish amounts of debt. In 1996, Adelphia's debt was 11 times its market capitalization, an off-the-chart number. (By contrast, Comcast's ratio was 1.28; Cox Communication's was 0.45.) Bond-rating agencies constantly subjected Adelphia to credit reviews. Shareholders paid a price. A Salomon Smith Barney analyst noted that Adelphia's debt "has caused the stock to trade at the steepest discount to estimated net asset value of any cable operator."

Stranger still, Adelphia began commingling revenues from its own cable operations, family-owned systems, and loan proceeds in an account referred to internally, according to documents filed recently with the SEC, as the "cash-management system." It was a lot of money. After Adelphia made a series of acquisitions in 1999, its annual revenues reached $3 billion. From time to time the Rigas family dipped into the account for personal business. The company says the Rigases tapped the account earlier this year to pay $63 million in margin loans. They used $4 million from the account to buy Adelphia stock. Another $700,000 went to pay for Tim's membership at the Golf Club at Briar's Creek on John's Island, S.C.

The independent directors now running the company say neither the unusual account nor the family's withdrawals were approved by the board. The Rigas family spokesman insists that none of it was hidden from the directors.

The Rigases didn't particularly care if investors shied away from Adelphia's stock or if bond-rating agencies called their debt junk. They cared about Coudersport. As Adelphia prospered, John Rigas became the town's biggest benefactor. He hired many locals and paid them well. Employees built suburban-style houses. The newspaper store started selling fancy coffee. A gym opened on Main Street. The Adelphia Christmas party became the "fancy-dress event in Coudersport, a chance to hobnob with the Rigases and socialize in suits over catered canapés," says Donald Gilliland, managing editor of the *Potter Leader-Enterprise*.

John combed the local papers and sent checks to down-on-their-luck families. "I'd always know when he did that because I'd get calls saying, 'Thanks for the article. I just got a check from John Rigas,'" says John Anderson, managing editor of the *Wellsville Daily Reporter*. People seeking favors camped out in Rigas' favorite restaurants, waiting for the CEO to arrive for lunch. He rarely turned anybody down.

Coudersport treated the Rigases like royalty, and they behaved accordingly. John now traveled in a Gulfstream jet, which Adelphia purchased from King Hussein of Jordan. At the Adelphia Christmas party one year, the orchestra played selections from the musical *Camelot*. It was John's favorite music, the conductor told the audience.

Doris rarely ventured into town, sending servants to do her shopping. When she was seen, she was in one of her Toyota minivans, an employee behind the wheel. But everyone felt her presence. The Rigases accumulated a dozen or so houses in Coudersport and the surrounding area. Doris had most of them painted brown and surrounded by split-rail fences. She also helped design Adelphia's buildings, including its brick-and-marble headquarters on Main Street, which locals call the "mausoleum."

No expense seemed to be spared. One day John asked Jimmie Bruzzi, the town dry cleaner, what he thought of Doris' work. "John," Bruzzi replied, "that woman is costing you millions."

"Well, sometimes it's worth it," Rigas replied. "Because when she's bothering [the contractors], she's not bothering me."

The boys, for their part, seemed to owe their allegiance more to the family empire than to the town. Michael was the only one who showed interest in community service. He worked 16-hour days and still attended Coudersport Rotary Club meetings. Tim, too, worked hard, jetting around the country negotiating acquisitions. He dressed well, had lots of girlfriends, and belonged to nearly 20 golf clubs. But when he was home, Tim would take John to church and Doris to her favorite restaurant, the Beef 'N Barrel.

James seemed more interested in having his own fiefdom. He spent most of his time running Adelphia Business Solutions, a telephone service company spun off from the parent. He flew coach and stayed in midrange hotels. (Sources tell *Fortune* that of all the sons, James was the least involved in Adelphia's financial weirdness.) Yet even James behaved like royalty at times. He built a baronial house on a hill above town that made the neighbors feel like serfs. "I didn't realize until now I lived in the cottage down the lane," one of them is said to have complained.

Even Ellen lived in high style—on the company tab, no less. The company says she and her venture capitalist husband lived rent-free in a Manhattan apartment owned by Adelphia. The corporation also put up $3 million in production money for *Songcatcher*, her critically acclaimed film about a musicologist. John reportedly walked out of the Coudersport premiere when two women kissed onscreen. (Ellen Rigas and her husband have paid the back rent on the apartment to Adelphia.)

It struck some of the locals that the Rigases were rather free with shareholder money. Teresa Kisiel, Coudersport's tax collector, couldn't help noticing that Adelphia paid its real estate taxes and those of the Rigas family with a single check. It was no secret that shareholders were footing the bills for a planned golf course. Tim and John told people it would have specially bred sheepdogs to chase away Canada geese.

Sometimes people in Coudersport even wondered whether all the spending was legitimate. But the thought would pass. It seemed as though everyone in town had benefited from John's largesse. "He's our Greek god," Shirlee Lette, a local newspaper columnist, told a visiting reporter.

Oren Cohen thought there was something about the family's spending that didn't add up. Then a high-yield-bond analyst for Merrill Lynch (and now a principal at Trilogy Capital), Cohen had followed Adelphia for a decade. He'd noticed that the Rigases were buying their own stock aggressively, but he couldn't figure out how they were paying for it. They didn't appear to have the cash themselves. John Rigas made $1.4 million in 2000. Michael, Tim, and James each took home $237,000.

The Rigases didn't have any sources of income outside Adelphia. They never sold their stock, and it didn't pay a dividend. Cohen was pretty sure their private cable systems weren't throwing off cash. John couldn't be selling that much honey at his farm. But every time Cohen tried to get an explanation, Adelphia rebuffed him. "If everything was on the up and up, the answer would have been, 'Oh, we bought it with family funds,'" recalls the analyst. "But that was never the answer. It was always 'We're not telling you.'"

Last February, Cohen noticed that the Rigases had bought or were committed to buying $1.8 billion of Adelphia stock and convertible bonds. At the time of the purchases the stock had been trading at about $40 a share. Now it was at $20. If John and his sons were using borrowed money, the Rigases were in trouble. It was time to call Adelphia again. "It seems to me the Rigases are $900 million or $1 billion in the hole," Cohen said to the head of investor relations. "How's this stuff being funded?" He got the brush-off.

On March 27, Cohen nearly shouted for joy when he spied a footnote on the last page of Adelphia's quarterly earnings press release. It said Adelphia was liable for $2.3 billion in off-balance-sheet loans to the

Rigas family. Near the end of a conference call that day, Cohen pressed Tim Rigas for details. Tim muttered something about family stock purchases and said he would provide details later.

That might have sufficed in the past, but it was just months after the disclosure of off-balance-sheet debt at Enron had led to the largest corporate bankruptcy in history. Adelphia's stock tumbled 35% in three days. The SEC began an investigation.

Things in Coudersport quickly spun out of control. John issued a statement acknowledging that "shareholders are looking for greater clarity and transparency." The stock continued to fall as Adelphia announced it would be restating earnings for 1999, 2000, and 2001. The company delayed filing its 2001 annual report to sort out its books. On May 15, John resigned as chairman and CEO.

Rigas was succeeded by interim CEO Erland Kailbourne, a retired Fleet Bank executive and Adelphia "independent" director. Kailbourne was a consummate Rigas family insider, an old friend from Wellsville, and a lot of observers suspected that John might still pull strings.

But the truth is, the independent directors were livid. They'd signed off on the lending agreements, but they thought the Rigases were buying more cable systems, not taking out what were essentially margin loans to buy Adelphia stock. John had made them look like fools. Kailbourne and the three other independent directors hired David Boies, the attorney who led the case against Microsoft, to look into Adelphia's books.

John did not object. Neither did Michael, Tim, or James, who resigned soon after their father. Boies sent in forensic accountants, who discovered that a $167 million bond purchase by the family hadn't been paid for. They also unearthed what appeared to be evidence of fraud. "Certain employees of the company may have prepared documents, including wire transfer receipts and bank-paydown and draw-down notices, . . . to support accounting treatment of this transaction as a cash transaction," Adelphia later explained in an SEC filing. *Fortune* has learned that five members of the accounting department who worked under Tim Rigas are now cooperating with federal prosecutors.

The independent directors also discovered that even after the disastrous March 27 conference call, someone in the family withdrew

$175 million from Adelphia's cash-management system to cover margin loans.

Adelphia's stock was soon worth pennies. The company was delisted by the Nasdaq because it didn't file its 2001 annual report. That triggered the default of $1.4 billion in Adelphia convertible bonds. Bankruptcy was all but certain. The company desperately needed a loan to stay afloat. But Wall Street wasn't about to lend it any more money as long as the Rigases were around. The family still held 100% of the company's class B voting stock. Technically they still controlled Adelphia.

The problem was that John Rigas didn't think he'd done anything wrong. The day after he resigned as chairman and CEO, he startled the independent directors by showing up at a directors' meeting. Surely, he told them, this mess could be sorted out and things would get back to normal. No, John, said his old friends, you and the boys have to go. Lawyers from Boies' firm tried to negotiate a severance package with John but couldn't reach an agreement. Finally the independent directors gave the Rigas family an ultimatum: Turn over your voting shares to us, or we'll resign and go public with everything we've uncovered. After an all-night negotiating session on May 22 in Coudersport, the Rigases finally relinquished control at 5 A.M. Adelphia got a $1.5 billion bank loan. CEO Kailbourne says he hopes to take Adelphia through Chapter 11 and come out with a viable company.

The story, however, isn't over yet. There's a three-way wrestling match going on between between the Rigases, the independent directors, and Deloitte & Touche, the company's auditor, over what people knew about Adelphia's finances and when they knew it. Predictably, the directors say Deloitte should have blown the whistle years ago, while Deloitte says the directors should have had better oversight. The Rigases, through their spokesman, say that both the directors and the outside auditors knew what was going on and didn't object.

John Rigas apparently still believes that he did nothing wrong. After weeks of silence, he told the *Buffalo News* that he'd been "depressed" lately and regretted disappointing "ordinary people." But his spirits were lifted by the hundreds of cards and letters he'd received from supporters. "It has been very inspirational to me and my family," Rigas told the paper. "I must say that most of the cards end with a message that is most meaningful and that is that 'You are in our prayers.' It does bring a tear to my eye."

If John Rigas showed up on Main Street in Coudersport tomorrow, some people would avoid him. Others might curse him. But the vast majority would pat him on the back and tell him to keep his chin up. They remember the checks, the Christmas parties, all the nice things he's done. Rigas knows that. But he hasn't been seen in town since everything fell apart at Adelphia. His friends say his health isn't good, and that must be part of it. But maybe there's another reason: He'd have to look everybody in the eye.

UPDATE

Soon after Leonard's story appeared in *Fortune*, John Rigas and his sons Timothy and Michael were arrested and charged with conspiracy to commit what a U.S. Attorney called "one of the largest and most egregious frauds ever perpetrated on investors and creditors." John Rigas was arrested on the morning of July 24 and led out in handcuffs, and television coverage of the event was widely credited with giving the stock market a boost that day. Prosecutors accused the Rigases of "systematically looting" Adelphia, and SEC officials said that the Rigases had overstated earnings and hidden $2.3 billion in debt from investors. The Rigases have pled not guilty to all the charges. Adelphia, meanwhile, sued the Rigases, and has apparently cut off all severance pay to John Rigas. Adelphia remains in business, but is still in Chapter 11.   —J.S.

LOSING A VIRTUAL FORTUNE

David Streitfeld

Los Angeles Times, May 2, 2002

AS THE LAST DAYS of 2000 ticked by, Critical Path Inc. President David Thatcher saw disaster rushing to swallow him.

Thatcher knew the software company was going to fall short of the $54 million in fourth-quarter sales it had promised Wall Street. The bad news would surprise analysts, disappoint investors and hammer the company's stock.

Desperate to avoid such a fate, Thatcher encouraged Critical Path's sales personnel to commit fraud. They persuaded an ex-colleague working at a small concert and sports ticket brokerage to sign a bogus contract for $2 million worth of Critical Path software.

The ticket broker was assured he would never actually receive the software, though Critical Path immediately booked it as a sale. A couple of days later, the software showed up on his desk. A Critical Path sales executive told him to throw it away.

While Enron Corp. and Global Crossing Ltd. have been grabbing headlines for financial chicanery, the tech community is quietly awash in its own accounting scandals. The number of high-tech companies issuing restatements—essentially admissions that previous revenue reports were more vapor than reality—has at least quadrupled since the early 1990s, according to New York University doctoral candidate Min Wu. Tech companies now constitute nearly 40% of all corporate restatements.

Restatements almost always damage or destroy investor confidence and spawn multiple lawsuits. In some cases, a restatement launches a company on its death spiral.

Clarent Corp., a Silicon Valley manufacturer of Internet telephone software, said in September that it had significantly overstated its revenue. Shares of Clarent, which traded at $178 two years ago, now are about 30 cents each.

Homestore.com, the Westlake Village real estate Web site, has restated its results for much of the last two years, shrinking them dramatically. The stock, which hit $120 during the dot-com boom, is trading at less than $3.

Quintus Corp., a business software maker based in the East Bay that had a market value of $1 billion, filed for bankruptcy protection after acknowledging that much of its 2000 revenue was based on "falsified documentation."

"Over the past several years, we have sued many tech companies, sought tougher sanctions, referred more cases to the criminal authorities, and yet people are still committing accounting fraud," said Helane Morrison, the SEC's chief in the Bay Area. "They just haven't stopped."

Few companies tried to get away with more than Critical Path. During its brief heyday, it was in the vanguard of high-tech upstarts that were supposed to destroy the dinosaurs of the "old economy." This was a pleasant fantasy that masked an ugly truth: Critical Path was a multibillion-dollar con game.

Thatcher, who pleaded guilty in February to securities fraud in U.S. District Court in San Francisco, told the judge that other members of the company's management were in on it. "The object of this conspiracy," he said, "was to report false revenues to meet Critical Path's predicted financial results."

In other words, the executives found themselves in the position of having to commit fraud merely to reach the revenue targets they had set themselves. Those targets offered the illusion that Critical Path was everything the media and analyst hype said it was.

"They used accounting to try to manufacture a reality that wasn't there," said Bill McGlashan Jr., who was brought in to run Critical Path last year after the fraud was exposed. "That's insanity. It's like, what were you thinking?"

Internet mania peaked only two years ago, but already it feels like another lifetime—an era when young entrepreneurs, often equipped with no more than a good story and a sincere desire to be rich, received tens of millions in funding from venture capitalists.

The resulting companies often were taken public before they had reaped enough revenue to buy a house in a middle-class San Francisco neighborhood, but that didn't matter. For a while, everyone made a fortune and looked like a genius.

COMPANY WAS HYPED AS A DIGITAL VISIONARY

Critical Path was founded in early 1997 by David Hayden, the former chief executive of Magellan, an Internet directory that tried and failed to compete with Yahoo! Realizing that e-mail was the oxygen of the Internet, Hayden formed Critical Path to provide corporations with one-stop communications packages.

By the time the company went public two years later, it was servicing 1.4 million mailboxes. With an estimated 245 million mailboxes on the Internet and the number rising rapidly, the company seemed poised for tremendous growth.

The analysts and the media certainly thought so. Gartner Group, a much-quoted consulting firm, estimated that two-thirds of all companies soon would be outsourcing their e-mail to firms such as Critical Path. *Forbes* magazine put Hayden on its cover as one of a dozen "digital visionaries." Hambrecht & Quist analyst Dan Rimer said the only way Critical Path could be in trouble was "if people suddenly decide to go back to using fountain pens."

In a sense, however, Critical Path's growth from the beginning was artificial. It acquired rights to service many of those 1.4 million mailboxes by giving equity stakes to their owners; for example, on-line broker E-Trade Group Inc. and phone company US West Inc. received 21% of the company.

This was a perfectly legal gambit used by many Silicon Valley start-ups, but there was only so much of the company that could be traded away. Critical Path had to find new ways to grow quickly, one reason it went public as soon as it could. It needed to raise money to buy other companies that immediately would boost its revenue.

Critical Path's initial public offering took place March 29, 1999, at a moment when Internet stocks were at their most glamorous. Investors ignored the fact that the company had revenue of only $897,000 in the previous year. Barbra Streisand asked for—and got—so-called friends-and-family shares, which enabled her to buy in at the offering price of $24.

It was a good deal: The stock rose 174% the first day, giving the company a valuation of $2.5 billion. At the IPO party, three employees were so giddy that they streaked. Maybe it was the four bottles of Dom Perignon sent by Streisand.

Within a few weeks, the stock jumped to $135. The gap between reality and expectations had become a chasm. At $135, the stock was factoring in expectations that Critical Path would service, and make at least a small profit from, every e-mail box on the Internet.

Employees, whose number would swell from 182 at the time of the public offering to 1,042 at the end of 2000, naturally were thrilled to be working at a hot company. Many programmed their computers to constantly display the stock price.

Employees knew they suddenly were rich—Hayden's stake alone was worth more than $300 million—but there were constant reminders about how fragile it all was. In May 1999, when a computer failure temporarily shut down many Critical Path mailboxes, the stock immediately dropped 7%.

Even before the stock was offered to the public, the board of directors had kicked Hayden upstairs. This followed another venerable tradition in Silicon Valley, where it's the founder's job to launch the company, not run it. Hayden used a little of his Critical Path wealth to buy, with television producer Norman Lear, one of the four surviving privately owned copies of the Declaration of Independence. The price: $8.1 million.

The task of turning Critical Path from a raw start-up into a truly successful company that would match its valuation fell to CEO Doug Hickey and to Thatcher, chief financial officer and, as of January 2000, president. Both were in their mid-40s, with sober backgrounds—Thatcher a former auditor for accounting firms Touche Ross and Price Waterhouse, Hickey a veteran tech executive—that would be reassuring to Wall Street.

It certainly started to seem like a real company, one former employee recalled. "Critical Path was started by a bunch of raver-hippie-engineer types, and they tended to hire their friends," said Mike Wertheim, a programmer. "Hickey was slick. He turned the company corporate. But people figured that was just what had to be done."

Hickey and Thatcher went on a spending binge, acquiring 10 companies from May 1999 to September 2000. Most of these companies had few real assets; in fact, four had liabilities that exceeded their assets.

At best, they were developing exciting technology that might work out well. That was enough to make them hot properties: Critical Path paid a total of $1.8 billion for them, nearly all in stock.

The acquisitions, along with other efforts, boosted the number of mailboxes the company serviced to 6.7 million in fall 1999 and then to 55 million early in 2000.

"I don't know if we are naive or what it is, but I've got to tell you, we really think we can touch virtually every Internet user in the world," Hickey told one Internet news site.

Forbes ASAP magazine voted Critical Path its No. 1 "ramp champ," saying that out of 100 fast-growing tech companies, it had the highest score in management, market opportunity, finances and competitive position. This was not, the magazine said, one of those companies "that are growing so fast that they spin out of control and crash."

Still, the pace was frantic. Thatcher told *Forbes ASAP* he had worked all night half a dozen times in the previous six months and logged 30,000 frequent-flier miles in one 15-day span. Employees were on call 24 hours a day.

The goal, one former employee recalled, was to do whatever was necessary to make the company look good. That would keep the stock price up.

"Financial statements usually tell you how successful a company's product is, but we wanted ours to look like advertising for the stock," said former Director of Engineering Steve Simitzis. "You would multiply your stock options by the day's stock price and just want the company to make its numbers to satisfy the market. You just wanted your net worth to continue to exist."

Those net worths could be considerable, as outlined in the company's 2001 proxy. Thatcher, who was paid $500,000 in 2000, made $5 million off his options. That was only a small part of his holdings: He had half a million additional shares in vested and unvested options. Sales chief William Rinehart was paid $210,000 and cashed in 200,000 options—every one that he could—for stock that was worth $10 million. An additional 200,000 options were scheduled to vest over the next several years. Chief Executive Hickey, who was paid $600,000 in 2000, had vested and unvested options for 1.2 million shares.

Of course, the size of any prospective windfall would depend on the stock price. And Wall Street by this point was beginning to want more than just growth. It wanted Internet companies to be profitable too. At a March 2000 investors' conference, Hickey promised both. "We'll achieve fourth-quarter profitability and at the same time achieve explosive revenue growth," he said.

But as 2000 wore on and the tech sector peaked, the canyon between the hype and the reality finally became unbridgeable. Those 10 acquisitions initially may have added to the bottom line—1999 revenue was up 1,700%, to $16.2 million, and 2000 was expected to easily clear the $100-million mark—but the new units proved hard to integrate. The mergers swelled the number of products the company offered, many of which had little to do with the one thing it really understood: e-mail management. The company eventually would have 77 facilities on several continents, becoming much too far-flung for its size.

It's not clear, and won't be until federal prosecutors have finished their investigations, exactly who might face prosecution at Critical Path besides Thatcher. Twenty-two people were dismissed by the company after it made its own internal investigation, but prosecutors aren't likely to pursue anyone below the executive level, a source said.

Timothy Ganley, former vice president of strategic sales, pleaded guilty last month to selling $31,885 worth of stock based on inside information about the fraud. Thatcher, meanwhile, is pledging cooperation and alleging conspiracy.

An attorney for CEO Hickey, who resigned early last year in the wake of the fraud revelations, said his client "did absolutely nothing wrong." Hickey relied on Thatcher to give him honest information, said Richard Marmaro of law firm Proskauer Rose, adding, "It's not the chief executive's job to go to the customer to confirm that revenue is real."

An attorney for Rinehart, the former sales vice president, didn't return calls. Rinehart was fired when the fraud was discovered.

Hayden, the founder, "has not been the subject of any criminal or SEC investigation," the company said.

If the "who" beyond Thatcher awaits the filing of new charges, the "how" and the "why" are more obvious. Software accounting is complex and vague, which makes it highly susceptible to abuse.

"A grocery store either sells $1,000 worth of groceries or it doesn't. At technology companies, it's not so simple," said Dennis Beresford, former chairman of the Financial Accounting Standards Board.

For one thing, software is small, lightweight and virtually cost-free to reproduce. It's often bundled with service contracts that last for several years, which brings up questions about whether the revenue should be recognized now or later. All those things make it easy to distort or fake sales in a way that would be impossible with bread or automobiles.

Several experts said high-tech accounting fraud almost always begins the same way: slowly.

"No one comes in to work and says, 'We're going to do a big fraud starting right now.' It's a continuum," said Charles Mulford, professor of accounting at Georgia Tech and author of *The Financial Numbers Game: Detecting Creative Accounting Practices.*

"What they think is, 'We'll do this right now, but I just know there's that big order down the road, and we'll make good on it.'"

During the second half of 2000, as detailed in court filings, Critical Path used just about every trick it could to improperly and illegally boost its revenue.

The first gimmick was a software swap, sometimes called a Barney deal in tribute to the purple dinosaur who proclaims, "I love you, you love me." Under accounting rules, the goods on both sides of the swap must be valued at fair-market prices.

Critical Path's swap was with Peregrine Systems Inc., a San Diego company at which Thatcher had once worked.

"To avoid the appearance that the transaction was a software swap, Critical Path and Peregrine prepared separate contracts for each purchase, each paid the full amounts owed, and made payments to each other on different days," Thatcher admitted in his plea agreement.

Thatcher admits that Critical Path didn't actually want what it was buying from Peregrine. The deal, he told the judge, "was driven by the need to report revenue"—$3 million worth.

Peregrine, based in San Diego, maintains that there were two separate transactions and that its accounting was appropriate. (The company said Wednesday that it was delaying reporting fiscal-year results "pending continued audit activities." Its shares dropped 50% to $3.45.)

A second deal was done with International Computers Ltd. ICL said it was owed $8.7 million by PeerLogic, one of Critical Path's many acquisitions, but was willing to settle the claim for $6 million.

Instead, Critical Path paid the full $8.7 million, and ICL paid back $2.7 million to Critical Path for software, according to Thatcher's plea agreement. Essentially, Critical Path paid ICL to buy its software — not only a gross violation of accounting rules but a crazy way of doing business.

ICL, a London division of Fujitsu Ltd., didn't respond to e-mails about the deal.

These and other improper deals added $9.7 million in revenue to Critical Path's third-quarter total, bringing it to $45 million. Wall Street, which had been expecting only $39 million, immediately sent the stock up $5 a share. Hickey used the occasion to raise fourth-quarter revenue estimates from about $50 million to $54 million to $56 million.

Two weeks later, on Nov. 2, Critical Path held a meeting for 100 investors and analysts. The company, Hickey said, was about to join "an elite group of profitable 'new-economy' companies."

THE WHOLESALE DECEPTION BEGINS

But if it was all smiles and sunlight outside, in the management suite there was gloom and recklessness. As the dot-coms began to fade, Critical Path lost about three-quarters of its value in the first 11 months of 2000. The easiest accounting tricks had been used in the third quarter. Now the wholesale deception began.

Critical Path sent $2.1 million in software to Storerunner Network, a struggling San Diego shopping site, despite the fact that Thatcher knew the chances of getting paid were essentially nonexistent. But he booked the shipment as revenue anyway. Storerunner filed for bankruptcy protection two months later.

Another customer was Education Networks of America, a Web resource for teachers that was interested in Critical Path's software and services but wasn't sure it could afford them. So Critical Path issued a side letter that gave ENA the ability to back out of the $2.2-million deal, according to Thatcher's plea agreement. Critical Path booked the revenue, even though ENA exercised its option to cancel.

Finally came the $2-million deal with Bestseats.com, the ticket broker.

When the Critical Path finance department, unaware of the fraud, asked the broker for proof he could pay for his $2-million purchase, he responded with an e-mail saying his firm had only $250,000 in capital. Before the finance department could see it, Thatcher changed the number to $12.5 million. Bestseats, which is based in the East Bay, declined to comment.

Even with nearly $10 million in sham revenue, Critical Path couldn't make its fourth-quarter sales goals, much less a profit. Total sales for the quarter were $52 million, $2 million shy of its low estimate. Instead of the promised profit, there was a net loss of $11.5 million. Analysts were upset, and the stock immediately lost half its value.

Two weeks later, on Feb. 2, 2001, the company said it had "discovered a number of transactions" that were improper.

Analysts were livid. Bert Hochfeld of Josephthal & Co. said he felt as if he had been raped. The stock fell 70% more, to $3. Lawsuits were filed. The company restated its revenue. The stock slid all year, bottoming out at 24 cents in September.

The SEC's chief accountant, Charles Niemeier, warned in February that even if a company strictly followed accounting rules, it still could face fraud charges if its filings distorted the company's true condition.

By that standard, a great number of tech companies might have reason to be worried.

"There was so much greed and so many get-rich-quick schemes," said Ram Shriram, a Silicon Valley financier and an early investor in Critical Path. "People did not take a long-term view of building businesses. Some not only cut corners but ran afoul of ethics and the law."

PAINFULLY BECOMING A REAL COMPANY

Critical Path says it finally has that long-term view. Hayden reassumed control after the fraud came to light; he and McGlashan, the new CEO, closed two-thirds of those 77 offices, cut the number of products and employees in half, settled the shareholder lawsuits and convinced most of the board that it was time to move on. Of the $1.8 billion paid for acquisitions, $1.3 billion was written off.

The Critical Path of two years ago wasn't a real company, McGlashan said in an interview in the company's new and cheaper offices next to the San Francisco–Oakland Bay Bridge. "There was no cash management, no budget. Nothing was ever integrated. Basic 101 stuff seemed to be missing."

Instead, according to the company's 2001 proxy, there were a lot of sweetheart deals for executives. A plane was leased from an aviation company that Thatcher and Hickey had invested in. Bonuses could approach or even exceed salaries, despite the fact that the company lost $79 million in 2000. The company lent CFO Larry Reinhold $1.7 million after he was hired in December 2000. One clause in the loan said he wouldn't have to pay either interest or principal if he quit. Saying he had accomplished "a great deal," Reinhold quit last August.

Critical Path would be a much harder place to commit fraud now. To take just one example, salespeople no longer approve contracts. The legal and finance departments do.

All the old management except for Hayden, who remains as executive chairman, and the chief technical officer are gone.

McGlashan doesn't miss them.

"It was a corporate culture based on people thinking they're going to be rich," he said. "The temptation, when billions are involved, becomes extraordinary."

Critical Path isn't very tempting anymore. Though the stock has recovered to about $2, only one analyst, Larry Berlin of First Analysis, still is tracking it.

"It's a viable company with a good product that has potential," Berlin said. "But it's not going to be a get-rich-quick scheme for anyone."

UPDATE

In September, Timothy Ganley, the former vice president of strategic sales for Critical Path, was sentenced to six months in prison and two years supervised release after pleading guilty to insider trading. Former sales executive Kevin Clark, meanwhile, also pled guilty to insider trading, admitting that he dumped more than $350,000 in company stock before news of the company's dubious accounting broke. Sales executive Jonathan Beck has pled not guilty to insider-trading charges. At press time, David Thatcher, who is cooperating with federal authorities, has not yet been sentenced. Critical Path is still in business. In early October, its stock was trading at 59 cents a share.   —J.S.

TOOTHLESS WATCHDOGS

Almar Latour and Kevin J. Delaney with Phillip Day in
Singapore and Phred Dvorak in Tokyo

The Wall Street Journal, August 16, 2002

HAMBURG, GERMANY—Gerhard Schmid, former chief executive
officer of MobilCom AG, last year began transferring 70.9 million
euros, or $69.5 million, from the publicly traded mobile-phone com-
pany to a firm owned by his wife. He didn't bother to inform Mobil-
Com's board. An internal report concluded that he broke German law
by failing to inform other executives and board members of those payments. So far, the money hasn't been returned to MobilCom.

The German authorities don't seem to mind. The German Financial Supervisory Authority says Mr. Schmid's actions don't fall under its
jurisdiction. The chief prosecutor in the state of Schleswig-Holstein,
where MobilCom is based, says there is no investigation into the matter.

Mr. Schmid argues that his misdeeds were mere technicalities. "So I
did something wrong but nothing happened," says Mr. Schmid, who,
along with his wife, owns 50% of MobilCom's stock. "It's like you're
going too fast on the street, but no accident happens. You learned that
you should not go too fast, but no one got hurt."

At a time when U.S. executives are being led away in handcuffs or
hauled before congressional committees, business scofflaws in the rest
of the world aren't hurting much at all. In most of Asia, Europe and
Latin America, regulations and enforcement are so weak that the
chances of conviction are slim. Legal systems are poorly equipped to
handle misconduct in the executive suite. And securities watchdogs
operate under budget constraints that make the U.S. Securities and
Exchange Commission look flush with cash.

For instance, Japan's Securities and Exchange Surveillance Commission, or SESC, has only about 364 employees, or about a tenth of the number at the SEC, which itself is widely considered understaffed. Unlike the SEC, Japan's SESC doesn't have the power to file civil suits or administrative actions. And it only brings about seven cases to criminal prosecutors a year, compared with the SEC's 50.

In Taiwan, the Securities and Futures Commission lacks the power to carry out its own investigations. The authorities who do have that power — local prosecutors and the national bureau of investigation — don't have much expertise in market and accounting fraud. Of the more than 300 cases the commission has turned over in the past five years, fewer than 20 have resulted in prosecutions, according to one senior regulator.

Meanwhile, Italy's center-right government last year actually decriminalized false accounting and made it a misdemeanor.

But such enforcement shortcomings could seriously undermine the growth and legitimacy of local capital markets. While the recent spate of accounting scandals has given U.S. business a black eye, vigorous prosecution of alleged wrongdoing could ultimately help persuade investors that it's safe to go back into the market.

There's little to reassure investors in many other countries. Frankfurt's Neuer Markt stock exchange, a Nasdaq-like market for up-and-coming companies founded in 1997, has been beset with scandal in the past two years. German investigators have opened probes into more than a dozen companies on suspicions of insider trading, misleading shareholders and fraudulent accounting. One investigation, involving Comroad AG, a supplier of technology for auto navigation, has resulted in charges against its founder. But almost all others have so far resulted in no action. Meanwhile, the Neuer Markt Nemax 50 index for growth stocks has plummeted 95% since its peak in March 2000.

"It's like the Wild West in Germany," says Ron Hoss, a salesman from Karlsruhe, who says he has lost nearly all of the 30,000 euros he invested in Neuer Markt stocks in mid-2000. "Executives made phony statements about their companies' earnings, but nobody does anything. If people get caught, they get nothing. But if I don't pay a parking ticket, they hunt me down."

The German Association for Shareholder Protection, a shareholder-rights group with 25,000 members in Germany commonly known as DSW, is campaigning for stricter enforcement of securities law. It regularly calls alleged abuses to the attention of the authorities. But "most cases we hand to the state prosecutor, more than 95%, end up not being investigated," says Jella Benner-Heinacher, the managing director of DSW. "The cases are often too complicated for prosecutors to handle. They've not been trained in these matters."

The case of MobilCom has been particularly galling for shareholders in the struggling company, whose stock is listed on the Neuer Markt and has lost about 97% of its value since peaking in March 2000.

In the 1990s, as stock-market investment began to catch on among Germans, Mr. Schmid was an entrepreneurial sensation. The son of a carpenter, he worked as a manager for a car-rental company after an early career as a professional hockey player and coach in Germany. Then, in the early 1990s, he was inspired by a chat with a salesman who wanted to install mobile phones in rental cars.

"It seemed like a huge market that nobody knew much about," Mr. Schmid recalls. "If you learned faster than others, you could hit it big." So he formed MobilCom in 1992 to provide wireless phone service in competition with Deutsche Telekom AG and others. MobilCom is now Germany's No. 5 mobile-phone company, with 4.9 million subscribers. The company's stock-market value hit a peak of 9.1 billion euros in March 2000.

"It's like WorldCom," says Mr. Schmid, wearing a black shirt and black trousers with gray sneakers. "They also grew big fast."

The CEO flew around Europe in a turbo-prop plane he dubbed "Idea." At one MobilCom Christmas party, Mr. Schmid says, he handed out 1,000-mark bills to employees (then equivalent to about $450). Drawing from leadership lessons he learned as a hockey coach, Mr. Schmid says, he tried to be a fair boss. When nonsmoking employees complained about the length of smoking breaks taken by colleagues, Mr. Schmid provided a clock for the nonsmokers to time those breaks. He told the nonsmokers they could take equivalent amounts of time off work.

His public profile grew. Last year, he served on a committee advising the German ministry of justice on corporate-governance issues.

Surfing the Internet in his office one day in early 2000, Mr. Schmid landed on a German Web site of France Telecom SA, which at the time was eager to obtain a license for third-generation, or 3G, mobile-phone services in Germany. He sent an e-mail to a France Telecom executive whose name he found on the Web site, asking whether the company wanted to team up with MobilCom. A day later, he got a call back: the French were interested.

After just two weeks of negotiations, France Telecom committed itself to paying as much as 10 billion euros to build a jointly owned 3G network with MobilCom in Germany and to pay 3.74 billion euros for a 28.5% stake in MobilCom.

It was 4 A.M. when the French side called him down to the lobby of the Ritz Hotel in Paris to sign the deal. He says he ordered a bottle of champagne to celebrate on the spot with the France Telecom people and his wife.

France Telecom's timing was unfortunate. Within weeks, shares in telecommunications companies were sagging all over Europe as investors began worrying about the huge amounts being spent on new networks and questioning whether those investments would ever pay off. MobilCom shares sank with the rest through much of 2000 and early 2001. German papers reported rumors that MobilCom was short of cash, though the company denied it.

Then something remarkable happened. Between mid-July and December 2001, MobilCom's thinly traded shares skyrocketed 85%, to 24 euros each from 12.99 euros, even as the Dow Jones Stoxx index of its European telecom peers declined 3.6%.

Investors began murmuring about a mystery buyer last summer and German papers in July reported that Mr. Schmid himself was increasing his stake. Both France Telecom's chief financial officer, Jean-Louis Vinciguerra, and smaller shareholders in MobilCom asked Mr. Schmid repeatedly to identify the buyer. He declined.

This February, Mr. Schmid finally announced the identity of the mystery buyer: Millennium GmbH, a company owned by his wife, Sybille Schmid-Sindram. Millennium had bought a stake of about 10%, according to MobilCom.

Mr. Schmid says that he didn't identify his wife as the buyer earlier because she had asked him not to do so. Nor was he legally required to do so. U.S.-style regulations mandating the disclosure of shareholders with stakes of 5% or more in companies listed on the Neuer Markt went into effect only on April 1 of this year.

The share buying wasn't the only link between MobilCom and the CEO's wife. An audit report by BDO Deutsche Warentreuhand AG, commissioned by MobilCom's supervisory board in March 2002, says that over a six-month period Mr. Schmid authorized the transfer of a total of 70.9 million euros from MobilCom to Millennium without seeking approval from MobilCom's other top executives or supervisory board.

Mr. Schmid says that 68.4 million euros were transferred to Millennium as part of an options program on MobilCom stock. He says the options were to be awarded to certain dealers and sales partners as an incentive for hitting sales targets.

MobilCom's board was aware of his intention to start a program, but it didn't authorize the issuance of new shares for holders who exercised options; the shares had to be bought on the open market, Mr. Schmid says. As it turned out, Millennium already owned enough MobilCom stock to provide shares to anybody who exercised options, he adds. The payments from MobilCom were intended to provide a financial cushion to Millennium should MobilCom shares rise sharply in value and spark the exercise of lots of options, Mr. Schmid says.

In its audit report, BDO offered one possible alternative scenario: that "payments were made to Millennium GmbH to enable it to purchase Mobilcom AG shares."

Mr. Schmid declines to speak officially for Millennium or for his wife. But he dismisses the notion that she would take MobilCom's money and use it to buy shares for herself. "She's independently wealthy," he says. "She has some 100 homes and condominiums she owns."

It isn't clear why there is a difference of 2.5 million euros between the sums cited by Mr. Schmid and BDO. When asked what happened to the 2.5 million euros, Mr. Schmid said: "It's an accounting error. That's not my job. It's stupid. Perhaps you should ask the financial officer." Thorsten Grenz, who was MobilCom's chief financial officer at the time of the payments and is now chief executive, declined to comment, according to a MobilCom spokesman.

In its report, BDO alleged that Mr. Schmid broke the law by authorizing the payments without informing other company officers and without having a legally binding contract with Millennium. Though a large chunk of the money was transferred by Sept. 7, 2001, Mr. Schmid and his wife signed a legally binding contract covering the payments only on Dec. 7, 2001, the BDO report says. Payments made before that date were "without legal grounding," the BDO report says.

After receiving the BDO report in May, MobilCom's supervisory board canceled the option plan and demanded the return of the money. So far, according to MobilCom, that money hasn't been returned. While he says that he doesn't speak officially on Millennium's behalf, Mr. Schmid says the money will be paid back if there is an agreement with France Telecom to secure MobilCom's financial viability.

At MobilCom's annual shareholder meeting on May 30 in Hamburg, the company's supervisory board chairman, Klaus Ripken, read the conclusions of the BDO report, saying, "Mr. Schmid has infringed his duties as chief executive under German share laws." Mr. Schmid apologized to the attendees. "I regret what has happened and will do everything I can so that it doesn't fall back on MobilCom," he said.

On June 21, MobilCom's supervisory board fired Mr. Schmid.

Anja Schuchhardt, a spokeswoman for the German Financial Supervisory Authority, says that the agency isn't investigating Mr. Schmid's conduct. She says the board's allegation that Mr. Schmid violated securities laws is an internal company matter and outside the jurisdiction of the financial watchdog. The BDO report "isn't relevant, isn't necessary for our purposes," says Ms. Schuchhardt.

Uwe Wick, the chief prosecutor in Schleswig-Holstein, MobilCom's home state, says he isn't investigating Mr. Schmid even though he has received several requests to do so. He declined to say who made those requests. Mr. Wick describes the requests as "settling of scores." In a brief telephone interview, Mr. Wick adds that he doesn't know much about the case.

Mr. Schmid is vague when asked to explain Millennium's activities. The BDO report says Mr. Schmid acquired the company in December 1997 and sold it to his wife in February 2001 for 50,000 marks. But during an interview, Mr. Schmid says he can't remember whether his wife bought the company from him or his lawyer. When asked about Millennium's purpose, Mr. Schmid describes it as a company "without activities." He says it has "not many" employees, then corrects himself, saying it has no employees. Later, he says the company serves primarily as a vehicle for his wife "to buy and sell shares tax-free." Such an arrangement is "normal in Germany," he says.

Ms. Schmid-Sindram—who wholly owns Millennium, according to her husband—declined to comment.

Mr. Schmid says he decided to pay Millennium to underwrite the option plan because two German banks had refused to do so. He concedes that he erred in not seeking approval from the MobilCom board. "I regret not following the formal rules," he says. But he argues that his actions didn't harm the company.

That is debatable. For one thing, MobilCom has been unable to recover the money paid to Millennium so far. It's not an insubstantial figure, considering that MobilCom reported a 2001 loss of 205.6 million euros on revenue of 2.59 billion euros.

In addition, when MobilCom's supervisory board criticized Mr. Schmid's actions in May, investors also took a hit: The stock price fell 13.5% on the day of that public reprimand.

By not disclosing that his wife's company was buying shares in MobilCom, he also deprived the market of information that might have been useful to other investors in assessing the company's value.

Now MobilCom's future is in doubt. France Telecom is in talks to restructure 5.8 billion euros of MobilCom's debt. But the restructuring won't proceed unless France Telecom reaches an agreement for it or another buyer to purchase the MobilCom stake controlled by Mr. Schmid and his wife. France Telecom warns that MobilCom could be forced into bankruptcy if no agreement is reached with creditors.

Mr. Schmid accuses France Telecom of complaining about his actions in an attempt to push down MobilCom's stock price so that the French company can buy the rest of the company more cheaply. France Telecom has repeatedly denied that charge.

Now that he has been ousted from the company he founded, Mr. Schmid says he is enjoying seaside walks with his wife. "I try to stop myself from talking about Millennium," he says.

UPDATE

MobilCom was able to avert bankruptcy, but only thanks to the intervention of German prime minister Gerhard Schroeder, who organized a government bailout of the company in order to bolster his chances in a tight campaign for reelection. MobilCom's new CEO said that despite the company's financial woes, it would continue investing heavily in a next-generation mobile network. No charges have been filed against Gerhard Schmid.   —J.S.

Part Two

Who Watches
the Watchmen?

If the biggest scandals of the past year and a half were not centered on Wall Street, they nonetheless could not have happened had investment banks and the Big Five accounting firms done the jobs they were supposed to do. Investors, perhaps naively, looked to accountants and Wall Street firms as objective arbiters, whose role it was to offer up impartial advice about which companies could be trusted and which could not. Instead, as the pieces in this section show in devastating fashion, neither the accounting industry nor Wall Street showed any objectivity at all. Instead of representing investor interests and carefully vetting companies that were looking to raise money, investment banks abandoned their watchdog function and gave their stamp of approval to even the most dubious of corporate strategies. Accountants, meanwhile, instead of acting as checks on executives who were trying to cook the books, often ended up helping them do so.

At its heart, the story laid out in the pieces that follow is one of fundamental conflicts of interest. Wall Street analysts who were supposed to be offering objective advice to investors were instead paid based on how much investment banking business they were able to generate, which gave them a clear incentive to tailor their recommendations to suit the whims of corporate CEOs. Accounting firms increasingly derived most of their revenue and profits from consulting contracts with the very firms they were supposed to be auditing. Since performing a tough audit was an easy way to get fired from a consulting job, it's not too surprising accountants ended up rubber-stamping dubious financial reports instead of challenging them. What's striking, in retrospect, is how obvious these conflicts of interest were—people have been writing stories about the corruption of Wall Street analysts, for instance, for years—and yet how little was done about them.

In part, as Jane Mayer shows in her profile of former SEC chair Arthur Levitt, that's because of the sheer lobbying power that Wall Street and the accounting industry can bring to bear. It's also, as Noam Scheiber suggests in his piece "Peer Revue," because the mechanisms that are supposed to allow accountants to regulate themselves simply don't work. On a deeper level, as Steven Rosenbush shows in his searing picture of telecom analyst Jack Grubman, investment banks and the companies they work with became locked in a mutually beneficial circle of vice. Jack Grubman was so far inside the telecom industry that it was impossible for him to be objective about it. He was not an independent arbiter, even if that's what he pretended to be. He was a major player in the industry he was supposedly evaluating. Unfortunately, in this, Grubman's case, while extreme, was hardly unusual, as Marcia Vickers and Mike France show in their piece "How Corrupt Is Wall Street?" (The answer, incidentally, is very.)

As Stephen Labaton and David Leonhardt make clear in their piece on insider trading, the Wall Street of the late 1990s was—as perhaps it always has been—a game in which the privileged few were playing by different rules. New York attorney general Eliot Spitzer has been trying to use his office to fix that, and as Michael Dumiak shows in his story, Spitzer's solutions have been surprisingly sophisticated and nuanced.

The downfall of Arthur Andersen, meanwhile, provided an occasion for two exceptional pieces. Anita Raghavan's profile of David Duncan, the Arthur Andersen partner who pled guilty to obstruction of justice in the Enron case, shows how easy it was to slip from aggressive accounting into breaking the law. And "Fall From Grace," by John A. Byrne, profiles Andersen's CEO, Joseph Berardino, and shows us a man who has not really come to terms with just what was wrong with the way his company did business. In a sense, Berardino's very inability to accept Andersen's responsibility may be all the explanation you need of what's wrong with the way Wall Street and the accounting industry did business in the bubble years.

THE ACCOUNTANTS' WAR

Jane Mayer

The New Yorker, April 22, 2002

NOTHING, IT HAS BEEN said, is duller than accounting—until someone is defrauded. And after every modern financial disaster—the stock-market crash of 1929, the bankruptcy of the Penn Central Railroad in 1970, the savings-and-loan crisis of the '80s, and now the bankruptcy of the Enron Corporation—investors have tended to ask the same question: where were the auditors?

Arthur Levitt, Jr., who was the chairman of the Securities and Exchange Commission under President Bill Clinton, believes that in the years leading up to Enron's collapse the auditors were busy organizing themselves into a lobbying force on Capitol Hill—one that has been singularly effective. Levitt, who issued a series of warnings about the accounting profession in those years, suggests that the aim of the so-called Big Five accounting firms—PricewaterhouseCoopers, Deloitte & Touche, Ernst & Young, KPMG, and Arthur Andersen, Enron's auditor—was to weaken federal oversight, block proposed reform, and overpower the federal regulators who stood in their way. "They waged a war against us, a total war," Levitt said.

Some have portrayed Enron's crash and the woes of Arthur Andersen simply as huge business failures. "There are always going to be bad apples," said Jay Velasquez, a former aide to Senator Phil Gramm, who is now a Washington lobbyist for the accounting profession, and who has fought increased regulation. Barry Melancon, who heads the American Institute of Certified Public Accountants, the profession's trade group, which has three hundred and fifty thousand members, fears that those who are trying to impose political solutions will overreact. "We live in a free-market system," Melancon told me. "Businesses fail. People are not infallible."

But Levitt casts the Enron story in starker terms. It is, as he puts it, "the story of the '90s"—a battle between public and private interests that is being fought at a time when there is more corporate money in politics than ever before. "This is about corporate greed," Levitt told me. "It is the result of two decades of erosion of business ethics. It was the ultimate nexus of business and politics. If there was ever an example where money and lobbying damaged the public interest, this was clearly it."

Levitt, who is seventy-one and has silver hair, exhibits a starchy correctness. He still seems bitter about his war with the accounting trade, and called one adversary "an oily weasel" and another "a sly mongoose" as he spoke about the influence of money on politics. "It used to be that if industries had a problem they would try to work it out with the regulatory authorities," he said, in his sleek office at the Carlyle Group, in midtown Manhattan, surrounded by mementos of years in public life. "Now they bypass the regulators completely, and go right to Congress." Their campaign contributions lend them clout. "It's almost impossible to compete with the effect that money has on these congressmen." Enron's campaign contributions and its political power have received much attention, but two of the top five accounting firms—Arthur Andersen and Deloitte—and the accountants' trade association actually spent more during the 2000 elections. "The money was enormous," Levitt said. "Look at the end result."

Not many years ago, Levitt was considered a consummate Wall Street insider, even an operator. In 1993, when President Clinton picked him to run the Securities and Exchange Commission, he was a centrist, a well-connected fund-raiser who had contributed to both parties. He had founded his own lobbying organization, the American Business Conference, to advocate the interests of small business on Capitol Hill. He was also someone with a knack for cultivating famous and powerful friends. In the 1960s, he joined a successful start-up New York firm as a stockbroker, and he eventually counted among his clients Leonard Bernstein, Aaron Copland, and Kenneth Clark. Three of Levitt's original partners were Sanford Weill, who became the chairman of Citigroup; Arthur Carter, now the publisher of *The New York Observer*; and Roger Berlind, who became a Broadway producer. (Levitt had his own ties to Broadway; his aunt was Ethel Merman.) Levitt thrived, too, and by the late '60s he was running Shearson Hayden Stone, which later became Shearson Lehman Brothers.

In 1977, after being asked to head a search committee for the next leader of the American Stock Exchange, he got the job himself. A few years later, he was thinking of investing in *The National Journal*, a policy-oriented magazine in Washington, when he learned of the publication's interest in acquiring *Roll Call*, a struggling newspaper on Capitol Hill. Levitt declined to invest in *The National Journal* but bought *Roll Call* himself, for about five hundred thousand dollars. Seven years later, he sold it for fifteen million dollars.

At the same time, Levitt was drawn to public life. He had grown up in a political household, the only son of Arthur Levitt, Sr., a Democrat who for twenty-four years was the New York State comptroller. Both his father and his mother, a public-school teacher in Brooklyn, were dependent on public pensions for their retirement, and they cared deeply about the protection of small investors.

When Levitt began his SEC job, he acknowledged the populist tradition of the Roosevelt Administration, which created the SEC in 1934, to insure the integrity of American financial markets. The agency's new Web site carried the motto of his most famous predecessor, William O. Douglas: "We are the investors' advocates." The SEC's basic requirement was that all publicly traded companies register with the agency and submit to annual independent audits. Douglas liked to say that the SEC was "the shotgun behind the door." But Levitt soon discovered that the agency's arsenal was no match for the bull markets of the '90s. The new economy spawned new accounting schemes that raised concerns almost from the start.

One early fight was over stock options. Many pointed out that the accounting convention that kept these expenses, unlike ordinary executive compensation, off the books was deceptive. It meant that investors could not see a company's real liabilities. Levitt recalls that when he took office the first thing that Senators David Boren and Carl Levin, who were both active in regulatory reform, told him was that he "had to do something about stock options."

Congress soon got involved in the stock-option fight, and the politicization of accounting became more apparent than ever. Supporters of Wall Street and Silicon Valley, including many ordinarily pro-regulatory Democrats, fought against changing the stock-option rules; one, for example, was Senator Joseph Lieberman, of Connecticut, a state with a large concentration of *Fortune* 500 companies, many of which are campaign contributors. More surprising, the accounting profession, rather than remaining neutral, joined forces with its clients to fight the change. Together, they exerted pressure on the organization that sets the rules for the accounting business, the Financial Accounting Standards Board, or FASB. "This was a defining moment for me," Levitt said. A lawyer who was with the SEC at the time says, "The accountants were going beyond good accounting. They were advocating a business position. They wanted to keep their customers happy. It was quite unseemly."

At first, Levitt played a hesitant role. In what he now regards as his "biggest mistake" at the commission, he, too, urged the FASB to back off. His rationale, he said, was a fear that, if the board tried to resist the anti-regulatory feeling then sweeping Congress, it would be crushed altogether. (Sarah Teslik, the executive director of the Council of Institutional Investors, an advocate for shareholders, is among those who argue that Levitt "wasn't the hero he makes himself out to be.") Levitt told me that the episode showed him that the accounting trade was undergoing a cultural transformation. Instead of overseeing corporate America, it was joining forces with it. "The kind of greed that produced Enron and Arthur Andersen was symbolized by the way the companies dealt with stock options," he said. "I realized something was wrong."

Until the Second World War, the American accounting industry had stayed close to its eighteenth-century roots in bookkeeping. But with the rise of information technology the accounting firms branched into consulting. During the 1990s, the Big Five doubled their collective revenues, to $26.1 billion. Their consulting practices, in particular, were hugely profitable, and brought in three times as much revenue as auditing did, according to a study soon to be published in *The Accounting Review*. Auditors started coming under pressure to attract non-audit business. At some firms, like Andersen, auditors' compensation depended upon their ability to sell other services to clients; equity partners began to be paid like investment bankers. Inevitably, there were conflicts between the independent role required of an auditor and the supplicant role of a salesman trying to expand services.

At Enron, for example, Andersen did consulting on taxes and on internal auditing. Both projects threatened to put the outside auditors in the awkward position of assessing their own company's work. The relationship was further compromised by the fact that Enron's management included many former Andersen employees, among them the company's president, vice-president, and chief accounting officer. Auditors were thus in the position of judging former colleagues—and prospective bosses.

More than a year ago, well before Enron's problems became public, an internal e-mail revealed that fourteen top Andersen partners had pointed out several of the financial schemes that eventually contributed to Enron's fall. In a discussion about retaining Enron as a client the partners considered whether Enron's "aggressive . . . transaction structuring" was too risky. It appears from the e-mail, however, that the partners' concerns were outweighed by possible future rewards. The e-mail noted that their fees "could reach $100 million per year."

"If you get too friendly and too relaxed, you can wind up nodding your head yes when you should be saying no," said Charles Bowsher, a former head of the General Accounting Office, who worked at Andersen for many years and has been retained to help reform the firm. "There's a lot of art in addition to science in accounting." Bowsher says that "most fraud flourishes in gray areas." But James Cox, a professor of corporate and securities law at Duke University, suggests that Enron's accounting gimmickry was black-and-white. "It was not even close," he said. "It was dead wrong."

Levitt said that, as the country's senior guardian of fair markets, he watched the transformation of the accounting profession with alarm. "The brakes on the worst instincts of the business community weren't working," he says. "The gatekeepers were letting down the gates." The number of audit failures afflicting corporate America was increasing; Lynn Turner, who served under Levitt as the chief accountant at the SEC, estimates that investors lost a hundred billion dollars owing to faulty, misleading, or fraudulent audits in the six years preceding Enron's crash. Many of the best-known corporations in the country were affected, among them Cendant, W. R. Grace, Sunbeam, Xerox, Lucent, and Oxford Health Plans. In fact, the number of publicly traded companies forced to restate their earnings went from three in 1981 to a hundred and fifty-eight last year, according to a doctoral thesis at New York University's Stern School of Business. (Barry Melancon, of the American Institute of Certified Public Accountants, calls concern over these numbers misleading, noting that they represent "fewer than one per cent of the audits performed.")

Shareholder lawsuits against the accounting firms proliferated. In response, the Big Five and their trade association united as a political force. According to the nonpartisan Center for Responsive Politics, between 1989 and 2001 accounting firms spent nearly thirty-nine million dollars on political contributions. The contributions were bipartisan, reaching more than half the current members of the House and ninety-four of a hundred senators.

By 1995, this investment had started to pay off. Congress passed the Private Securities Litigation Reform Act, making it harder for shareholders to sue businesses and their auditors when the businesses failed. The legislation was championed by the Speaker of the House, Newt Gingrich, as part of his Contract with America. "What we were after was trying to get rid of the frivolous, meritless cases," said Mark Gitenstein, a lawyer and lobbyist who helped shape the legislation. "We convinced Congress that you needed a system that did a better job of screening the marginal cases from the serious ones." The resulting legislation, Professor Cox said, reversed "eighty years of federal procedure."

At first, Levitt tried to fight the private-securities bill, but when it became clear that the federal regulators couldn't compete with the accountants' clout in Congress, he looked for a compromise. "It was a case where the industry had more power than the regulators," he said. Then, as now, there were approximately seventy-five lobbyists for every member of the House and Senate; in the Gingrich era, they were more integrated into the lawmaking process than ever before. Jeffrey Peck, a former Democratic Senate aide who was then the head of Arthur Andersen's Washington lobbying office and is now an outside lobbyist for the firm, says that after this fight there was "really bad feeling" between Levitt and the profession. "It was as if two people had gone out on a first date and had a bad time," he says. "But the rules required them to keep dating."

Levitt told me that he has always been proud of his ability to create consensus, and in the spring of 1996 he tried to involve the profession in reforming itself. He urged the big accounting firms to strengthen their oversight system and toughen discipline for transgressors. He proposed giving investors and other members of the public a bigger role. But, he said, the accountants resisted, and progress was made only after "huge fights."

Rules governing auditors' independence hadn't been updated in two decades. To examine the growing number of questions about conflicts of interest, Levitt created a new board, whose membership was divided between independent business leaders and people from the accounting industry. "They were constantly deadlocked by differences of opinion," Levitt said, and added, "When I asked for support, I never got it. I never heard in any speech they"—the accountants—"gave the words 'public interest.' They were so stilted, and terse, and nonproductive—I realized it was an industry that completely lacked leadership."

The accounting industry hired Harvey Pitt, who was known as one of the smartest and most aggressive private-securities lawyers in the country. Pitt responded to Levitt's call for greater public oversight by arguing, in a lengthy white paper, that the accounting firms were better off policing themselves. "The staff regarded his white paper as a kick in the stomach, because it was so one-sided and confrontational," Levitt said. One SEC official recalls that Pitt made the negotiations over the new board "the most horrible ever," and Lynn Turner says, "It was doomed from day one."

Pitt, who was appointed by President George W. Bush to succeed Levitt as chairman of the SEC, said, "There was a lot of misperception about what the white paper said. For some reason, early on people seemed to get in their mind that I opposed what Levitt did" to reform accounting. "I tried to give him my own help on a personal basis."

In the summer of 1998, Levitt received a report about a problem in Pricewaterhouse's Tampa office. According to the report, nine executives there had made eighty investments in companies that they were supposed to be auditing—a violation of the most basic independence standards. Under the SEC's direction, the firm initiated a company-wide investigation. To the shame of the entire profession, it turned up more than eight thousand such violations. The SEC fined Price-waterhouse two and a half million dollars, and called for an investigation into compliance with independence rules at the rest of the Big Five firms; Levitt asked an independent group, the Public Oversight Board, which had been created after the Penn Central collapse, to undertake this task.

Levitt also took his battle public; in the fall of 1998, he gave a speech that attacked the "numbers game." He said, "Accounting is being perverted. Auditors who want to retain their clients are under pressure not to stand in the way." He explained, "Auditors and analysts are participants in a game of nods and winks. . . . I fear we are witnessing an erosion in the quality of earnings, and therefore the quality of financial reporting." In conclusion, he said, "Today American markets enjoy the confidence of the world. How many half-truths and accounting sleights of hand will it take to tarnish that faith?"

The Public Oversight Board, made up of major business figures, was supposed to act as the profession's conscience. But in May, 2000, before its investigation could be completed, the POB's head, Charles Bowsher, received a letter from officials at the American Institute of Certified Public Accountants, which finances the board, announcing that it would "not approve nor authorize" funding for further investigations. Bowsher, who had himself been a high-ranking officer with Arthur Andersen before becoming the head of the General Accounting Office, says that he was shocked; the industry was effectively stopping the investigation. Melvin Laird, a former Secretary of Defense, who was the longest-serving member of the POB, called it "the worst incident in my seventeen years." Barry Melancon, the head of the trade association, defended the association's position. "We were never opposed to the concept," he told me, referring to the investigation. "We just felt the POB was undertaking a project that it couldn't define."

At the same time, the SEC was uncovering a huge case of accounting fraud involving the garbage-disposal company Waste Management: Arthur Andersen had put an unqualified seal of approval on numbers that the government said it either knew or should have known were misleading. As if in anticipation of the revolving-door conflicts at Enron, practically every CFO and CAO in Waste Management's history had come from Andersen. SEC enforcement documents from the investigation reveal something else: at least two of the partners who were singled out for scrutiny by the SEC remained in influential positions at Andersen while being investigated, and both have now surfaced in connection with the Enron affair. (One executive, Robert Kutsenda, who was later barred by the SEC from auditing public companies for a year, was placed in charge of redesigning the firm's policy on which documents to retain and which to shred, an issue in the Enron case. Kutsenda and Steve Samek, who was also investigated in the Waste Management case but not publicly sanctioned, were among those involved in the discussion of whether to retain Enron as a client. None of the executives involved in the Waste Management matter were fired by Andersen, which last year agreed to pay a seven-million-dollar penalty to the SEC, without admitting or denying guilt, after it was charged with fraud. In addition, two of the Andersen partners targeted by the SEC in the fraud case now serve on the profession's standard-setting board, the FASB.)

By 2000, Levitt, faced with what he calls the Big Five's "fortress mentality," had initiated a series of meetings with the firms at which he insisted that they needed to do more to police themselves. Levitt's message, Turner told me, was that the firms could either cooperate with an investigation into their compliance with independence rules or "we'll issue the subpoenas tomorrow—take your pick."

In the spring of 2000, the SEC announced that it planned to draft new rules that would greatly restrict accountants' ability to consult for the same companies they audited. Arthur Andersen reportedly argued that this would cut its market potential by forty percent, and vowed to fight back. A June meeting in Deloitte's New York headquarters with the heads of the three firms who most vehemently opposed the new rules "was so icy you could have stored cold meat in that room," Turner says. The heads of Andersen, Deloitte, and KPMG joined Melancon on one side of a conference table. (Pricewaterhouse and Ernst & Young were more supportive of Levitt, and didn't attend.) Levitt and two SEC officials were on the other. When Levitt made it clear that he intended to move forward, Andersen's chief executive, Robert Grafton, declared, "This is war."

"It was unbelievable, just unbelievable," Turner recalled. "They all went after Arthur. They made clear that everything was fair game." Turner says that the attitude of the firms was "You know we're going to win anyway in the end, so why not save us the expense, and give up now?"

"As soon as I left that meeting," Levitt told me, "it was clear the fight was going to Capitol Hill." Such clashes over commercial interests are commonplace in Congress, but "this wasn't about legislation," he said. "It was about SEC rule-making—we're supposed to be an independent agency. I'd never seen anything like it at the SEC."

During this period, Levitt said, he got a letter from Representative W. J. (Billy) Tauzin, of Louisiana, the chairman of the House Energy and Commerce Committee, who has received more than two hundred and eighty thousand dollars from the accounting industry over the past decade. The letter consisted of four pages of pointed questions. In a not very veiled threat, Tauzin asked how many violations Levitt and the other members of the SEC would have if their stock holdings were subjected to the independence rules being proposed for the accountants. He also demanded that Levitt produce proof that non-audit consulting undermines auditors' accuracy. "It was a shot across the bow from the industry," Levitt says. "They were saying, 'If you go forward, expect a lot of pain.'"

In the following weeks, he said, Tauzin "badgered me relentlessly. He knew what the accountants were doing before I did. He was working very closely with them. I don't mean to sound cynical, but is it because he loves accountants?" At one point, relations between the two men grew so bad that Levitt hung up on Tauzin, because he felt that "his words and his tone were threatening."

Tauzin was not alone. In the four weeks after Levitt announced his intention to go through with the proposed new rules, forty-six more congressmen wrote to him questioning them. Data from the Center for Responsive Politics show that in 2000 the accountants contributed more than ten million dollars to political campaigns and spent $12.6 million on federal lobbying. Arthur Andersen alone nearly doubled its lobbying budget in the second half of the year, to $1.6 million. Among the lobbyists hired by the industry were Vic Fazio, a former congressman; Jack Quinn, a former Clinton White House counsel; Ed Gillespie, a former

Bush campaign adviser; Patrick Griffin, Clinton's former congressional liaison; Dan Brouillette, a former aide to Tauzin who is now an Assistant Energy Secretary; and a number of other former Hill staff people.

Now, however, Tauzin has joined in the public outrage toward Enron and Andersen; in a House hearing that he chaired, he called the case "an old-fashioned example of theft by insiders, and a failure of those responsible for them to prevent that theft." He told me that money hadn't influenced his earlier defense of the accountants. "Donations have never bought anybody any slack with this committee," he said. "I'm not saying that contributions don't have the power to corrupt. They do. But I always assume people contribute to me because they like the work I do."

By early fall of 2000, Levitt says, he began to hear another kind of threat: lobbyists told him that if he didn't back off there would be a push to cut the SEC's funding. "They were going to place a rider on our appropriations budget," Levitt said, still sounding as if he could not believe it. Jay Velasquez, a lobbyist for the accountants at the time, confirmed this. "You have to consider all your options," he said. "There is no doubt that the rider was a consideration. In these battles, everything is on the table." Henry Bonilla, a Texas Republican with an anti-regulatory temperament who is a member of the House Appropriations Committee, was prepared to attach the rider. Bowsher, the former GAO head, says that such threats were once unthinkable. "In the old days, the SEC was off limits to that kind of pressure. It was a place the private sector respected. Nobody, nobody, would have thought about asking Congress to cut the budget."

Representative Tom Udall, a Democrat from New Mexico, says that his staff urged him to sign a widely circulated letter to Levitt opposing the proposed rules, because so many of his colleagues had. "There's sort of a herd mentality," he said. He refused; he knew Levitt slightly, through mutual friends in Santa Fe. "Levitt was out to solve these things before people realized there was a problem. That's the sign of a leader. But the special interests have such a hold on members of Congress that they were able to stop a lot of things."

Levitt initiated a nationwide series of public hearings about accounting abuses, fighting back as if he were involved in a political campaign. Damon Silvers, an AFL-CIO official who supported the SEC's position, recalls that "Levitt looked like a figure from some old movie—he was sitting at a huge desk at the SEC with a bank of phones, talking on several lines at once."

But by then Levitt's eight-year term at the SEC was about to expire, and the accounting-industry supporters developed a new strategy: they started to oppose the rule's substance on procedural grounds, arguing that there hadn't been enough time for public hearings. "Of course, we knew that by calling for more time it would mean the end of Levitt," one lobbyist said.

With the accounting firms threatening to take the SEC to court if he went ahead with the rules, Levitt tried to strike a deal with the three firms who opposed him, at which point the two firms who had previously supported him turned against him. That night, one aide recalled, Levitt gave up. "I lost it," Levitt said.

In the end, he kept negotiating, and the SEC agreed to let the firms continue to consult for the companies they audited. But the firms agreed to disclose the details to investors. "I knew it wasn't enough, but I thought we'd be overruled by Congress in one fashion or another," Levitt said. "The part of me that was insecure wanted a bird in the hand."

Almost exactly a year later, Enron's outside auditor, Arthur Andersen LLP, a company whose image had virtually defined Midwestern probity, made an astonishing admission. During the previous three years, when it had vouched for Enron's financial statements, the company's net income had actually been inflated by almost six hundred million dollars. In a financial market where stocks plummet if corporate earnings fall a penny short of projections, Enron was forced to reveal that its profits had been off by about twenty percent over three years. As early as 1997, Andersen had known that Enron was inflating its income. But when Enron declined to correct the numbers Andersen certified them anyway. Within six months, Enron had filed for bankruptcy and Andersen had been indicted on charges of obstruction of justice for destroying documents related to its Enron work. Investors lost an estimated ninety-three billion dollars, a sum nearly equal to the amount of the economic-stimulus package that President Bush requested for the entire country. In the year before Enron's crash, Andersen had collected a million dollars a week from Enron for its expertise. More than half of that, Andersen acknowledged, in compliance with the new SEC rule, was for non-auditing work.

"If these reforms had been in place earlier, we wouldn't have had an Enron," Lynn Turner told me. He laughed, but the laugh sounded a little forced as he spoke about Congress's newfound interest in reform. "Maybe the congressmen were listening more than I thought—we just weren't giving them enough money," he said.

Not long ago, Levitt was called to testify before Congress about what went wrong at Arthur Andersen. "It was a play within a play," he told me. He said that he has little hope for meaningful change in the profession, despite all the bills under consideration, and despite commitments from Harvey Pitt, his successor at the SEC. Before Enron collapsed, Pitt promised the accountants "kinder and gentler" treatment than Levitt had shown them, but he has since sharpened his rhetoric and proposed a great many reforms. Pitt told me that his work for the accountants has made him better able to persuade them to change their ways because, "to put it bluntly, I know where the bodies are buried." But Pitt dismissed Levitt's approach—separating auditing from consulting—as "a simplistic solution to a complex problem," and told me that he thought it could prove counterproductive. "A firm that does only audits may be incompetent," he said.

"That's the same argument that the accountants put forward," Levitt said with a sigh. "I didn't accept it then, and I accept it even less today. I have to conclude it's specious. It's very sad. The Administration is missing a glorious opportunity to reform this industry."

UPDATE

Although a number of the reforms that Arthur Levitt pushed for have not yet been enacted, the passage of the Sarbanes-Oxley Act in July effected the biggest changes in the accounting industry in more than half a century. Sarbanes-Oxley created a new quasi-governmental board to regulate auditors, which will replace much of accountants' current self-regulation. Auditors are now prohibited from performing many non-audit activities, including many consulting activities, and companies now have to rotate their auditors every five years.   —J.S.

PEER REVUE:
HOW ARTHUR ANDERSEN
GOT AWAY WITH IT

Noam Scheiber

The New Republic, January 28, 2002

GIVEN THE BY NOW well-publicized lapses of its most notorious client, it came as something of a surprise this month when Enron's auditor, Arthur Andersen, passed its triennial peer review "without qualification." A release on the company's Web site does note three mysterious "issues" raised by the reviewing firm, fellow accounting giant Deloitte & Touche, but adds that they were "not deemed significant enough to affect the opinion." The implication, as a *Washington Post* article on the matter concluded, is that "the investing public can have confidence in audits performed by [Andersen]."

A more precise parsing of Deloitte & Touche's findings, however, would be that investors can have confidence in Andersen's audits—as long as they don't have the misfortune to have invested in Enron, or any other company whose audits by Andersen proved controversial. The reason is that when accounting firms review each other's work, they generally exclude any audits where litigation may be pending. (Such litigation is not uncommon: Over the last five years Andersen alone has been sued for its handling of inflated earnings at Waste Management, Inc. and Sunbeam Corp.) It's as if a college student's grade point average were determined only after excluding all the classes in which he'd done poorly.

Of course, any review of Andersen that excludes Enron—the largest corporate meltdown in history—is for all intents and purposes useless. So, days after the results were publicized, Charles Bowsher, head of the

Public Oversight Board, the organization responsible for overseeing the accounting industry's peer-review process, ordered that the issues highlighted by Enron's case be examined retrospectively. But Bowsher's decision ultimately misses the point. The real scandal of Andersen's peer review isn't that Enron wasn't examined; it's that even if it had been, Andersen would still have earned a passing grade.

When Congress passed the Securities Act of 1933 it decided—under pressure from the major accounting firms—to forgo active regulation of the industry. Instead, it merely drew broad guidelines and relied largely on the industry to apply them. But the attempts at self-regulation produced one weak regime after another: the American Institute of Certified Public Accountants' (AICPA) Committee on Accounting Procedure in 1939; AICPA's Accounting Principles Board in 1959; the Financial Accounting Standards Board in 1973. None reduced accounting fraud to an acceptable level.

So in the late 1970s the major accounting firms made a final effort to stave off real government oversight, proposing a system of peer review in which each firm would have its audits scrutinized by another firm once every three years. The process is supposed to ensure that a given accounting firm has appropriate quality-control procedures in place—everything from how it selects employees for a given assignment to how it attracts and retains clients—and that it adheres to those procedures when conducting its audits. For instance, "they might try to find examples where one of the managers on the audit had a disagreement with management, brought it to a partner, and see how it was handled," explains University of Chicago accounting professor Roman Weil.

Overall, the triennial review must examine enough cases to cover between 3 percent and 6 percent of a Big Five firm's total audit hours over the previous year. (Amazingly, the two years prior are off-limits.) And though within that range the peer reviewer has broad discretion over which audits to examine, there are certain categories of audits that must be included: an audit that involved several of a firm's different offices; an audit of a public entity like a municipal government; an audit of a company's employee-benefits plan.

What the peer review doesn't include is anything that might ordinarily be thought of as a reasonable fail-safe: say, picking an audit at random, reworking the numbers from scratch, and seeing if those numbers jibe with the original audit. "They're not tracing transactions," Weil concedes. On the rare occasion that a peer-review auditor actually does examine another auditor's paperwork, the point is not to do a so-called reaudit, but simply to make sure that the numbers documented by the original auditor look plausible. The problem with this is that accounting is notoriously dependent on judgment calls—what future economic benefits are likely to be derived from a given asset, whether losses can be characterized as one-time or recurring, etc. Since the logic behind these judgment calls never actually makes it into the final documentation, there's no way for a reviewer to gauge their soundness. "All that they're looking at is whatever the people that did the audit happened to record," explains Douglas Carmichael, a former vice president of AICPA (the industry's standard-setting body) and an accounting professor at Baruch College. Worse, Carmichael points out, even when a reviewer has reason to suspect that the original auditor failed to scrutinize something, the original auditor can always claim that he or she applied the necessary scrutiny and plead guilty to the relatively minor offense of "failing to document."

In fact, these are exactly the sort of problems that arose prior to Arthur Andersen's last peer review. In 1997 Andersen had discerned that Enron's stated earnings of $105 million actually looked more like $54 million when accounted for properly. But when it pointed this out to Enron's financial officers, they protested that the error was less than 8 percent of normalized income—that is, income averaged over several preceding years—and was therefore acceptable under a widely invoked "materiality" provision. (The idea is that auditors are not responsible for errors so small they might plausibly fall below their radar screen.) Andersen relented and signed off on the original $105 million figure. When Deloitte & Touche completed its peer review the following year, it would have had no way of exposing this bit of sophistry, assuming it even examined the Enron audit. Without being privy to the logic behind the decision, "the peer reviewer [would not have been] in a position to challenge the judgment the auditor applied," complains one former Securities Exchange Commission (SEC) official. Not surprisingly, Deloitte & Touche obliged with a passing grade.

Since then, we now know, Enron's accounting has gotten progressively shadier. For example, the company created dozens of special partnerships specifically to hide hundreds of millions of dollars in debt from investors and credit-rating agencies. And Andersen's auditing, it seems, has deteriorated as well. Last Thursday the company admitted it had destroyed numerous documents relating to Enron, some of which may well have disclosed this shell game. Ironically, part of what a peer reviewer is supposed to do is determine whether a firm's documentation policies make sense. But since a peer reviewer only actually looks at existing documents (rather than, say, generating his own documents for comparison), beyond very obvious omissions it's difficult to determine what kinds of documents a firm might have thrown away. Indeed, says the former SEC official, there's little reason to expect that Deloitte & Touche would have suspected any improper document shredding at Andersen—let alone looked into what the shredded documents contained—even if it had examined the Enron audit. Thanks to Enron's spectacular collapse, this task will now fall to Congress, the Justice Department, and the SEC.

Enron is an egregious case, but it's less an anomaly than an extreme example of the efforts at "earnings management" that have become quite common in corporate America in recent years. During the 1990s Wall Street grew so fixated on analysts' quarterly-earnings expectations that failing to meet them by even a single penny per share could send a company's stock price tumbling. So, rather than disappoint the market, companies took to fudging their numbers. Some tried Enron's materiality gambit, albeit in less brazen ways. Others tried what's known as "revenue recognition," whereby a company records sales in one quarter even though it won't actually receive payment until the next. (The recently humbled Microstrategy made this particular "microstrategy" famous.) But perhaps the most widespread approach was what's known as "big bath accounting." That's when a corporation inflates profits by writing off years of future expenses as a one-time "restructuring cost."

Of course, once everyone realized that so many companies were bending the rules to meet expectations, it became all the more damning to fail to meet them. As one stockbroker told the *Harvard Business Review* last year, "Things must be pretty bad if Cisco can't manage to come up with one lousy penny." Companies that still fell short of expectations were punished even more severely, raising the stakes even higher and encouraging companies to bend the rules still further. This vicious

cycle had accelerated so much that, according to a recent study by the
Levy Institute Forecasting Center, an economic research and consulting group, corporate earnings for the S&P 500 may have been inflated
by as much as 20 percent at the height of the boom.

For their part, the Big Five auditors were loath to blow the whistle.
After all, over the last two decades the big accounting firms have taken
to viewing their auditing services as "loss leaders" that get them in the
door, at which point they can sell their clients far more lucrative consulting services. But with big consulting contracts on the line, it isn't
exactly in an auditor's interest to begin questioning his client's math.
That left peer review as the only line of defense.

As the lax standards of the peer-review regime demonstrate, the system wasn't designed to catch any of this. But even if it had been—and
there are reports that the SEC is negotiating with the industry over a
tough, new self-regulatory body—the Big Five accounting firms would
probably have been no more inclined to expose one another than they
were to expose companies like Enron. Part of the reason, no doubt, is
the sense that one hand washes the other. If Deloitte & Touche lets
Andersen off easy, presumably Andersen will be inclined to do the same
when it comes time to conduct its own review. But it goes deeper than
that. Indeed, over the years the Big Five firms—down from the Big
Eight as recently as 1989, and the Big Six as recently as 1997, as the
result of mergers—have often behaved less like competitors than corporate partners. Among other things, they all belong to the same insurance
pool. That means any time one of them has to cough up a wad of cash
to settle a potential fraud case, it raises the insurance premiums for the
other four. With that kind of incentive why would any of them ever rat
on the other?

To make things even cozier, the Big Five firms have created a network of extremely close relationships between their in-house lawyers.
According to an October 2000 *BusinessWeek* article, the general coun-
sels of the Big Five accounting firms meet in New York once every six
weeks to talk shop over lunch. Among the topics of conversation? How
best to avoid audits that might require one firm to cast doubt on the work
of another. This arrangement paid off for Deloitte & Touche in 1991.
That year a little-known New Jersey thrift named Fidelity Mutual Savings and Loan Association discovered that one of its vice presidents had

spent the previous 16 years defrauding it to the tune of $6 million. Confused at how this minor detail escaped its auditor's attention, Fidelity hired rival firm KPMG to investigate. Roger Ham, the lead investigator, concluded that the scam was only possible because of numerous failings on the part of Deloitte & Touche. Indeed, his initial report used some form of the word "failure" no fewer than ten times. But rather than accept that judgment, Deloitte's general counsel (again, according to *BusinessWeek*) simply picked up the phone and called his counterpart at KPMG. The final "revised" report contained not a single mention of "failure."

With this kind of chumminess, it's no mystery why no major accounting firm has ever received a failing peer-review grade. And even when a review, like Andersen's this year, contains qualifications, they're usually quickly forgotten: As soon as the next triennial review is completed, the previous one is removed from public display. When I called AICPA to get a copy of Andersen's 1998 peer review, a spokesman there told me, "We shred 'em, get rid of 'em" once the new one is done. Sounds like a pretty good suggestion for the entire peer-review process.

INSIDE THE TELECOM GAME

Steven Rosenbush in New York, with Heather Timmons in New York, Roger O. Crockett in Chicago, Christopher Palmeri in Los Angeles, and Charles Haddad in Atlanta

BusinessWeek, August 5, 2002

TELECOM HAS BEEN a disaster for just about everyone. Investors have lost some $2 trillion as stock prices have tumbled 95% or more from their highs. Half a million workers have lost their jobs during the past two years. Dozens of debt-laden companies, from Winstar Communications to Global Crossing, have collapsed into bankruptcy. And on July 21, the sector sank to a once-unimaginable low when World-Com Inc., the company that embodied the industry's power and promise, filed the largest bankruptcy claim in U.S. history.

Yet a small group of CEOs and financiers managed to save the family silver before the house burned to the ground. Philip F. Anschutz, founder of ailing local and long-distance upstart Qwest Communications International Inc., reaped $1.9 billion from company stock sales since 1998. Former Qwest CEO Joseph P. Nacchio sold $248 million worth of stock before he was pushed out of the scandal-plagued company in June. Global Crossing founder Gary Winnick sold $734 million of his shares before his company filed for bankruptcy in January. And former WorldCom CEO Bernard J. Ebbers borrowed some $400 million from his company before he was ousted in April—and that loan remains to be repaid.

What do these execs have in common? They were all central players in a tight-knit telecom clique that dominated the communications industry in the second half of the last decade. Individually, some of these men were well known, but the ties among them are little understood even today. The group was linked through Salomon Smith Barney's telecom analyst Jack B. Grubman, the son of a Philadelphia municipal worker who rose from his blue-collar roots to become one of the most powerful players on Wall Street. He helped raise money for Qwest, Global Crossing, and WorldCom, recommended their stocks to investors, attended board meetings, and was elbows-deep in working with them to plot strategy.

Grubman's influence stretched far beyond the three companies that have collapsed in scandal in recent months. According to Thomson Financial Securities Data, Salomon helped 81 telecom companies raise $190 billion in debt and equity since 1996, the year the Telecommunications Act was passed to deregulate the telephone industry. In return, Salomon, part of Citigroup, received hundreds of millions in underwriting fees and tens of millions more for advising its stable of telecom players on mergers and acquisitions. Grubman himself was paid about $20 million a year.

So powerful was Grubman in his heyday that he could direct development of the telecom industry. Like junk-bond king Michael Milken at the height of his power in the 1980s, Grubman's word was good as gold. He could raise millions for start-up players, win investor support for a proposed acquisition, or boost a company's stock price. On Mar. 14, 2000, for example, he raised his price target for Metromedia Fiber Network, which Salomon had taken public, and its shares surged 16%, to about $46. MFN filed for bankruptcy in May. "Jack orchestrated the industry," says analyst Susan Kalla of investment company Friedman, Billings, Ramsey Group Inc.

Individual investors may have jumped at Grubman's picks because they thought he was doling out impartial advice on his favorite stocks— the traditional job of Wall Street analysts. But Grubman's interests were deeply conflicted, and he came to personify the blurred lines between research and investment banking in the boom. More than any other telecom analyst, he was actively involved with the companies he covered. Many critics felt that made it impossible for him to be objective about those companies' prospects. For example, he helped Anschutz recruit Nacchio as Qwest's chief executive in 1997, and he aided Global Crossing's Winnick in his $11 billion acquisition of Frontier Communications in 1999. Could Grubman then step back and make critical assessments about Qwest and Global Crossing for investors?

In the wake of the telecom meltdown, Grubman is facing more intense scrutiny than ever before. As the telecom bubble began deflating in 2000 and 2001 and other analysts began to warn that the industry was straining under the weight of excess capacity and enormous debt, he continued urging investors to load up on shares of Qwest, Global Crossing, WorldCom, and others. In March, 2001, Grubman issued a "State of the Union" report in which he wrote: "We believe that the underlying demand for network-based services remains strong. In fact, we believe that telecom services, as a percentage of [gross domestic product], will double within the next seven or eight years." Now, investors are questioning whether Grubman was motivated by his true opinions—or by the millions of dollars he received from supporting his telecom clique.

Grubman, 48, knew he was crossing a line few analysts dared traverse. But he forcefully defended his dual roles. In a 2000 profile in *BusinessWeek*, he said he was the model of the modern Wall Street analyst. "What used to be a conflict is now a synergy," he said at the time. "Someone like me, who is banking-intensive, would have been looked at disdainfully by the buy side 15 years ago. Now, they know that I'm in the flow of what's going on." At the time, Sanford Weill, Citigroup's chairman, voiced support for Grubman's activities, though he said analysts have to maintain their objectivity as stockpickers or "they will lose their credibility." Both men declined to comment for this story.

Grubman's credibility was strained even at the time. In the 2000 article, *BusinessWeek* reported for the first time that Grubman had lied on his official Salomon biography for years—claiming he had graduated from the prestigious Massachusetts Institute of Technology when his alma mater was really Boston University. He admitted the discrepancy at the time. "At some point, I probably felt insecure, and it perpetuated itself," he said. He also claimed to have grown up in South Philadelphia when he really was from Oxford Circle in the northeast part of Philadelphia. Both are blue-collar neighborhoods. But South Philly is a more historic neighborhood, the stomping grounds of singer Frankie Avalon and movie boxer Rocky Balboa, and would hold more appeal for a one-time amateur boxer like Grubman.

Despite such issues, Grubman was able to wield his influence in the telecom industry, which benefited his inner circle. When analyst Vik Grover of Kaufman Bros. LP questioned Winstar's prospects in January, 2001, Grubman blasted him in a research note issued later that day. "We believe this is highly irresponsible of the analyst since they do not have coverage of [Winstar], nor did they speak with senior management," he wrote. He also chastised Grover during Winstar's quarterly conference call on Feb. 1. That helped buoy Winstar's stock—but only for several weeks. Short of cash, the company, under CEO William Rouhana, filed for bankruptcy two months later, in April. The National Association of Securities Dealers is investigating whether Grubman's recommendations on the stock violated its standards for stock analysts.

Nowhere was Grubman's loyalty more evident than with WorldCom. Other Wall Street analysts, including Daniel P. Reingold of CS First Boston, stopped recommending the stock last year because of its deteriorating long-distance business and slowing growth rate. Yet Grubman reiterated his "strong buy" regularly in 2001 because, he said, it had the "best assets in the telecom industry." Grubman didn't downgrade WorldCom to a "neutral" until Apr. 22, when the company slashed its revenue targets for 2002. By that time, WorldCom's shares had dropped about 90% from their peak, to $4.

Grubman's allies may have benefited from his actions in other ways. According to a lawsuit filed by David Chacon, a Salomon broker who was fired in 2000, Grubman doled out shares in hot initial public offerings to Ebbers, Nacchio, and several other telecom executives to win investment banking business. Ebbers allegedly received stock in broadband provider Rhythms NetConnections Inc. at the time of its initial public offering in 1999. When the upstart's stock soared 229% in the first day of trading, Ebbers cashed out for a $16 million profit, according to the suit. If Chacon's allegations are true, Salomon may have violated securities regulations that bar investment banks from paying individuals for banking business. Salomon denies the assertion.

Now, Grubman's entire network is unraveling. The Securities and Exchange Commission is investigating Qwest for alleged accounting improprieties in what has become a criminal probe. Global Crossing is under investigation by the Securities and Exchange Commission, the FBI, and two congressional committees. WorldCom faces scrutiny from the SEC, the Justice Dept., and the House Energy & Commerce Committee. WorldCom has admitted to a $3.8 billion accounting error in its financial statements. A spokesman says the company "supports the investigators and wants them to get to the bottom of things so we can all move forward." Qwest and Global Crossing have denied any wrongdoing. Global Crossing execs were not available for comment. A spokesman for Qwest says, "We worked with [Grubman] as we would any analyst."

Grubman is under the microscope, too. Besides the NASD, he is being investigated by New York Attorney General Eliot Spitzer and U.S. Attorney James B. Comey in Manhattan. He was called before the House Committee on Financial Services on July 8 to explain his role in the WorldCom accounting scandal—and was hammered by legislators. "We have an independent analyst who is neither independent and apparently can't analyze," said Michael E. Capuano (D-Mass.). "My major fear is that you'll get away with it." Salomon has supported Grubman, although Citigroup said in July that it would support a ban on analysts participating in many investment banking activities.

Grubman has defended his actions before Congress and elsewhere. He said that he helped Qwest, Global Crossing, WorldCom, and others raise billions of dollars because he saw a brilliant future for the telecom industry. He thought a rapid deployment of broadband connections to businesses and consumers around the country would lead to a surge in Internet traffic that would require the creation of new networks with vast amounts of capacity. He admits he was wrong in his analysis. But he says he was not motivated by conflicted interests. "I am saddened by the events that have brought us here," he told congressional probers on July 8. "I am sorry to see investors suffer losses. I am sorry to see employees laid off."

No question, the damage caused by Grubman and his circle of insiders is threatening to undermine the health of the telecom industry. While Grubman and his allies encouraged investors to cough up the billions of dollars needed to make huge new capital investments in fiber-optic networks and broadband connections, it's now clear that that vision of the future was wildly hyped. Billions in investments are going to waste, as little as 3% of new long-distance networks are being used, and investors are fleeing the sector. Even once-stable players are suffering. On July 23, local-phone giant BellSouth said WorldCom owes the company $75 million to $160 million, contributing to a 15% drop in BellSouth's stock price that day.

The crisis could relegate the U.S. to second-class status in the communications industry. In the 20th century, U.S. phone services were the envy of the world, reaching 95% of the population and operating with 99.999% reliability. They played a crucial role in the U.S.'s economic development and even served as a strategic asset in World War II, thanks to innovations such as early wireless communications. But in recent years, the rollout of high-speed Net access and other services has been led by other nations, such as South Korea and Japan. As telecom companies cut back on capital spending, it will be harder to catch up. "The U.S. is already behind, and will likely fall further behind as telecom companies find it extremely difficult to raise funds in the near term," says James Glen of Economy.com.

Already, the fallout is brutal. The $2 trillion in losses that telecom investors have suffered is twice the damage caused by the bursting of the Internet bubble and on a par with the savings-and-loan crisis of the late 1980s. Bank exposure to the telecom mess is tens of billions of dollars. Worse, the investigations into WorldCom, Global Crossing, and Qwest, layered on top of the Enron scandal, are dealing a huge blow to investor confidence. They've led the entire stock market down as the Standard & Poor's 500-stock index has tumbled 29% so far this year.

It wasn't supposed to turn out this way. The incestuous telecom players had a legitimate business idea: making the U.S. industry the most competitive in the world. Deregulation in 1996 allowed any company, including long-distance players such as AT&T and WorldCom, to move into the local telephone business and compete against the Bells. One of the first success stories was MFS Communications Co., which was started in the early 1990s by execs from construction giant Peter Kiewit & Sons in Omaha. MFS built local phone networks around the country. After WorldCom decided to move into the local business in 1996, it bought MFS for the then-unheard-of price of $10 billion.

It was a windfall for everyone involved. Top MFS execs, such as James Q. Crowe and Royce J. Holland, made tens of millions apiece. WorldCom's banker, Salomon Smith Barney, reaped tens of millions in fees. Even WorldCom shares rose, which is unusual for a company that plays the acquiring role in a deal. But the company had a key supporter: Grubman, who endorsed the deal.

The temptation to keep using the formula was irresistible. MFS execs left WorldCom to set up new telecom companies. Crowe created long-distance data upstart Level 3 Communications Inc., and Holland created local-service competitor Allegiance Telecom Inc., both of which received funding from Salomon and glowing recommendations from Grubman. "These guys decided they should all jump on the Net bandwagon. They were all trying to tap markets as quickly as possible before others jumped in first," says telecom analyst Glenn Waldorf of UBS Warburg.

Grubman and the telecom execs argued that the market could easily absorb all the new capacity. At one road show after another, from the meeting halls of San Jose, Calif., to the dining rooms of plush Manhattan hotels, Crowe stood before audiences, charming them with the bearing and voice of a senior military official. He argued that the telecom sector was going through the same sort of changes that had spawned successful start-ups in the software and computer industries. He said that "silicon economics" would allow upstarts such as Level 3 to offer more capacity at lower prices than mature rivals such as AT&T. And the demand for these networks would soar as voice communications gave way to e-mail, pictures, video—even holograms, Crowe said. Investors ate it up, and the shares of these companies soared.

Before long, the line of entrepreneurs waiting for funding stretched out the door. Salomon funded upstarts Qwest, Global Crossing, Teligent, Winstar, Rhythm, Williams Communications, Focal, and dozens more. "WorldCom delivered such success that Grubman had [other telecom executives] mimic [WorldCom's approach]," Kalla says. "He would put them up on the pulpit at his conferences, where they were the keynotes. It was just very well orchestrated."

Meantime, Grubman was becoming a star. He rose from humble roots—his father was a construction manager for the city of Philadelphia, and his mother worked in a dress shop. A math whiz, he worked at AT&T from 1977 to 1985, doing quantitative research, among other things, and then jumped to Wall Street. But it was moving to Salomon in 1994 that gave him the chance to become the most powerful analyst in his field.

His formula for his success was to grow increasingly close to the managers at the telecom companies he was covering. He recruited execs, helped plot strategy, and advised on mergers. For example, he helped Ebbers launch WorldCom's hostile bid for MCI in 1998, which resulted in the $43 billion acquisition. In his congressional testimony on WorldCom, Grubman revealed that he had attended "two or three" board meetings at WorldCom at the company's headquarters in Mississippi. Rival analysts chafed at Grubman's chumminess with the execs he was covering. "He'd get on a company's conference call and just start talking about what he thought about the company," says one analyst. "We all had questions for the company, and he was asking them 'so, how about that dinner last night, huh?'"

The relationships in Grubman's network go back years. Clark McLeod sold his long-distance upstart to MCI in 1990 for $1.25 billion, pocketing $50 million. Then, in the mid-1990s, Grubman and the bankers at Salomon helped him launch a new company called McLeod Communications, raising $3.4 billion for construction of a 31,000-mile telephone network. McLeod, a Midwesterner who handed employees copies of his book *This Way Up*, boldly promised that revenues would hit $11 billion by 2007. Grubman maintained a buy rating on the company—right until it declared bankruptcy in January of this year with $1.8 billion in revenue.

At first, no one ever worried about whether these telecom upstarts were making money. Even older telecom players, such as MCI and Sprint, needed years to invest in their network. MCI didn't turn profitable for more than a decade. When Grubman helped them raise money in the late 1990s, the Internet bubble was in full swing, and claims that rising data traffic would allow them to become profitable someday sounded believable. The unspoken assumption was that they would be acquired anyway by the likes of WorldCom, AT&T, or one of the Bells.

These assumptions were shaken when the Internet bubble burst in March, 2000. As one dot-com after another went bust, the growth of data traffic slowed. Network utilization on all the new optical telecom networks fell to just 3%, and prices started plunging 50% a year. The capital windows quickly slammed shut.

Telecom executives realized that they could never deliver on their promises of revenue growth of 20% or more. But rather than come clean to investors, an alarming number of them resorted to misleading accounting practices to preserve the illusion of stability. In the first six months of 2001, Qwest sold $857 million worth of network capacity to Global Crossing and other carriers. It also bought $450 million worth from Global Crossing and other carriers. That helped Qwest's revenue rise 12% for the first half of the year. Without those deals, Qwest's revenue would have increased only 7%.

Such deals may have allowed senior management to cash out before the bubble finally burst. In May of last year, Winnick sold $123 million worth of Global Crossing stock. That same month, Anschutz sold $230 million worth of Qwest stock. The SEC is investigating both companies.

With investors losing trillions of dollars and dozens of telecom players in bankruptcy, there are growing calls for tough action against those responsible. Grubman, certainly, will face more scrutiny. New York Attorney General Spitzer has subpoenaed his research records, e-mail, and other documents. If Spitzer finds wrongdoing, Salomon may have to pay a fine or even discipline Grubman. The U.S. Attorney's investigation could even result in criminal charges.

Two years ago, Grubman claimed he was creating a new model for Wall Street analysts. Today, it's a model that Grubman—and most telecom investors—may wish they had never heard of.

After months of pressure, Jack Grubman finally resigned from Salomon Smith Barney in mid-August. He did not walk away empty-handed. His severance package was worth a reported $32 million. Grubman came under more fire when a congressional committee revealed that Salomon had funneled shares in hot IPOs to telecom executives with whom the company was doing business, including most notably WorldCom's Bernie Ebbers. One memo from Salomon showed that, in at least two cases, Grubman was informed which executives got IPO shares, further evidence of just how porous the so-called Chinese Wall between investment banking and research really was.

HOW CORRUPT IS WALL STREET?

Marcia Vickers and Mike France, with Emily Thornton,
David Henry, and Heather Timmons in New York and
Mike McNamee in Washington

BusinessWeek, May 13, 2002

WHEN DEBASES KANJILAL, a Queens (N.Y.) pediatrician, picked up his phone in early 2001 to call lawyer Jacob H. Zamansky, he had no idea he would whip up a full-fledged hurricane on Wall Street. Kanjilal claimed he lost $500,000 investing in Infospace Inc., an Internet stock he says his Merrill Lynch & Co. broker urged him not to sell when it was trading at $60 a share. By the time he sold, it was down to $11. Zamansky filed a novel arbitration claim against Merrill in March, 2001, in which he argued that its star Net analyst, Henry Blodget, had misled investors by fraudulently promoting the stocks of companies with which the firm had investment banking relationships. That lawsuit led directly to an investigation by New York State Attorney General Eliot Spitzer, who stunned Merrill and its Wall Street brethren three weeks ago when he made public some shocking e-mail exchanges between Merrill analysts and bankers.

That was just the start. Now, Spitzer is investigating Salomon Smith Barney, Morgan Stanley Dean Witter, and at least three others. The Securities and Exchange Commission has launched a probe into practices at 10 firms, while the Justice Dept. is pondering an inquiry of its own. And plaintiffs' lawyers are advertising for clients and filing new suits daily.

The widening scandal has plunged Wall Street into crisis. The resulting furor is more thunderous than the one unleashed by Michael R. Milken's junk-bond schemes in the 1980s, the Prudential Securities limited-partnership debacle in the early '90s, or price-fixing on the Nasdaq later in the decade. In part, that's because many more individuals lost money in the recent market collapse than in earlier scandals.

But uproar over the relationships between analysts and their investment banking colleagues has also grown because it comes on the heels of several other scandals that raise big questions about how Wall Street operates. Already, probes are under way into Wall Street's shady initial public offering allocation practices, as well as its crucial role in setting up and selling the partnerships that led to Enron Corp.'s collapse. Worse, execs at many firms may have made a bundle investing in the partnerships, even as those same firms advised clients to hold Enron stock virtually until it went bankrupt. It all makes Wall Street seem rigged for the benefit of insiders as never before.

The damage goes way beyond the tattered reputations of the firms and their beleaguered analysts. The entire economy depends on the financial system to raise and allocate capital. And that financial system, in turn, is built on the integrity of its information. Should investors lose confidence in that information, it could deepen and prolong the bear market, as wary investors hesitate to put money into stocks. And it could easily put a damper on the economy if companies are less willing—or less able—to raise capital on Wall Street. "One of the precious things we have is the integrity of the financial markets. If that changes it could have dramatic repercussions on the dollar, on domestic inflation, on the economy," says Felix G. Rohatyn, former managing director of Lazard Frères & Co.

Wall Street has always struggled with conflicts of interest. Indeed, an investment bank is a business built on them. The same institution serves two masters: the companies for which it sells stock, issues bonds, or executes mergers; and the investors whom it advises. While companies want high prices for their newly issued stocks and low interest rates on their bonds, investors want low prices and high rates. In between, the bank gets fees from both and trades stocks and bonds on its own behalf as well, potentially putting its own interests at odds with those of all its customers.

But in recent years, those inherent conflicts have grown worse, as the sums to be made by overlooking them have grown enormous. That's because since the repeal of Depression-era banking laws, megabanks such as Citigroup and J.P. Morgan Chase are allowed to do everything from trading stocks to lending money and managing pension funds.

Chinese walls—jargon for the strict separation of the different lines of business conducted under the same roof—were supposed to keep the bankers honest and free from corruption. But a series of scandals since the early 1980s has eaten away at those foundations. The final blow, however, was the tide of money that flooded over Wall Street during the great tech bubble. Between the last quarter of 1998 and the first quarter of 2000, the tech-heavy Nasdaq market index soared from 1,500 to more than 5,000. Many investors made out like bandits. So did the investment banks. During the same period, according to Thomson Financial/First Call, Wall Street earned $10 billion in fees by raising nearly $245 billion for 1,300 companies, many of them profitless tech outfits that later blew up. The bubble burst in the spring of 2000, wiping out more than $4 trillion in investor wealth. "The fact is that a bubble market allowed the creation of bubble companies, entities designed more with an eye to making money off investors rather than for them," wrote famed investor Warren E. Buffett in his annual report to Berkshire Hathaway shareholders last year.

Staking their claim in the gold rush, Wall Street firms ramped up in the late '90s, hiring hordes of analysts, many of them inexperienced. New investment bankers were hired as well. A feeding frenzy set in as rivals fought to grab a big share of the market to bring companies public. At the same time, a new cult of equities came to life, as individuals invested in stocks as never before. True, many investors ignored common sense. Still, as analysts applauded stocks, trumpeting their picks on CNBC and other media, investors bought. "Investors took everything at face value, which was understandable. There wasn't a lot of information, and it was of varying quality," says Michael E. Kenneally, cochairman and chief investment officer at Bank of America Capital Management Inc.

Only now are the ugly details of the conflicts at play being laid bare. In some of the e-mail turned up by Spitzer, analysts disparage stocks as "crap" and "junk" that they were pushing at the time. The e-mails are so incendiary that they threaten to thrust Wall Street into the sort of public-relations nightmare that Philip Morris, Ford, Firestone, and Arthur Andersen have endured in recent years. All the ingredients are present:

publicity-hungry attorneys general, packs of plaintiffs' lawyers, and potential congressional hearings. "The last thing the industry wants is . . . the drip-drip-drip of new stories every week," says Howard Schiffman, a former SEC Enforcement Div. lawyer now practicing privately in Washington.

More explosive documents may be on the way. Both Spitzer and the SEC are seeking from more than a dozen firms papers and e-mail related to analysts' recommendations and their potential conflicts of interest. While nobody knows what evidence will emerge, other firms will have their own smoking guns. And analyst pay is likely to emerge as a hot-button issue. Zamansky, for instance, claims that he has seen contracts from investment banks promising analysts 3% to 7% of all the investment banking revenues that they help to generate.

That would be clear proof that analysts were being paid to help the firms' banking clients, often at the expense of investors who expected objective advice.

The financial implications of this mess are enormous. Based on the evidence that has already emerged, Merrill is facing potential fraud claims by every retail investor who purchased any stock that Blodget & Co. may have insincerely recommended. If analysts covering other industries at the firm harbored similar doubts about the companies they hawked, the number of claimants will expand exponentially. Should other financial firms have similarly embarrassing documents in their files, Wall Street could easily be facing billions in potential liability. In a report released on Apr. 24, as the fiasco was unfolding, Prudential Financial analyst David Trone estimated the issue could cost Merrill alone $2 billion.

Heads could roll, too. If prosecutors conclude that firms are guilty of systemic fraud—rather than harboring a small group of rogues—research directors and other high-ranking execs could be vulnerable. That's why the way analysts were paid is such an explosive issue. In egregious cases, criminal prosecutions are possible. Although regulators have never thrown an analyst in jail for fraudulently recommending a stock, experts say that could happen if public outrage flames high enough. Spitzer, whose tough New York securities statutes give him unusually broad power to file criminal suits, says he won't stop short of structural reform. "I'm continuing to negotiate [with Merrill]," he told

BusinessWeek on May 1. "They've been fruitful discussions, but negotiations can break down over a range of things. At this moment, we have significant issues that have not been resolved."

Over the long run, a risk bigger than legal penalties could be new restrictions that Spitzer or others place on the way investment banks do business. On May 8, the SEC is scheduled to approve new rules forcing analysts to limit and disclose contacts with investment banker colleagues. But there's good reason to question whether these steps will be enough to satisfy the industry's critics—some of whom seek a separation between investment banking and analysis. At the moment, such radical change is a long shot. But if the Democrat-controlled Senate latches on to the analyst issue, it could trigger embarrassing hearings or proposals for more stringent rules. "Other shoes will drop," says one securities-industry lobbyist. "If [Salomon's Jack] Grubman or [Morgan Stanley's] Mary Meeker turns up [in similar evidence], the sky is the limit" for this issue. "It has big legs."

It was never much of a secret that analysts who work at investment banks often work against investors. Sell ratings now make up less than 2% of analysts' recommendations, up from around 1% during the bull market, according to First Call. Analysts are under pressure from the companies they cover, as well as from big institutional clients who may own the stock, to give positive ratings. Michael Mayo, senior bank analyst at Prudential Financial, recently told the Senate Banking Committee that he had been exhorted to stay bullish throughout his career, from both his former employers and the companies he covers. Otherwise, he said, he doesn't get the same access that others do, which gives him a harder time making nuanced stock calls. "It's like playing basketball with one hand tied behind your back," says Mayo. Analysts also need to shine in surveys such as *Institutional Investor*'s annual rankings, in which money managers vote for their favorite stockpickers, so they spend too much time lobbying clients rather than crunching numbers. "Analysts get focused on saying what they think the client wants to hear to win the vote," says Henry J. Herrmann, chief investment officer at Waddell & Reed Inc., a money manager.

The biggest factor now contaminating the system is compensation. To an ever-increasing degree, analysts' pay is tied to how much investment banking business they bring in. According to a Merrill memo released by Spitzer, Blodget detailed how he and his team had been involved in 52 investment banking transactions from December, 1999, to November, 2000, earning $115 million for the firm. Shortly thereafter, Blodget's pay package shot up from $3 million to $12 million. Charles L. Hill, First Call's director of research, says that when he was a retail analyst 20 years ago, if he helped investment bankers with a new client, he would get a small reward at year's end: "But it was the frosting on the cake. Now, it is the cake."

It would be an exaggeration to say analysts alone are to blame for Wall Street's woes. There's a much deeper problem involving everyone from credulous investors to deal-happy investment bankers and execs looking to fatten their wallets. "It's finally dawning on people that this incentive system we've given managers based on the value of stock options has encouraged management to puff up their companies a lot," says Robert J. Shiller, an economics professor at Yale University and author of the 2000 bestseller *Irrational Exuberance*.

Even so, experts say a lot of the corruption oozing from Wall Street has to do with an erosion in investment banking ethics and practices. It goes clear back to 1975, when fixed trading commissions were ended. Until then, investment banks had been able to make big bucks off pricey trading commissions. Slashed commissions meant the firms were forced to derive more revenues from investment banking business. "There's a real sense of sadness over what has happened in investment banking. It's not about what's right for a client, it's all about jamming a deal down a client's throat," says an ex-analyst who recently joined a hedge fund.

Consider Enron, which has paid $323 million to Wall Street in underwriting fees since 1986, according to Thomson. Goldman, Sachs & Co. pocketed $69 million of that, while Salomon made off with $61 million, and Credit Suisse First Boston took $64 million. Indeed, two of CSFB's investment bankers, after helping to design Enron's off-the-books partnerships, sat on one of the partnerships' boards. According to a complaint filed in Houston Federal Court on Apr. 8, investment bankers generated megaprofits from secretly investing in Enron's hidden partnerships. Meanwhile, many analysts continued recommending the stock to the bitter end: 11 out of 16 analysts who follow Enron had buys or strong buys less than a month before the company's bankruptcy filing.

Enron may be an extreme example. Still, in the past, tradition and ethics played a large role in keeping investment bankers loyal to their corporate clients. Indeed, Wall Street itself used to have much more of an interest in guarding its reputation. Says Jay Ritter, a finance professor at the University of Florida: "These days, bankers are far more focused on short-term profits than on their long-term reputations."

That's likely to get worse as investment banking business continues to dry up. The amount being raised in initial public offerings is way off its 2000 highs. Now there are far fewer mergers and follow-on offerings taking place. Because of this, it's unlikely that Wall Street, after all its hiring during the tech bubble, can sustain its profitability. Goldman Sachs estimates that five of the top investment banks on Wall Street will have to get by on $2 billion less than the $16 billion in net revenues they racked up in 1999. If investment banks roll back to 1999 staffing levels, Putnam Lovell Securities estimates that banks will have to shrink their payrolls by 5%—putting over 13,000 out of work.

But no matter how much Wall Street shrinks, its credibility must grow again. Firms have already taken some steps, such as eliminating direct reporting by analysts to investment bankers. But the Street and the SEC still must hammer out a solid, enforceable code of conduct. And if strong reforms in how analysts are compensated aren't pursued, focusing on increased disclosure will do little to end the abuses. Beyond that, regulators may need to go after the firms' top brass—the folks who set the procedural as well as ethical tone. And the Street should take great pains to monitor itself in an effort to restore investors' confidence. "If Wall Street knows what is good for it and what is good for this country, it will very definitely clean up its act," says Rohatyn. Adds George H. Boyd III, head of equities at New York's Weiss, Peck & Greer: "This is an industry of trust; it's one of its key assets. If [Wall Street] loses it, it is going to have to invest in getting [that trust] back and putting in the controls to rebuild it. Without that trust, there's nothing."

Merrill Lynch apparently knows this. At its annual shareholder meeting on Apr. 26, Chairman and CEO David H. Komansky took an unprecedented stand on the analyst debacle, saying: "We have failed to live up to the high standards that are our tradition, and I want to take this opportunity to publicly apologize to our clients, our shareholders, and our employees." Other apologies may follow, as firms desperately try to assuage potentially litigious investors and unyielding regulators. But for Wall Street, just saying sorry at this stage may prove to be too little, too late.

STREET SMART

Michael Dumiak

US Banker, July 2002

T H E T H I N G T O K N O W about Eliot Spitzer is that he uses the whole court.

Whether he's up early swatting tennis balls the morning after a grueling workday or dogging some of the nation's most influential power brokers, people who know him say he sees his options well. He's not afraid to use any move that might bring an advantage, expected or otherwise.

This worked during Spitzer's mythmaking Untouchable gumshoe turn this spring, which blew the lid off Wall Street's interest-conflicted analyst community and gained a $100 million settlement with Merrill Lynch. Spitzer's barnstorming approach is recasting his New York State Attorney General's office as a force to be reckoned with. It's an example for other legal eagles watching with interest as he turns what can be a backwater post into something with national clout. Spitzer leaped to prominence using a series of well-planned, executed and timely maneuvers—drawing a bright spotlight from *BusinessWeek* and *Time* to the British national press to papers in Singapore and Poland—and has gone from scraping into his first term to a budding candidate for governor. He's got definite interest in the financial sector and is set to keep pushing these hot buttons. Others like him are going to wade in.

In other words, Spitzer's going to be around for a while.

So, what's he want?

To hear Spitzer tell it, nothing special—just a little boardroom accountability. He ticks off a laundry list of dirty corporate dealing, from bogus audits to bogus investment advice. "Whether it was Vinson & Elkin in its capacity as counsel for Enron; Tyco, or GE, the multitudes of restatements, the unending supply of situations where there has been some failure to abide by the appropriate standard of behavior—it should be a wake-up call," Spitzer says. "The lesson for all market actors should be we've got to challenge ourselves more aggressively."

In the deregulated, laissez-faire world hatched by Ronald Reagan and completed by Newt Gingrich's GOP House class of '94, exactly what challenges is this 43-year-old New Yorker talking about? Like any cagey pol would say, Spitzer's not convinced there needs to be a ton of new rules. He has said repeatedly that he doesn't have a "master plan" for financial reform. But sources say, even if he doesn't bring a big agenda to the minutiae of economic policy—a flip side to the GOP's hero in economics, Senator Phil Gramm—it would be a mistake to think Spitzer is merely reacting to events, that he has no vision. The probe leading to the Merrill settlement took 10 months to prepare; it was exhaustive. It hinged on an 80-year-old state law, the Martin Act, that had long been forgotten somewhere in a dusty Albany law book—a good example of using the court, examining options before taking action.

Spitzer's former law partner and mentor Lloyd Constantine—who was Spitzer's boss during a long-ago internship in the attorney general's office and went on to head up Spitzer's transition team in 1998—says his protégé knows finance inside out, having once advised plenty of Wall Street firms. "He constantly did work which involved the securities markets during his four years with our firm," Constantine says. "He knows the turf." Prior to that, Spitzer spent two years with high-powered law firm Skadden, Arps—ironically counsel to Merrill Lynch during the settlement negotiations. Constantine says Spitzer knows he's now running in open field. "With something as obscure as the Martin Act, you can virtually touch upon any securities transaction in the United States because of the nexus to New York," he says. It's the same with antitrust.

And while Spitzer is circumspect about what he'd like to see, there's no mystery about how he views his post. It's an activist, pro-consumer position, looking to live up to its billing on his campaign site as the "People's Lawyer." When he ran for office in 1998, following a failure to get out of the pack in the Democratic primary four years earlier, Spitzer—

not the first politician to do so—declared his allegiance to *Mr. Smith Goes to Washington*. The state attorney general, he said, should be "our Jimmy Stewart in Albany." That's music to hard-luck investors' ears.

During his bruising '98 battle with GOP incumbent Dennis Vacco, Spitzer held to his activist ideas, even as Vacco attacked him as a liberal shark and left-leaning Democrats hit him for being too conservative. On the campaign trail Spitzer said that he's for affirmative legislation, in antitrust, securities, civil rights, the environment and medical care. He promised aggressiveness in going after airlines keeping smaller competitors out of upstate markets and hospital mergers that reduce competition. "I would have stopped the Bell Atlantic–NYNEX merger," he told one paper.

Well, maybe, or maybe not. Ma Bell's a hard target. But there is no doubt Spitzer thinks big and follows a plan. Why would the financial industry get a free pass? "He has the ability to become an extraordinary presence in this particular area," former New York mayor Ed Koch says. "It's an area that everybody now realizes has not been looked at and has cost the public billions of dollars."

So maybe in certain areas new rules are needed, Spitzer allows. He was pleased by a recent reform-minded speech from Goldman Sachs chairman Henry Paulson, and applauds new rule-making by the New York Stock Exchange and National Association of Securities Dealers that cracks down on analyst conflicts of interest. "I also agree with [Paulson] that we should separate auditing and consulting," Spitzer says. "We should separate compensation for analysts from the investment banking side."

SILVER SPOONS

What makes him stand out is that Spitzer is an unlikely populist with a patrician's résumé.

Spitzer grew up in the leafy Riverdale section of the Bronx, attending Horace Mann, which isn't exactly public school. The son of wealthy New York real estate developer Bernard Spitzer, he went on to Princeton and then Harvard Law, clerking with U.S. District Court judge Robert Sweet. He spent a year with law firm Paul, Weiss, Rifkind, Wharton & Garrison before embarking on a six-year stint as a Manhattan assistant district attorney. He spent $4 million of his own money in his limp race for state attorney general in 1994; Spitzer was then dogged by criticism that his rich father was underwriting his 1998 effort.

So from appearances, Spitzer belongs to the very elite he is causing such a headache. "He's from a rich family. Good schools. A high-powered lawyer. He's not going to be intimidated by some guy who sells stocks and bonds," says Maurice Carroll, the Quinnipiac University polling institute director. This gives him an advantage in dealing with someone like Merrill's David Komansky.

The deal Spitzer cut with Merrill is textbook for the man, sources say. He's deliberate in his planning, like the marathon runner he's been, and then relentless in action.

It wasn't until January that his office got to the meat of the Merrill matter, and once Spitzer got it, he got going. "Get me the damn e-mails—all of them," he told an aide. These e-mails showed Merrill analysts excoriating the same firms, in language anyone can understand, that they were touting as good buys to the public. Merrill was also handling investment banking duties for these firms. "You get your first e-mail and say, man, this is great stuff," he says. "When you get your tenth, you come to the realization that the first wasn't an aberration. When you realize that this talk was pervasive, you say, 'Wow, this is really proof.'" Spitzer's office sifted through tens of thousands of e-mails.

Merrill's admitted no wrongdoing as part of the settlement, and maintains the e-mails were, as ex–Atlanta Brave John Rocker once said, "taken out of context." Still, Komansky had to take a hit over the affair and, in showing that he'll use whatever means necessary—public hearings, subpoenas, indictments, you name it—Spitzer set the table for further Street concessions. "He's created a fundamental shift in the way Wall Street does business," says Andy Collins, a bank analyst at U.S. Bancorp Piper Jaffray. "He's gone after one of the big conflicts of interest. There have always been a lot of conflicts of interest in investment banking, so it shouldn't come as any surprise."

Some argue these are moderate steps. "Had he actually called in [Merrill analyst] Henry Blodget for public hearings under oath, and had Blodget done what most criminal defense lawyers would tell him that he had to do—namely, take the Fifth—you would have had headlines all over the country," Columbia University securities law expert John Cof-

fee says. "To most of the American public that means you are the equivalent of a Mafia gangster. Or worse, an Enron executive. The stigma
that would have created would have been enormous."

But Tom Brown, hedge fund manager and longtime Street critic—a
former analyst himself, he was forced out by DLJ for refusing to compromise his research in order to be a rainmaker—thinks Spitzer's a sell-
out and won't be around long. "He's a one-trick pony," Brown says. "It
was all about getting a deal done and saying he scored a victory." He says
the Merrill deal's mild, and other settlements will be milder unless
Spitzer finds more smoking guns. "We're not seeing a reformer in the
making; we're seeing a politician in the making," Brown says.

TAKING PUNISHMENT

In the vortex after the settlement, Spitzer got it all different ways. But
he's used to being beaten up. His campaign against Vacco wasn't for the
faint of heart. He won by a blip; his opponent cried election fraud and
contested it in the courts for a month. Vacco went as far as to call on
then-mayor Giuliani to get cops to knock on tens of thousands of voters'
doors to confirm they were real people. That's hardball.

Having been through that, he's now in shape for a fall re-election
run. "He's so home free that we haven't bothered to ask approval or dis-
approval," Quinnipiac pollster Carroll says, in what is no doubt disturbing news for Spitzer's opponent, Dora Irizarry. While it's early days yet,
a Marist College poll gives Spitzer a 39-point lead. Even though he's
annoyed much of Wall Street—few bankers will talk about him on the
record, and plenty say unprintable things off the record—it's not like
they can weigh in decisively by bankrolling Irizarry, either. "He's already
rendered himself persona non grata to the industry—there's not much
point in seeing the industry as a source of political capital, as other attorney generals have," Coffee says. Carroll agrees, pointing to his personal
resources. "If Wall Street decides collectively that 'we're not going to
give this guy any money, he's giving us angst,' then he can just write a
check," Carroll says.

If he's got the state GOP on notice, Spitzer's got the attention of
regulators now, too. The field is altered. "He raised the conflict-of-
interest issue more visibly than anyone else has, and that produced self-

corrective reforms all over the industry," Coffee says. "The rules of both the NASD and NYSE went through without serious opposition. If it hadn't been for Spitzer, there would have been some real fighting by the industry over those reforms." Spitzer has taken some heavy flak for doing what many bankers, and many politicians, think is the Securities and Exchange Commission's job. Spitzer agrees. "If they do it, that will be great and I wouldn't need to be there. In the absence of an appropriate regulatory presence, we have the jurisdiction to step in," he says.

The SEC's not going to cop to being red-faced over the affair. It has said it appreciates the help; it has moved to take action and now has five ongoing conflict-of-interest investigations. SEC chief Harvey Pitt and Spitzer have met and have made nice in public. But Coffee and others say there's no doubt the SEC was embarrassed by the black-and-white baldness of the Merrill e-mails. "The SEC has to do something, even if it's more theatrics than real reform," Coffee says, adding that other conflicts—analysts who, for example, sell short companies they rate as strong buys—remain. "The SEC is in the unaccustomed position of being the observer on the sidelines to significant reform implemented by others."

Given these results, sources say Spitzer's unlikely to back off; though he won't shed much light on the future, he's clearly thinking about it. "I was never persuaded that spinning off research was the right thing to do," he says. "If five years from now we've been incapable of insulating the role of the analyst, then people may say we have to do that."

Roy Smith, a finance professor at New York University and former Goldman Sachs general partner, says financiers don't know quite what to make of him. "He's never been a player before," Smith says, describing Spitzer as a rising, scrappy and determined politician who has made himself a player and raised important long-term questions. "If the SEC seems slow or too understanding of the firms it regulates, has room now been created for other regulators to jump in to create a kind of regulatory arbitrage?" It's too early to tell. "When the public is aroused by apparently flagrant abuses, the door now seems open for state officials to issue subpoenas and begin their own investigations. If this should continue to happen in the future, then the SEC's power and influence in this important zone of its responsibility might be seriously eroded," Smith says.

Democratic sources are sure Spitzer's going to run for governor. If Carl McCall or Andrew Cuomo loses to GOP incumbent George Pataki, Spitzer's the leading candidate for 2006. That would likely mean a respite from his financial-world dealings—sources say the governor's mansion isn't really a good place to take direct action in that regard. A jaded banker might think, Well, four more years and this do-gooder Spitzer show will be over. He might even be right. Even so, four years is a long time—and Spitzer's shown he can pull rabbits out of a hat in a hurry.

UPDATE

After Eliot Spitzer succeeded in his case against Merrill Lynch—which paid $100 million to settle charges that its analysts had pushed stocks they privately regarded as "junk"—he turned his attention to other investment banks and their clients. In September, Spitzer filed a civil suit against five telecom executives, alleging that they had given Salomon Smith Barney investment-banking business in exchange for shares in hot IPOs, shares that they quickly sold for hefty profits. Spitzer also claimed that Salomon had kept the stock prices of these companies artificially high by touting their prospects, giving the executives a chance to dump hundreds of millions of dollars in stock. In early October, Spitzer and SEC Chairman Harvey Pitt announced that they would be working together to come up with a way of pushing Wall Street firms to make fundamental changes in the way they allocate IPO shares and manage the conflict of interest between research and investment banking.   —J.S.

WHISPERS INSIDE. THUNDER OUTSIDE

Stephen Labaton and David Leonhardt

The New York Times, June 30, 2002

THEY'RE BACK. INSIDER-TRADING investigations, which haunted Wall Street nearly a generation ago as prosecutors pursued Ivan F. Boesky and others, have returned to center stage.

Early this month, Samuel D. Waksal, the former chief executive of ImClone Systems, a biotechnology company, found himself sitting in a jail cell next to a man accused of selling drugs. Last week, on the *The Early Show* on CBS, Martha Stewart had to answer questions about an investigation into her trades before the anchor allowed her to make a chicken-and-shredded-cabbage salad. And on Friday, the Securities and Exchange Commission announced an insider-trading case against the Carreker Corporation, a Dallas company whose vice president for investor relations tipped off his brother, a broker, who then tried to profit in advance of a news release on declining earnings, prosecutors say.

Suddenly, SEC officials are combing intently through piles of trading records involving huge numbers of stock sales by executives and others privy to confidential information. In particular, they are looking for cases against executives tied to the accounting and disclosure problems that have tainted a growing number of the nation's largest corporations.

In recent years, investigations focused largely on the small fish of Wall Street and corporate America, often because cases were easier to make against them. But investors have grown so disgruntled that prosecutors are now searching aggressively for any and all illegal profiteers during the precipitous decline in the stock market.

"One of the things we look at in every accounting and disclosure case is whether those involved in any misconduct were selling stock," said Stephen M. Cutler, director of the enforcement division at the commission. "One also has the sense that everyone in the current climate is sensitive to breaches of public trust by officers and directors, so it should come as no surprise that courts are more sensitive to these issues as well."

Mr. Cutler said the commission was imposing tougher penalties in an effort to restore confidence to the markets. It is no longer willing to automatically assess a penalty equal to only twice the ill-gotten gain as the price for a defendant who voluntarily acknowledges illegal trading. The agency is also stepping up efforts to bar officers and directors who are guilty of illegal insider trading from working for publicly traded companies.

It is too early to tell how many scandals will be uncovered this year. But the investigations are all but certain to fall short of the sweeping post-bubble reckoning that many outraged investors and laid-off employees appear to want. The reason is simple: the overwhelming number of executives who struck it rich shortly before their stock plummeted probably did so without breaking any laws at all.

Because they awarded enormous piles of stock options to top executives, boards have enabled them to accumulate vast wealth by selling small portions of their holdings regularly. In late 2000, in one of his final acts as chairman of the SEC under President Bill Clinton, Arthur D. Levitt persuaded the commission to adopt a rule that permits executives to set prearranged schedules for their stock selling, further insulating them from insider-trading charges.

The commission wanted to allow executives to sell stock without taking advantage of what they knew. As part of its so-called safe harbor approach, the SEC is expected to soon require companies to make public such prearranged trading plans.

"If a 55-year-old executive has most of his entire estate in his company's stock, most advisers would tell him he's got too many eggs in one basket and he should liquidate," explained Otto G. Obermaier, a former United States attorney in Manhattan who is now at Weil, Gotshal & Manges. "He ought to be entitled to do so without fear that he winds up trading as earnings go down and he is accused of insider trading."

Still, many executives have sold a lot of stock since 2000, either with an inkling that it was overvalued or to diversify generous compensation packages of stock and options in a well-timed way. They did so even as they continued to make predictions about their companies that would prove to be badly exaggerated in 2000 and 2001.

Consider the 25 companies whose executives and other employees have sold the largest amounts of stock since the start of 2000—a list compiled by Thomson Financial, the research company. Among the 25—including AT&T, Dell Computer and Microsoft—the median decline in stock price over that same period, through May, has been 65 percent, a larger drop than even the Nasdaq composite index has suffered.

So even as profits have all but disappeared, layoffs have spread and long-term investors have taken a beating, many executives have walked away with rewards worthy of a bull market.

At AOL Time Warner, where shares have fallen 80 percent since the beginning of 2000, Stephen M. Case, the chairman, has sold $100.4 million of stock over the period, according to Thomson. One vice chairman, Ted Turner, has sold $79.1 million, and another, Kenneth J. Novack, has sold $34.7 million. Richard D. Parsons, the chief executive, has sold $35.3 million worth of stock.

The sales were "consistent with their regular selling patterns," said Edward Adler, a spokesman. He added that all top executives continued to hold large amounts of company stock and were suffering along with other investors.

WorldCom, which the SEC accused of accounting fraud last week, did not make the list of 25. But an executive at the center of the inquiry, Scott D. Sullivan, the former chief financial officer, sold $44.1 million of WorldCom stock from 1997 to 2000, when the shares were worth many times what they are now. Because the trades do not appear to have taken place during the period for which the SEC is alleging fraud, Mr. Sullivan's profits may be safe.

Burned investors aren't waiting for the outcome of the inquiries by the authorities, however. Led by some of the largest institutional investors, they have filed class-action lawsuits against current and former executives at companies like Enron and Global Crossing. Unless they are settled, as they often are, those cases may present the first legal tests of the safe-harbor provision put in place by the SEC nearly two years ago.

For many investors and employees, the most galling examples are those in which executives clearly failed but walked away with millions.

Few companies offer a sharper contrast than Ariba, a software company in Sunnyvale, Calif., near the center of Silicon Valley. The company went public in June 1999 amid the Internet mania, promising to create Net marketplaces where companies could buy and sell goods. When analysts talked excitedly about the future of "B2B"—business-to-business electronic commerce—they often mentioned Ariba.

Ariba's stock soared above $150 in early 2000 and, after falling more than two-thirds, recovered to an all-time high of $168.75 that September, as its executives offered an enticing vision of the future.

"We're seeing an incredible amount of demand out there," Keith J. Krach, the chief executive, said in April 2000. Three months later, he told Dow Jones Newswires, "This marketplace is red hot." And in October of that year, he said, "Profitability is imminent."

It never arrived. Ariba's software had bugs, and its B2B marketplace attracted fewer users than the company had projected. When it announced a newly aggressive accounting method in 2001, investors worried that the company was exaggerating sales, and the stock fell sharply. The company has laid off hundreds of workers, and in its most recent fiscal year reported a $2.7 billion loss.

But Mr. Krach and his colleagues have done well. In 2000 alone, as he was making some of his optimistic pronouncements, Mr. Krach sold $167.4 million worth of Ariba stock, according to Thomson. Overall, insiders have sold more than $850 million of stock since the start of 2000.

"I find it appalling," said Glenn Luksik, a former Ariba shareholder from Columbus, Ohio, who is a plaintiff in a class-action lawsuit filed against the company last year, related to Ariba's initial public offering.

"Has big business always been like this, with all of these inside deals?" Mr. Luksik asked.

Lauren Ames, an Ariba spokeswoman, said that most of the executives who sold large amounts of stock no longer worked at the company, and that Ariba was a much stronger company today than a year ago. Mr. Krach, now chairman, was unavailable to comment, Ms. Ames said.

Ariba's case may be extreme, but there appear to be dozens of cases in which insiders legally sold millions of dollars of shares shortly before the stock price sank.

Now some people are asking whether trading rules should change again, this time making it more difficult for executives to accumulate vast wealth from a temporary blip in their company's stock price. Regulators or corporate boards could, for example, require executives to hold their options and shares for years.

Huge stock-option grants "put great incentives on the short term," said Peter G. Peterson, a former secretary of commerce who is now on a private-sector committee trying to devise better guidelines for corporate governance. "Maybe we'd get the long-term point of view if the holding periods on stock options were longer so that there was not the incentive to manage earnings in the short term."

The committee, set up by the Conference Board, a business-backed research group in New York, plans to make its proposals later this year.

To many investors, however, a voluntary guideline is not enough. They say the worst transgressors should be sent to prison.

Yet for investigators, building cases will not be easy. The SEC regulations adopted 20 months ago made it easier for executives to sell stock without fear of being prosecuted for illegal insider trading. The rule has yet to be tested in court.

On one level, insider trading is easier to prove than complex accounting or financial fraud.

"This is not securities law litigation," Mr. Obermaier said. "This is basically cops and robbers. The issue is, 'Did you get the information and did you trade on it?'"

But the rules that have been laid down by the SEC and by several court decisions, though largely favorable to prosecutors, still require the government to prove that an investor made a trade with particular knowledge of confidential information, a high burden under any circumstances. That difficulty has led investigators in some cases, like the one pending at ImClone, to also look at whether some of the principals in that case may have violated other laws, like making false statements or obstructing justice.

The main tools of prosecutors in combatting insider-trading abuses are the broadly worded securities-, mail- and wire-fraud laws, which give wide latitude to the authorities in building cases.

During the Wall Street scandals of the late 1980's, a group of law-makers, regulators and defense lawyers tried to come up with a statutory definition of insider trading. But the effort, led by Harvey L. Pitt, failed for a variety of political reasons, and it now turns out that Mr. Pitt, who last summer became the SEC chairman, may be better off for having failed.

Supporters of an explicit statutory definition argued that it was a matter of basic fairness. Investors, they said, are entitled to know clearly what kind of information is proper, or not, to trade on.

"A legitimate businessman," Mr. Pitt said in 1989, "is entitled to know what the rules of the game are before he gets carted off to jail."

But opponents of that proposal, including some enforcement officials at the time, said there was a downside. They said that innovative lawyers and creative traders would be able to circumvent any statutory prohibition and that no law could anticipate all kinds of improper trading.

One reason for the debate was a split in the courts over how far prosecutors could go in charging insider trading. For decades, it was settled law that a corporate executive could not trade on confidential information, but a debate raged over whether the law also covered outsiders, like lawyers, research analysts and printers, who were privy to confidential information. With mixed success, prosecutors had tried to make such cases under the so-called misappropriation theory, which held that corporate outsiders who gained information by virtue of a special relationship could not "misappropriate" that information to personal gain.

The Supreme Court largely settled the issue in 1997, when it upheld the insider-trading conviction of James H. O'Hagan, a Minneapolis lawyer who tried to capitalize on his law firm's representation of Grand Metropolitan in its tender offer for Pillsbury nine years earlier. While Mr. O'Hagan's law firm was working for Grand Met, he bought call options and shares of Pillsbury stock. When the tender offer was announced, he sold the options and stock, making a profit of more than $4.3 million.

A federal appeals court had tossed out his conviction because Mr. O'Hagan was neither an employee nor a fiduciary of Pillsbury. But the Supreme Court reversed, saying in effect, that anyone who gains inside information under conditions in which that person knows it is supposed to remain confidential may not use it for trading.

The decision contained important restrictions, but it did not bar all kinds of insider trading. Someone who obtained confidential information innocently—by finding a document on the street, for example— could still trade on it. Moreover, the court required prosecutors to show that the trader knew or had reason to know that the information was coming from a confidential source. That, combined with the SEC rule changes in 2000, has all but eliminated the calls for a statutory definition of insider trading.

The recent scandals suggest that the rules and the earlier cases have done little to deter trading on insider information. "I'm amazed," Mr. Obermaier said, adding, "It's always surprising when people of substance, as opposed to street criminals, believe that they can capitalize on something that society has said is an impermissible action."

ACCOUNTABLE: HOW A BRIGHT STAR AT ANDERSEN FELL ALONG WITH ENRON

Anita Raghavan

The Wall Street Journal, May 15, 2002

FOR MOST OF his life, David Duncan played by the rules.

He graduated from high school with honors after losing his father at 18. Joining Arthur Andersen LLP out of Texas A&M University, he rose to become one of its youngest partners. So valued was his work that he was feted before 2,000 of his fellows at the firm's annual partners' meeting in New Orleans last October. He was earning more than $1 million a year by last January, when Andersen abruptly fired him for destroying documents related to the audit of Enron Corp.

Mr. Duncan's friends now struggle to understand the events that led to his pleading guilty last month to obstruction of justice. They know him as a family man, who arrives like clockwork each Sunday for the 8:25 A.M. service at his local church, always sitting in the same pew.

To some, Mr. Duncan's career symbolizes what went wrong with the accounting firm itself. Emboldened by success, amply rewarded and pushed by an ever-demanding client, they theorize, he chose to go with the flow, acquiescing in Enron's questionable maneuvers and basking in the glow that came from a cozy relationship with the energy giant.

There is "no question David Duncan was a client pleaser," Andersen lawyer Rusty Hardin told jurors in the current federal trial against the accounting firm.

Mr. Duncan's struggle to please both Andersen and Enron comes through in memos provided to congressional investigators. They show him sometimes pressing the Enron point of view with Andersen's Professional Standards Group, and sometimes appearing to be less than fully forthcoming with members of that group.

Now Mr. Duncan is giving his side of the case on the witness stand in Houston, as the federal government's star witness in its prosecution of Andersen. Yesterday, he stated publicly for the first time that he had destroyed Enron audit documents because of rising fears of a federal investigation.

In a decade-long relationship with Enron, the last five years as partner in charge of the account, Mr. Duncan developed close ties to the client company. His office was in an Enron building. He and Enron's chief accounting officer, Richard Causey, often lunched at a place called Nino's, and they attended Masters golf tournaments together.

This clubby relationship, while initially underpinning Mr. Duncan's success, finally led to his undoing. Accounting-standards specialists at Andersen warned that Enron's treatment of its partnerships was questionable. But Mr. Duncan at times hewed to his client's wishes and sparred with his partners to help the company realize its goals.

Mr. Duncan sprang into the spotlight in late October. That's when he led an effort to shred tons of Enron-related documents as regulators were closing in.

It was a tense time at the firm. Senior partners were holding conference calls focused on finding a way to avoid restating Enron's earnings for the first two quarters of 2001, because of the accounting for certain partnerships. On Oct. 12, Mr. Duncan was forwarded an e-mail from an Andersen lawyer saying people should be sure to follow the firm's policy on document retention. Ten days later, in a meeting with Enron people, Mr. Duncan was briefed about a request for information that Enron had received the week before from the Securities and Exchange Commission.

The next day, Mr. Duncan called an urgent meeting of his staff, where he ordered them to get in compliance with the document-retention policy. Mr. Duncan testified this week that he gave the instruction knowing it would result in the destruction of documents. Andersen has said the result was a frantic effort between Oct. 23 and Nov. 9 to get rid of sensitive documents, the basis of the guilty plea Mr. Duncan has entered.

To people who've known him since childhood, it's an astonishing turn of events. "This kid was ambitious—he was going to go places," says

Don Branham, his political-science teacher at Forest Park High School in Beaumont, Texas.

Mr. Duncan had lived in Beaumont barely two years when his father, Dewey, died suddenly. By all accounts, the Duncans were a close-knit family. Friends say his father, manager of Houston Chemical Co.'s Beaumont plant, would arrive at the plant a little late most days just so he could have breakfast with his wife and children. David would go duck hunting with his father, and fishing with him in the Louisiana wilds.

He also received his early impressions of the corporate world from his father, who was focused on meeting the needs of his customers at Houston Chemical. "The management background that David grew up around would teach you to follow the company's policy—to be innovative but to work within the company's structure," says a friend of the family.

James F. Jackson, his pastor in Beaumont, thinks Mr. Duncan's background would have made him reluctant to be confrontational with a demanding client. "He is not the kind of person in a business meeting to be disrespectful," Mr. Jackson says, calling Mr. Duncan "a good man who got caught up in a bad situation." He says Mr. Duncan has since told him he regrets not fighting harder to push Andersen to drop Enron as a client when the accounting firm reviewed its relationship a year ago.

Mr. Duncan followed his father's footsteps to Texas A&M, becoming an "Aggie," a breed of graduates known in business circles for a strong loyalty and work ethic. Texas A&M also was a source of future Andersen accountants. Wooed by an A&M graduate who headed the firm's Houston audit practice, Mr. Duncan joined Andersen in 1981.

There he met people who would later play key roles at Enron. Among them: Mr. Causey and Jeffrey McMahon, who became Enron's treasurer and then president before resigning last month. D. Stephen Goddard, another Aggie, later served as a mentor to Mr. Duncan. And the firm was where he met his wife, Peggy, whom he married in 1992.

But in 1992, after 11 years at Andersen, the rising star was lured to the natural-resources company Freeport-McMoRan. He didn't get along with the executive he worked for there, however, and in nine months he was back at Andersen. His fling with another outfit didn't stall his ascent. He made partner in 1995 and two years later became the "global engagement partner" for one of Andersen's biggest clients: Enron.

Enron's executive ranks were populated with accountants, many of whom had worked at Andersen and seemed eager to push accounting to new frontiers. And Enron's hard-charging executives weren't averse to telling Andersen's people how to do their job.

In 1999 Enron Chief Financial Officer Andrew Fastow approached Mr. Duncan about a "special-purpose vehicle" the CFO wanted to set up. It turned out to be LJM, a partnership that, it was revealed last fall, had brought Mr. Fastow millions of dollars in compensation and helped Enron hide millions in debt off its balance sheet.

Mr. Duncan consulted Andersen's Professional Standards Group, the firm's source of advice on tricky accounting issues. It balked. "Setting aside the accounting, idea of a venture entity managed by CFO is terrible from a business point of view," wrote Benjamin Neuhausen, a member of the standards group, in an e-mail to Mr. Duncan on May 28, 1999. "Conflicts of interests galore. Why would any director in his or her right mind ever approve such a scheme?" he wrote.

Mr. Neuhausen also told Mr. Duncan the standards group would be "very uncomfortable" with Enron's recording gains on sales of assets to the Fastow-controlled entity or immediate gains on any transactions.

"I'm not saying I'm in love with this either," Mr. Duncan replied in a June 1 e-mail, referring to the recording of gains. "But I'll need all the ammo I can get to take that issue on."

Mr. Duncan told the standards-group member that "on your point 1, (i.e. the whole thing is a bad idea), I really couldn't agree more." But he made clear the issue was by no means dead. He said he had told Mr. Fastow that Andersen would sign off on the transaction only if Mr. Fastow got chief-executive and board approval at Enron, among other things. Enron ultimately approved setting up the partnership, with Mr. Fastow in charge.

Andersen's total fees from Enron for auditing, business consulting and tax work were $46.8 million that fiscal year, ended Aug. 31, 1999. The next year the fees leapt to $58 million. They were between $50 million and $55 million in fiscal 2001.

Mr. Duncan's profile rose at Andersen. He and his wife and three children moved to a neighborhood called Willowick in Houston's affluent Memorial area. At times he shared his feelings with old friends, such as James Benjamin, head of Texas A&M's accounting department. Mr.

Benjamin says Mr. Duncan would talk about the "challenge he was facing as a result of the complexity of Enron and the types of transactions they were doing and the difficulty of having comfort with its accounting."

Mr. Duncan was an advocate for his client as well. In March 2001, Carl Bass, a Houston-based member of Andersen's Professional Standards Group, was removed from the Enron account. That didn't please Mr. Bass's boss, John Stewart, who complained to a senior partner. Mr. Duncan called Mr. Stewart about the matter on March 12. He told of a negative view of Mr. Bass on the part of two Enron executives, Mr. Causey and John Echols, according to notes that Mr. Stewart took and that have been handed over to congressional investigators. In other words, Mr. Duncan told Mr. Stewart he didn't drive Mr. Bass's removal—Enron did.

Last summer, as Mr. Duncan sought advice from the standards group on the outside equity needed for joint ventures, he hinted at the challenges he faced. If the standards group and Enron were "miles apart," Mr. Duncan said, according to e-mails given to congressional investigators, "I may need a whole different tact [sic] from a client management perspective. If this is what you believe to be the case, we probably need to talk fairly urgently so I can start managing Enron's expectations way down from where I believe they are as soon as possible."

Mr. Stewart told Mr. Duncan the two sides indeed were "pretty far apart." The subject evidently remained unresolved two months later. Mr. Stewart responded to an e-mail from another auditor by calling it "deja vu all over again." Mr. Stewart declined to be interviewed.

At one point, Mr. Duncan appears to have avoided telling Andersen's Professional Standards Group about a decision he and his team made. In late 2000, he approached the group about the accounting treatment for four Enron special-purpose entities known as Raptors. Mr. Duncan, putting forth Enron's view, was asking if Enron could lump the entities' financial results together, allowing profits from two to offset losses from others. This would mean the loss Enron reflected on its financial statement would be less than if the entities were treated individually, Mr. Duncan testified yesterday.

Mr. Bass, then still a member of the standards group, opposed the idea. Mr. Duncan testified at the Andersen trial yesterday that he himself "was sympathetic" to Enron's view when the issue first arose, though it took a while before he became convinced. In early 2001, "we decided to accept the client's position" with some modifications, he said.

Mr. Duncan testified that to his knowledge, nobody got back to Mr. Bass to tell him that the team auditing Enron wasn't following Mr. Bass's advice.

Last fall, the auditors revisited the issue because losses in the Raptors were potentially going to force Enron to restate first- and second-quarter earnings. The audit team sent memos documenting the late-2000 discussions to members of the standards group. They didn't mention that Mr. Bass had disagreed with Enron's treatment. Mr. Bass "recalled the issue and wanted the memos to document that he had disagreed with this approach," Mr. Duncan testified yesterday. So last Oct. 12, the memo was amended to reflect Mr. Bass's original position.

By this time, the pressures facing Mr. Duncan were multiplying. Mr. Stewart, the standards-group member, asked him about "LJM1," which, Mr. Stewart observed, must exist, since there was an LJM2, according to statements Mr. Stewart provided to congressional investigators. Mr. Duncan left Mr. Stewart with the impression that LJM1 just wasn't an issue.

A few days later, Mr. Stewart pressed the issue again on a conference call with some members of the Enron audit team. According to statements Mr. Stewart gave to congressional investigators, he asked what LJM1 was and if it met "nonconsolidation" tests—that is, whether Enron could legitimately avoid consolidating LJM1's results with Enron's own. A special-purpose vehicle doesn't have to be reflected in a company's financial statement if an independent party owns at least 3% of it.

Mr. Duncan assured him LJM1 met the test, according to the statements Mr. Stewart gave to congressional investigators. People close to Mr. Duncan say he believed that it did.

That night, Debra A. Cash, a member of Mr. Duncan's team, called Mr. Stewart. Although she had been silent on the conference call earlier in the day, she told Mr. Stewart her silence didn't mean she agreed with Mr. Duncan, according to statements given to congressional investigators. It was the first time Mr. Stewart had heard this.

After Enron collapsed, says Mr. Duncan's pastor, Mr. Jackson, the accountant spoke about the pressure Enron had put on him. "He basically said it was unrelenting," Mr. Jackson says. "It was a constant fight. Wherever he drew that line, Enron pushed that line—he was under constant pressure from year to year to push that line."

UPDATE

In part thanks to David Duncan's testimony, Arthur Andersen was convicted of obstruction of justice, effectively dooming the firm. Oddly, though, his testimony may have made any future case against Enron executives more difficult, since Duncan testified that there was nothing fundamentally illegal in Enron's accounting methods. At the time this book went to press, he had not yet been sentenced.   —J.S.

FALL FROM GRACE

John A. Byrne

BusinessWeek, August 12, 2002

THE DAY AFTER WorldCom Inc. admitted cooking its books to the tune of $3.8 billion, former Andersen Worldwide CEO Joseph F. Berardino was glued to the TV set watching CNBC's coverage of the shocking news. Berardino had good reason to be riveted to every development: WorldCom was a major audit client of the firm he had recently quit.

Like the rest of the world, Berardino watched in outrage. But in his case, the ire was directed at the media, which he believed was exaggerating the story. "They were talking down the market," says Berardino with disgust. Four weeks later, the beleaguered telecom provider filed the largest bankruptcy in U.S. history.

Berardino seems clueless as to how Andersen could have failed to detect the fraud at WorldCom, which occurred over five consecutive quarters. "In a quarter, you're typically not looking at that kind of detail," he says. "It's shocking. It just blows your mind. But why was that stock down to $1 already? It's because some investors did their homework."

Of course, many are wondering if Berardino, who resigned in disgrace as CEO in March, had done his. At 51, he finds himself exiled from an industry that consumed him for nearly 30 years, a mere bystander to a national debate that will result in the most sweeping reform of the profession he worked in all of his adult life. When Berardino ventured to California in June to give a speech on reform, the

San Jose Mercury News ran his photo with the caption: "Why would you listen to this man?"

It is not an irrelevant question. Berardino, after all, was at the helm of a legendary firm when it was convicted of obstruction of justice, the same firm that stamped its approval on the dirty books of Sunbeam, Waste Management, Enron, Global Crossing, Qwest, and WorldCom. The scandals that enveloped those corporations alone have cost investors more than $300 billion and have put tens of thousands of people out of work.

The collapse of Andersen represents an unimaginable failure of leadership and governance. It raises questions about the anachronistic governance structure imposed by a private partnership, a structure better suited to a local enterprise than a global organization. In many ways, Andersen was more like a loose confederation of fiefdoms covering different geographic markets than an integrated company. Checks and balances were few and frequently ineffective. Insular and inbred, Andersen was unable to respond swiftly to crises or even to govern itself decisively. It took the firm five months to elect Berardino as CEO. Once in office, he was unable to fire a partner without a two-thirds vote of Andersen's 1,700 partners around the world. Even as the firm was engulfed in turmoil, some partners squabbled over who should be its public spokesman. If it was the head of Andersen's U.S. business, rather than Berardino who was CEO of the worldwide firm, perhaps the crisis could be confined to America, some thought.

For the firm Berardino once led, the end has been swift. By September, the 89-year-old Andersen expects to have no more than 3,000 employees on its ever-dwindling payroll as it phases out of business. The Andersen name is likely to live on in the popular culture as Watergate did, a shorthand way to refer to a certain kind of scandal. Already, it has become the butt of countless jokes and cartoons. A minor league baseball team in Portland, Ore., for example, recently held an Arthur Andersen appreciation night by stationing document shredders throughout its stadium and handing out receipts with inflated ticket prices.

Berardino's fall from grace has been just as swift. In the space of 15 months, he has gone from being CEO of a $9.3 billion global partnership with 85,000 employees in 84 countries to a pariah in his industry. Although many of the accounting scandals that helped bring the firm

down began festering long before he became CEO, Berardino's emphasis on growth over audit quality, his reluctance to walk away from big
clients with questionable accounting, and a stunning ignorance of
potentially crippling issues all contributed to the firm's undoing. He
claims that he was never told the most basic outlines of the Enron con-
troversy until it erupted into the news.

At times, Berardino, who made an estimated $3 million a year as
CEO, seems to focus more on his personal losses than those of the
shareholders and employees who lost investments and jobs because
Andersen failed in its duty. "I paid the price," he says in a near whisper.
"I lost my job. I lost my firm. I've got less money today than I had as the
newly elected CEO [in 2001]. I lost my partner capital. I lost my retirement. I don't have any stock options. I may never work again."

And he seems able to accept only limited responsibility for the catas-
trophe. "Somewhere north of one person sunk this firm, but it wasn't
85,000 people. Do I bear responsibility? No question. Nobody had to
ask me to step down, O.K.?" But he also blames forces outside of Andersen for the wave of accounting scandals currently afflicting the market.
He points to shareholders who invested in companies without examining their filings and to board members who were disengaged and failed
to ask the right questions.

The story of what went wrong at Andersen and how a seasoned professional like Joe Berardino could become blind to the problems goes
well beyond a few botched, albeit giant, audits. It involves a fundamental change in the firm's culture and a breakdown in the values of an
industry that once prided itself on serving the public good.

Just 20 years ago, Andersen, along with its brethren in the Big Five,
were auditors above all else. Highly trained specialists, they relied on
their professional ethics to help manage the tricky business of judging
and sometimes countermanding the clients who paid the bills. But then
in the '80s came the rise of the management-consulting business, a
broader, less quantitative, and more lucrative line of work that involved
a much higher degree of salesmanship. Slowly, auditing went from
being the soul of the firm to a loss leader used to attract and retain the
consulting contracts. Just as the vast riches represented by stock options
helped corrupt ethics at some corporations, consulting helped push
Andersen and its rivals off course. "The culture of the company changed

because it got deeply involved in the consulting business," says Paul A. Volcker, former Federal Reserve Board chairman.

The conflict played out at Andersen with especially devastating effect because of the divorce in 2000 of the firm's consulting and auditing arms. The culmination of 11 years of acrimony, the split left the auditing firm smaller, weaker, and less profitable. The onus shifted to creating a new consulting practice and building revenue. "There is no question in my mind that Andersen took its eye off the ball," adds Volcker. "Their compensation practices were based on how much revenue you could generate."

There is no better example of that than Enron Corp., which was paying Andersen about $1 million a week in fees by the late 1990s. Back then, Enron was lionized in the press and among management gurus for its radical business model, just the kind of fast-growing client Andersen was desperate to cultivate. At Enron, Andersen's consulting revenues exceeded its audit fees for the first time in 1999. The following year, Enron paid $27 million for Andersen's consulting services and $25 million for audit work.

Were those consulting fees enough to cause Andersen to lower its guard? Berardino says not. He says the auditing fee was so huge to begin with that if the firm were vulnerable to being swayed, that alone would have been enough. And, he says, that didn't happen.

But regardless of whether the fees played a role, it's clear that Andersen's work at Enron had been compromised long before the energy giant's final flameout. As head of Andersen's U.S. audit practice for nearly three years before becoming CEO in January, 2001, Berardino had helped to lead an exercise that evaluated the "risk profile" of each of the firm's 2,500 audit clients. During that review, Andersen grouped its clients into four categories: maximum, high, moderate, and low risk. Enron was one of some 50 clients deemed "maximum risk," while 700 more were considered "high risk."

That alone should have been enough to put Enron front and center on Berardino's radar, but that did not happen. There were plenty of other signs of trouble, signs that Berardino says never reached him. In February, 2001, Andersen partners in Chicago, worried about Enron's aggressive accounting, were actively debating whether to retain Enron as a client. Meanwhile, Andersen's audit team at Enron was having increasingly heated internal conflicts. A senior Andersen partner, Carl E. Bass, who had been sent in to monitor the high-risk audit, strongly objected to Enron's accounting. Berardino paid a call on Enron CEO Jeffrey K. Skilling and Chief Accounting Officer Richard A. Causey that same month at Enron's Houston headquarters. Berardino says it was strictly a meet-and-greet, that he didn't confer with the Andersen audit team on the Enron account before the visit, didn't know about the conflicts over the accounting, and never discussed them with Enron. He says it's a coincidence that within weeks of his visit, Bass was removed from his oversight role, at Enron's request. "If that kind of issue isn't important enough to get to Berardino's desk, then what is?" asks Allan D. Koltin, CEO of the Practice Development Institute, a consulting firm that specializes in the accounting industry. "He either knew and chose to look the other way or he had to be the most incompetent CEO in America."

Bass was a member of Andersen's Professional Standards Group, an internal team of accounting experts that reviewed and passed judgment on tricky accounting issues facing local offices. He found plenty to keep him busy at Enron, where he had once helped audit the books. In a Dec. 18, 1999, e-mail, Bass documented a conflict over how Enron should account for the sale of options owned by one of the partnerships managed by Enron Chief Financial Officer Andrew S. Fastow. If the Andersen team had accepted Bass's advice, it would have resulted in a $30 million to $50 million charge to Enron's earnings. An Andersen practice director in Houston, however, overruled Bass, who continued to object to other accounting transactions over the next couple of months. Andersen was the only one of the Big Five where a local partner could overrule the Professional Standards Group.

In retrospect, the system for airing such conflicts at Andersen seemed designed to ensure that top executives never learned of them. Instead, they were handled several layers down in the organization by people with clear and strong incentives to maximize revenues. Berardino denies that the system was faulty. "I probably wouldn't have done anything differently than the team," he says. Why? Berardino thought Andersen could manage the risks. He says the firm walked away from hundreds of clients, especially after the risk assessment pointed up dicey ones. But he acknowledges that the rejected clients tended to involve smaller fees and engagements. "It was hard to start with the big ones," he says. "We had to learn how to walk before we could run."

Even with Andersen in its death throes, there's an air of unreality at the firm, a gross misreading of the events that led to its downward spiral. Partners there will still argue that Berardino was not combative enough in defending Andersen from the Justice Dept., which they claim was hell-bent on destroying the partnership. "He probably should have been a street fighter and told them they were a bunch of liars who weren't interested in the public good," says Aldo Cardoso, a Paris-based partner who is acting CEO of Andersen Worldwide. "The Justice Dept. is responsible for the collapse of the financial markets because they caused our collapse."

That's in contrast to the prevailing view outside the firm. Berardino "never said he took full responsibility for this," says Arthur W. Bowman, a longtime industry observer and founder of *Bowman's Accounting Report*. "That was the problem with everyone at Arthur Andersen. They are all so arrogant that none of them wants to take responsibility."

When Berardino joined the firm's New York office in 1972, it was with a sense of mission. Founded by a Northwestern University accounting professor in 1913, Andersen stood for integrity. Just months after Arthur Andersen set up shop in Chicago, the president of a local railroad insisted that he approve a transaction that would have inflated earnings. Andersen told the executive there was "not enough money in the city of Chicago" to make him do it.

In the spirit of the company's founder, Berardino saw himself as a public guardian. An early role model was Pete Kennedy, a patrician partner from Berardino's hometown of Garden City, N.Y., who taught him to stand his ground. An audit was not merely a collection of numbers, Kennedy insisted, but a position that had to be intelligently made and defended.

Berardino climbed the firm's ladder, becoming a partner in 1982 and acquiring such top-notch audit clients as Merck & Co. and Colgate-Palmolive Co. But over the course of nearly 300 presentations to audit committees, he says he found directors far too complacent and disengaged: "Nobody fell asleep, but many of them didn't understand the business. They just sat there and received reports," he says. "Some directors just don't want to know. They might have to do something about it."

While Berardino focused on his auditing work, a profound change was unfolding inside his firm and the other major auditors. Much of Andersen's growth was coming not from accounting and auditing but rather from a wide array of consulting work, from installing information technology systems to advice on tax avoidance. One recent study in *The Accounting Review* showed that the consulting practices of the Big Five accountants brought in three times as much revenue as auditing in the 1990s.

No firm was more successful in consulting than Andersen, which boasted the largest and fastest-growing network of consultants in the world. Indeed, it led to concern in Washington that high-profit consulting work was compromising audits, which were quickly becoming a commodity service. In some cases, by taking over the internal audit functions of some clients, Andersen and its Big Five rivals were effectively auditing their own work.

In the fall of 1998, Securities and Exchange Commission Chairman Arthur Levitt Jr. went public in an attack on the industry. "Accounting is being perverted," he said. "Auditors and analysts are participants in a game of nods and winks." He urged new rules to restrict the ability of the accounting firms to consult for the same companies they audited. At a meeting between the SEC and three accounting-firm CEOs in June, 2000, Andersen's then–Chief Executive W. Robert Grafton was said to declare: "This is war."

It fell to Berardino, as head of Andersen's U.S. audit practice, to broker a compromise with the SEC, which he did in late 2000. It is a testament to his political skills that Berardino is viewed in Washington as a conciliator who forged a compromise pact, while at Andersen he was viewed as the man who stared down Levitt and won. After all, the deal he struck merely led to public disclosure of audit and consulting fees, not a prohibition from signing consulting contracts with audit clients. Levitt says he considers Berardino to have been far more reasonable to deal with than his rivals. "He was different," says Levitt. "He was civil, measured, and thoughtful."

Berardino's handling of the crisis helped him gain election as chief executive in January of 2001, with 90% of his partners' votes. "It was the dumbest reason to elect a person CEO," says Lynn Turner, former chief accountant of the SEC. "They should have elected someone who realized that their customer was the investing public and who could deliver high quality audits."

But while Berardino may have reached a truce in Washington, he was grappling with a highly divisive war inside Andersen. Once consulting had eclipsed auditing in profitability, by 1984, the consulting partners began getting restless. They wanted their pay to reflect the success of their business, which was driving Andersen's growth. The dispute led to warring factions inside the firm that ultimately became so toxic it would rend Andersen in two. In 2000, an arbitrator ruled that Andersen Consulting, with $9.4 billion in annual revenues, could break free merely by paying $1 billion and changing its name. (It is now called Accenture.)

The decision was a huge setback. The auditors, some expecting a payment as high as $15 billion, were shocked. "There was so much anger, and the leadership was obsessed with what was going on," says a former partner. Overnight, Andersen went from being the world's largest professional-services firm to the smallest of the Big Five accountants. Concedes Berardino: "It was a major distraction."

That led Berardino to shift the emphasis even more strongly toward building revenues by rebuilding the consulting practice. The firm's long-held beliefs, known as "the four cornerstones," were to provide good client service, produce quality audits, manage staff well, and produce profits. But as the pressure to bring in more money grew, some partners began to grouse that the four cornerstones had become "three pebbles and a boulder." Berardino acknowledges those complaints. "Some of our partners thought that that was happening," he says. "I didn't."

The focus on consulting left little time to ponder the quality of the firm's audits. "When Berardino would get up at a partners meeting, all that was ever reported in terms of success was dollars," says Barbara Ley Toffler, a former Andersen partner from 1995 to 1999. "Quality wasn't discussed. Content wasn't discussed. Everything was measured in terms of the buck," adds Toffler, who is writing a book with former *Business-Week* editor Jennifer Reingold. "Joe was blind to the conflict. He was the most aggressive pursuer of revenue that I ever met."

Berardino soon found himself consumed with one crisis after another. In May, 2001, he agreed to pay $110 million to settle shareholders' claims in an accounting scandal at Sunbeam Corp. A month later, he paid nearly $100 million more to settle similar claims at Waste Management Inc. and $7 million to settle the SEC case for its role in approving Waste Management's fraudulent audits. In both cases, Andersen did not admit guilt. Berardino has no explanation for how his firm could have been so lax.

The garbage hauler was an early example of Andersen collecting more for consulting than auditing. That disturbing pattern would continue. Last year, Qwest Communications International Inc., now under investigation by the SEC and the Justice Dept., paid Andersen $10.5 million for consulting and $1.4 million for its audit. The telecom provider has said it overstated revenue for 1999, 2000, and 2001 by $1.2 billion.

When Enron hit in the fall of 2001, Berardino tried to contain the crisis by showing up on Capitol Hill and admitting to some mistakes. He rushed off to meet with the audit committees of more than 20 Andersen clients, hoping to persuade them to stay. It wasn't until early March, when he was awakened in the middle of the night in a Tokyo hotel room, that he realized the entire firm could be vulnerable. Andersen's lawyers told him then that the Justice Dept. was inclined to indict the firm. "The indictment was enough to kill us," he says. "That's what we told them."

Berardino says he worked frantically to turn the Justice Dept. around. He got Volcker, hired in February, to create an independent oversight board to revamp the organization and announce reforms that would transform Andersen into a pure audit firm and lead to a new management team. But on Mar. 14, Justice went through with an indictment for obstruction of justice. The very next day, Berardino says, he offered to step down during a conference call with Andersen's 18 directors. But they insisted that he stay. "I said, 'At some point, we may want me to do this. I don't want you guys meeting in bars worrying about it.'"

On Mar. 26, he finally resigned. Berardino says it was a sort of Hail Mary pass to get Justice to reconsider. It didn't work, and on June 15, a jury in Houston convicted the firm of obstruction of justice, though not of accounting fraud.

Berardino still commutes from his home in Greenwich, Conn., to his office on the 12th floor of a Manhattan skyscraper twice a week. But when a partner sticks his head in the door these days, he's not there to talk about business. Instead, he's likely to be saying a final good-bye. Some partners tell him that when they tuck their children into bed at night, they have to reassure the kids that they're not going to jail. "It's devastating," says Berardino. "You find out who your friends are at your wake."

He is vague about his future. "A lot of people come up to me and say, 'I feel so sorry for you,'" he says. "This will sound Pollyanna-ish, but I now know who my friends are. I now know what I'm made of. My integrity is intact."

Maybe so. But history is likely to judge his performance harshly.

UPDATE

Arthur Andersen's conviction for obstruction of justice effectively destroyed its business. All of the firm's nearly 1,300 clients moved to other accounting firms, and as of August 31, it was barred from auditing publicly traded companies. Andersen has not declared bankruptcy, but its only real business at this point consists of handling existing lawsuits and running a single training facility in Illinois.   —J.S.

Part Three

What Went Wrong,
and How Do We Fix It?

Greedy CEOs, corrupt investment bankers, shady accountants: these were certainly the key players in the scandals of the past few years. But they were only able to wreak as much havoc as they did because the system had, in some important sense, broken down. Capitalism clearly encourages the pursuit of self-interest, but in a healthy capitalist system there are a host of mechanisms that are supposed to make the pursuit of self-interest socially, as well as personally, beneficial. We've already seen how some of those mechanisms—investment advice and auditing—were corrupted. But it's also the case that investors in general were far less vigilant than they should have been, while regulators found themselves ill-equipped to deal with the proliferation of enormously complex financial instruments and accounting strategies. This final section offers pieces that take more of a big-picture look at what went wrong and at what needs to be done to make things right.

What's inarguable, it seems, is that the corruption of the past few years cannot be separated from the bull market and its evolution into a stock-market bubble. In "What's Wrong?" David Wessel shows how bubbles generate corruption as an inevitable by-product. Investors, made giddy by the constant rise in stock prices, stop paying close attention to the stories they're being fed. And the demand for new opportunities is so intense that even obviously shady deals are suddenly welcome. In recent years, the impact of the bubble was magnified by companies' affection for stock options. Stock options originally seemed like an excellent way of aligning the interests of CEOs with the interests of shareholders, since they ensured that a CEO could only get rich if he got the stock price up, which is what shareholders want. But as Thomas A. Stewart argues, in practice stock options encouraged CEOs to adopt risky strategies that might pump up the stock price in the short term while weakening the company in the long term. The more volatile a stock price is, the more valuable a stock option becomes. As a result, investors found themselves holding stocks whose value oscillated wildly.

At the same time, it'd be a mistake to let investors off the hook. They were the ones, ultimately, who approved those stock-option packages. And as P. J. O'Rourke, Michael Kinsley, and Michael Lewis all point out, in different ways, investors were also the ones who bear the biggest responsibility for letting CEOs run wild. In fact, as Kinsley suggests, it's telling that we didn't hear any complaints about corporate corruption until after the stock-market bubble burst. Lewis and O'Rourke, meanwhile, both suggest that the scandals have at least forced investors to spend some time scrutinizing income statements and balance sheets instead of just watching the stock-market ticker. In the end, O'Rourke argues, even the best regulations can't save investors from themselves. That said, in their respective pieces, Irwin M. Stelzer and the team of Joseph Nocera and a host of *Fortune* writers offer up a healthy mix of suggestions for regulatory reform and for self-imposed changes in corporate America and on Wall Street. As the title of Nocera's piece suggests, what we've seen is a case of "system failure," and systemic change is in order.

WHAT'S WRONG?

David Wessel

The Wall Street Journal, June 20, 2002

EVERY DECADE HAS KING-SIZE corporate villains. In the 1970s, Robert Vesco was indicted for looting the Investors Overseas Services mutual funds. In the 1980s, arbitrageur Ivan Boesky and junk-bond inventor Michael Milken went to jail.

But the scope and scale of the corporate transgressions of the late 1990s, now coming to light, exceed anything the U.S. has witnessed since the years preceding the Great Depression.

Enron Corp.'s top executives reaped hundreds of millions as the company collapsed. Arthur Andersen LLP, Enron's auditor, was convicted last week of obstructing justice. Tyco International Ltd.'s lionized chief executive is charged with tax evasion and accused of secret pay deals with underlings. Cable giant Adelphia Communications Corp. admitted inflating numbers and making undisclosed loans to its major shareholders. Xerox Corp. paid a $10 million fine for overstating revenues. Dynegy and CMS Energy Corp. simultaneously bought and sold electricity in transactions with no point other than pumping up trading volumes. Merrill Lynch & Co. paid $100 million to settle New York state charges that analysts misled investors, and other Wall Street firms are now under scrutiny.

"I've never seen anything of this magnitude with companies this large," says Henry McKinnell, 59, chief executive of pharmaceutical maker Pfizer Inc.

Why is so much corporate venality surfacing now? Is there more of it, or is more attention being paid? Did a few executives lose their ethical moorings in the exuberance of the 1990s? Or did a few notorious offenders break rules that many others merely bent? Is the entire system of corporate governance and regulation flawed? Or was the system abused by a few cleverly diabolical executives who deserve, as Treasury Secretary Paul O'Neill puts it, "to hang . . . from the very highest branches?"

The answer, put simply: A stock-market bubble magnified changes in business mores and brought trends that had been building for years to a climax. The victims: the very shareholders the executives were supposed to be serving.

One culprit was stock options, which gave executives huge incentives to boost near-term share prices regardless of long-term consequences. No CEO pay package seemed to strike any board of directors as too big.

These incentives helped turn the widely practiced art of earnings management—making sure profits meet or barely exceed Wall Street expectations—into a gross distortion of reality at some companies.

And the institutions that were created to check such abuses failed. The remnants of a professional ethos in accounting, law and securities analysis gave way to getting the maximum revenue per partner. The auditor's signature on a corporate report didn't testify that the report was an accurate snapshot, says Mr. O'Neill. He says it too often meant only that a company had "cooked the books to generally accepted standards."

The current sordid chapter in the history of American business opened on Aug. 14 last year when Jeffrey Skilling quit as chief executive of Enron Corp., an unmistakable sign that all was not well inside one of the country's most-admired corporations.

Enron is "the private sector's Watergate," says John Coffee, a Columbia University securities-law professor. Although not all politicians were crooks, Watergate bred a virulent cynicism about government among the public, the press and even some politicians. That cynicism persists 30 years after the White House–blessed burglary of the Democratic National Committee's office.

Enron and all that followed threaten to do the same to American business. "I have had a lot of e-mail from shareholders who seem to have gone off the deep end and think all corporate executives are crooks and all accountants are sheep, just as some think all Catholic priests are pedophiles," says mutual-fund manager James Gipson of Clipper Fund. "None of those statements are true."

Measuring the volume of corporate skullduggery precisely is difficult. The SEC opened 570 investigations last year. That's more than in any of the previous 10 years—but just 10 more than in 1994. More than 150 companies restated their earnings in each of the past three years, an acknowledgment that they had misinformed investors. That's more than triple the levels of the early 1990s, but represents only one of every 100 publicly traded companies.

One view, a staple of speeches by chief executives and government officials, underscores that only a small fraction of companies and executives stand accused of wrongdoing. It's the "a few bad apples" analysis. Treasury Secretary O'Neill, former chief executive of Alcoa Inc., talks of "a very small number compared to all the enterprises out there."

Pfizer's Mr. McKinnell, who serves as vice chairman of the Business Roundtable's corporate-governance task force, cautions against generalizing from "eight or ten companies who allegedly behaved in ways that are incomprehensible . . . and deserve what they're getting." Securities and Exchange Commission Chairman Harvey Pitt, who has been practicing securities law in and out of government for 35 years, chides business reporters by recalling how the reporting of muckraking journalist Lincoln Steffens created a "crime wave" in the 1890s at a time when the actual number of crimes was falling.

For this camp, the smart response is to punish the miscreants severely and tinker with the parts of the system that are broken, taking care to avoid hasty changes with unintended consequences. "Things aren't as broken as they appear to be," says Mr. McKinnell.

But there's another view: The headline-making cases are symptoms of a broader disease, not exceptions, and a regulatory apparatus that isn't up to the challenge. "A few bad apples? Looks like we've got the whole peck here," says retired federal judge Stanley Sporkin, the SEC's enforcement chief in the 1970s.

"Everybody did this," says economic historian Peter Temin of the Massachusetts Institute of Technology. "The people who got in trouble are those who are most at the edge. Enron didn't get caught. Enron got so far out on the edge that it fell off."

To this camp, the reasonable response is broader legislation and tougher regulation on the scale of the 1930s laws that created the SEC and the modern regulatory regime.

The "irrational exuberance" so famously flagged in 1996 is an essential part of explaining the 1990s. When the man who coined the term, Federal Reserve Chairman Alan Greenspan, talks informally with business and other groups, he says the greediness of human beings didn't increase in the 1990s. What increased, he says, were the number of opportunities to satisfy that greed. The run-up in stock prices meant there was more to grab.

Revelation and outrage always follow the bursting of a bubble. The cycle is immutable. "At any given time there exists an inventory of undiscovered embezzlement," economist John Kenneth Galbraith wrote in *The Great Crash of 1929*. "This inventory—it should perhaps be called the bezzle—amounts at any moment to many millions of dollars. . . . In good times people are relaxed, trusting and money is plentiful. But even though money is plentiful, there are always many people who need more."

Mr. Galbraith continues: "Under these circumstances the rate of embezzlement grows, the rate of discovery falls off, and bezzle increases rapidly. In depression all this is reversed. Money is watched with a narrow, suspicious eye. The man who handles it is assumed to be dishonest until he proves himself otherwise. Audits are penetrating and meticulous. Commercial morality is enormously improved. The bezzle shrinks."

Mr. Gipson, the mutual-fund manager, says, "There is a tendency during boom times for even honest people to shift their moral compasses, and there is a belief that everyone else is doing it. It's when the music stops, if you will, and the scrutiny goes up that the over-the-top cases become apparent."

Stock options were supposed to solve a problem of the past: entrenched corporate management that wasn't serving shareholders—the indictment that corporate raiders made with such ferocity in the 1980s.

"Today, management has no stake in the company," raider Gordon Gekko says in his speech to shareholders in the 1987 movie *Wall Street*. "Where does Mr. Cromwell [the CEO] put his million-dollar salary?

Not in Teldar stock. He owns less than 1%. You own the company. That's right, you, the stockholders. You are being royally screwed over by these bureaucrats with their steak luncheons, hunting and fishing trips, their corporate jets and golden parachutes."

The solution, widely embraced in American business, was to use stock options to link executives' and shareholders' interests. It sounded reasonable: Executives would benefit if they managed companies in a way that lifted share prices.

It didn't work as intended. A soaring stock market rewarded executives not for good strategic management, but for riding the roller coaster. And when the stock price dipped below the exercise price—essentially making the options worthless—some companies simply revised the terms or, in Wall Street jargon, "reloaded" them.

Even worse, the incentives to do almost anything to increase the stock price were huge. And the incentives weren't to increase profits and share prices over a decade or two, but rather to increase profits—never mind if they have to be restated later—just long enough for executives to cash out, often without ever risking any of their own money to buy shares in the first place.

Stock options, Mr. Pitt says, were "a device that was supposed to align shareholder and manager interests—and actually 'disaligned' them." Not all executives were swayed, of course, but an ill-designed compensation system pushed them in the wrong direction.

Of course, corporate executives aren't supposed to be monarchs. All sorts of checks and balances have been established during the past century: accountants, lawyers, securities analysts, investment bankers, audit committees, regulators, even the press.

None of the abuses that have been exposed in the past 10 months were committed by chief executives who worked alone to steal shareholders' money. "In every one of these cases," says Mr. Sporkin, the former SEC chief, "you have professional assistance."

This exposes one of the problems that have plagued corporate capitalism since its inception. "When the laws or regulations fail to protect investors, corporate insiders—whether managers or owners—tend to expropriate," economists Gene D'Avoilio, Efi Gildor and Andrei Shleifer asserted in a paper they presented at a Federal Reserve Bank of Kansas City conference last summer.

Perhaps the rules were inadequate; that's still being debated. But there is little debate about the failure of the professionals who are supposed to see that rules are obeyed and executives are honest.

The decay of professionalism—and codes of ethics that distinguished a profession from a job—intensified in the 1990s, but it didn't begin then. Reflecting on his 23 years in corporate management, Mr. O'Neill recalls a parade of Wall Street professionals who came to his office with plans for "new and exotic" financial maneuvers to reduce his company's tax bill or report debt levels in ways "not clearly prohibited by the tax code or law," but not designed to illuminate corporate operations, either.

"They get," he says, "into an ethical vacuum space."

The shortcomings of accounting firms are now well exposed. The duplicity of some highly paid Wall Street analysts is documented in internal e-mails that are now public. The acquiescence of the lawyers inside Enron and Tyco, as well as the readiness of lawyers to clear increasingly aggressive corporate tax shelters for other companies, is readily apparent.

This disturbing pattern is the biggest reason why the abuses of the 1990s can't easily be dismissed as the fault of a few flawed human beings. "The professional gatekeepers were greatly compromised by finding they could make tremendous profits by deferring to management," says Columbia's Mr. Coffee.

But not one of the instances of egregious abuse of shareholder interest could have occurred if the CEO had simply said, "No!"

The climate made it commonplace. The incentives were perverse. The watchdogs were sleeping. But not every company did it. What distinguishes those that did from those that didn't?

Mr. Gipson, the mutual-fund manager, divides offenders into two classes: the "confirmed crooks" who deliberately and willfully ripped off shareholders, and the "morally marginal who went right up to the line of acceptable behavior" and then "when the line was moved found themselves on the other side."

Treasury Secretary O'Neill makes a similar point: "A little lie leads to ever bigger ones in lots of cases without a recognition on the part of the perpetrator that they ever told a lie, even when it gets grotesque. They say, 'If only I had another 12 months . . .'"

At Harvard Business School, the citadel of corporate management, the faculty uses case studies of heroes and villains in an effort to inoculate students against the temptations they will inevitably confront.

"Maybe," says a member of that faculty, Richard Tedlow, "we ought to think about CEOs and other managers as fully formed human beings, not as people who focus on one variable and who check their personalities at the coat rack. Some of what was going on was people doing exactly what the incentives suggest that they do: Give me a lot of stock options, and I'll make the stock go up.

"But something is missing," he adds. "Life is lived on a slippery slope. It takes a person of character to know what lines you don't cross. That part of the equation of corporate management hasn't had the emphasis it should have had in the last decade or two."

The excesses of the 1920s and the spectacular crash of the stock market in 1929 led to the creation of modern financial regulation, from bank-deposit insurance to the ban on insider trades, in 1933 and 1934. Despite the obvious parallels, this is a different time. The U.S. is not in an economic depression, nor does George W. Bush see himself as Franklin Delano Roosevelt's heir. The debate over how to repair the system is just beginning to take form; this week saw competing legislative and SEC proposals to tighten oversight of accountants.

The nature and dimensions of the reforms depend on factors that aren't knowable. How many more Enrons and Tycos remain unreported? How swiftly will corporations, boards of directors, the New York Stock Exchange, the National Association of Securities Dealers and other self-regulatory organizations move to reassure investors? And, most important of all, how much longer will the stock market languish?

ENRON DEBACLE HIGHLIGHTS THE TROUBLE WITH STOCK OPTIONS

Thomas A. Stewart

Business 2.0, March 27, 2002

A FEW WEEKS AGO, I was talking with the CEO of a global media company about—what else?—Enron. He's a friend, a former neighbor. We were discussing the spectacle of Enron executives dumping stock as the company tanked. The amounts were huge: more than $1 billion worth, reportedly. I had found myself outraged and protesting that managers shouldn't own so much stock, then caught myself short: That's theologically incorrect. We *want* managers to own stock, because we want them to "think like owners" and "be in the same boat with shareholders." But the image I had was of rats leaving a ship—or the crew shouldering passengers out of the way in a race to the lifeboats.

"Help me out," I said to my ex-neighbor.

Yes, the dumping was stinky, he agreed, albeit apparently legal. I wondered if my gut anger came from the fact that these people acquired their shares via options. Ordinary shareholders paid cash money; executives picked up shares from in-the-money options, never putting their own money at risk. In the same boat, but with a free ticket.

"You know," he said, dropping a small bombshell, "options aren't the same as stocks. The securities behave differently." The value of an option, he went on, varies not just with the value of the underlying asset but also with the asset's volatility. Other things being equal, the more volatile a stock, the more valuable the option. "It's elementary Black-Scholes," he said, referring to the standard model for pricing options, named for Fisher Black and Myron Scholes. (Scholes and Robert C.

Merton shared the 1997 Nobel Prize for the work; Black, who died in 1995, would almost certainly have joined them in Stockholm.)

In other words, if you're an executive with lots of stock options, it's in your interest to make decisions that increase risk and hence increase the amount by which a stock's value jumps around. That incentive is strengthened because you're playing with someone else's money. Since the option costs you nothing, you're more likely to play fast and loose than you would be if the money were your own and hard-earned. One could test this proposition empirically by standing at a spot equidistant from a savings bank, a Charles Schwab office, and a casino, handing out $1,000 bills to passersby, and seeing where they go. Or (slightly more efficiently) you could do what I did, which was call another former neighbor, Stephen Bryan, a professor of accounting at the Babcock School of Management at Wake Forest University who has been studying stock-based compensation of CEOs. Bryan went into Standard & Poor's ExecuComp database and looked at 1,100 companies. He first got a measure of how lavishly (or not) they bestowed options by calculating the number of options granted to the CEO as a percentage of total shares outstanding. He then measured the volatility of their stocks—the beta—by comparing the returns for each company with those for the market as a whole. Then he set the two against one another, to see if there was a correlation between outsize options grants and volatility.

Blackjack. Bryan told me: "The correlation between beta and percent is about 0.12 to 0.14, depending on the correlation method (Pearson or Spearman), but both are highly significant in a statistical sense." As a rule, the more you load the CEO up with options, the more volatile the company's stock is. One could object that this might just be a function of certain industries. Maybe high-tech companies, which tend to give out a lot of options, are inherently more volatile than banks or utilities. To check, Bryan ran the numbers for companies in industry groups. Blackjack again. For example, within the software industry, companies that give their CEOs the most options have higher betas than the others; that correlation is 0.23. The trend holds true similarly in the chemical industry, where the correlation is 0.18. In a few industries, the correlation is too low to be significant, but in no industry is it both negative and significant.

So we have evidence that, in companies where the chief executive has a big incentive to rock the boat, the boat rocks. That still doesn't prove he rocked it. As Bryan points out, the cause and effect might be reversed: Conceivably, managers in volatile businesses could negotiate for option-heavy compensation packages as a way to deal with the fact that they work in a risky neighborhood. Maybe, but common sense — the behavior of those passersby we gave a thousand bucks to — suggests that shareholders are getting splashed because management is jumping up and down on the gunwales.

It's not necessarily bad to encourage risk-taking among managers. Indeed, a venerable criticism of hired-hand managers — dating back to the seminal analysis by Adolf Berle and Gardiner Means in the 1930s, called *The Modern Corporation and Private Property* — is that salaried managers can be too risk-averse because their self-interest is best served by overly cautious behavior that protects job security. (Remember the expression "No IT manager was ever fired for buying IBM"?) Stock options started to become popular in the 1950s partly to encourage managers to behave more like entrepreneurs. But those were modest grants — a thousand shares, maybe two or three thousand — piddling to today's CEOs.

Any shrink will tell you there's a difference between risk-taking and thrill-seeking. Prudent risks are what capital is for. But when stock option grants get as humongous as they've become, the CEO's incentive is no longer to maximize the value of the stock. It's to maximize the value of the option — and that can be a completely different, and ugly, thing.

HOW TO STUFF
A WILD ENRON

P. J. O'Rourke

The Atlantic Monthly, April 2002

EVERYONE BLAMES TOO LITTLE regulation for the Enron mess, but maybe the culprit was too much.

Beyond a certain point complexity is fraud. It's the Airline Ticket Price Axiom. Am I getting the best deal on my airline ticket? How could I know? To map the labyrinth of airline-ticket pricing structure I would have to spend a greater value in time, at the minimum-wage billing rate, than the value of the money I'd save. Or it's the *Finnegans Wake* Postulate. We all know that Joyce, the old soak, was just scribbling a learned version of what Jack Nicholson typed in *The Shining*.

Maybe "complexity is fraud" doesn't apply to mathematics or the physical sciences. Nevertheless, when someone creates a system in which you can't tell whether or not you're being fooled, you're being fooled. This is true in the intellectual food chain from the fine arts, literature, and sociology on down.

And Enron was pretty far down there among the cunning weasels of ratiocination. What Enron was doing, what caused investors to embrace it in a rapture of baffled awe, was hiding debt. Several friends of mine who work in finance tried to give me a simplified model of the kind of thing Enron would do: Enron would have some business in which it had invested a lot of money. But that business wasn't making a profit. Enron would form a partnership with outside investors. The partnership would buy the business. But almost all the money to buy the business would be lent to the partnership by Enron, usually in the form of stock.

Enron would count the sale of that business as income and count the loan to the partnership as an asset. The unprofitable business would disappear from Enron's financial statement, because under accounting conventions, if a mere three percent of capital is brought into a partnership from outside a corporation, then the corporation doesn't have to carry that partnership on its books. Enron's liabilities were turned into black ink.

Enron engendered these partnerships with wild fecundity and in many variations; but some of the most important of them, to stay vital, depended on a high market price for Enron stock. Meanwhile, Arthur Andersen auditors were standing by reciting the only joke that makes accountants laugh:

"Q. What's two minus two? A. Whatever the client wants it to be."

I've got to hurry and hire Arthur Andersen before everyone in the firm gets sent up the river to Club Fed. I'm going to tell my new accountants, "I had this expensive divorce. But I figure you can list it as an asset. Because, believe me, no matter what that divorce cost, it was worth it."

Enron was, by the common if not by the legal definition, defrauding the people who bought its stock. Is there something in the American capitalist system that encourages such fraud? Yes: the regulations against it. Generally accepted accounting principles consist of 144 standards, each requiring a volume of explication. Title 17 of the Code of Federal Regulations, covering commodity and securities exchanges, is 2,330 pages long. Federal tax law runs to 3,778 pages, with an additional 12,888 pages of IRS tax code regulations.

There are plenty of places to hide in this vast briar patch of dos and don'ts. Enron broke the rules of ethics. But the corporation's worst sins seem to have been lawful: the Gordian partnership ties, the tales of profit and growth enhanced for dramatic effect, the taxes avoided by sending revenues on vacation to the Cayman Islands, the freezing of employee 401(k)s in the ice-cube tray of the company's own stock, the auditing firm with about half its Enron fees gained from provision of other accounting services, so that Arthur Andersen accountants were cooking the very books that Arthur Andersen auditors were expected to swallow. And so on. According to *The Economist*, even Kenneth Lay's eleventh-hour stock sales may not have violated SEC regulations, because Lay was selling the stock to repay personal loans from the corporation; hence insider-trading restrictions did not (for reasons known only to someone who reads and marks with Hi-Liter pens all 2,330 pages of Title 17) apply.

Enron was supposed to be a supporter of marketplace deregulation. In a January 21 *Newsweek* article, "Who Killed Enron?" Allan Sloan wrote,

At a dinner I had with [the former Enron CEO Jeffrey] Skilling in the late 1990s, he was like a religious zealot who couldn't stop repeating his favorite mantra . . . There are rolling blackouts in the Midwest? Deregulate. Some energy companies look like they're price gouging? Deregulate more. And if salad dressing had dripped onto my tie? . . . You get the picture.

But Jerry Taylor, the director of natural-resource studies at the Cato Institute (which really favors deregulation), points out that Enron lobbied for strict price controls on rates charged for access to power grids. Except when Enron lobbied otherwise, in places such as Texas and Louisiana, where Enron had bought those power grids. Then legislators were urged to let grid owners do what they liked. Bill Keller, the author of a January 26 *New York Times* column titled "Enron for Dummies," wrote, "Enron believed in reducing regulation of Enron."

And so believes every other regulated industry. This is why regulated industries set out to "capture" their regulatory bodies. Usually the tranquilizer guns and large nets work well. On the front page of the January 28 *Wall Street Journal* a headline read FEDERAL REGULATOR OFTEN HELPS BANKS FIGHTING CONSUMERS.

The Cato Institute's president, Ed Crane, calls generally accepted accounting principles "skewed in favor of management, not investors." Of course they are. Enron's management paid Arthur Andersen $25 million in auditing fees in 2000. I paid H&R Block $80. The SEC allows an astonishing conflict of interest in large financial-services firms that can make fortunes doing investment banking for corporations and then make more fortunes advising me to buy stock in those corporations and taking a commission when I do. The so-called Chinese wall between the two sides of the business is as effective as the one that

Genghis Khan walked through the gates of in the thirteenth century. Enron stock reached a high of $90.75 in August of 2000. According to *The Wall Street Journal*, only one Wall Street analyst put a "sell" recommendation on it before the price fell below $10. And this despite a damning article in the March 5, 2001, *Fortune* (when Enron stock was trading at $70) by Bethany McLean, who called Enron's business activities "impenetrable to outsiders" and "mind-numbingly complex" and said, "As for the details about how it makes money, Enron says that's proprietary information, sort of like Coca-Cola's secret formula."

Regulation creates a moral hazard. We don't understand finance, but it's regulated so we're safe. "Regulation," Jerry Taylor says, "dulls the senses that you would take into an unregulated situation. If you hear screaming in the middle of the night, you assume it's hot sex, not murder."

Regulation of the marketplace isn't bad. The problem is, rather, that the regulation we have now is too good—at least in its intent. Our regulatory bodies strive to create honest dealings, fair trades, and a situation in which no one has an advantage over anyone else. But human beings aren't honest. And all trades are made because one person thinks he's getting the better of the other, and the other person thinks the same. And you will always have an uncle who's heard about a merger on the golf course, whereas I've got an uncle who gets his inside information at the OTB parlor.

Regulation would be better if its goal were not to ensure probity in finance but to rake muck. Get all the dirty laundry out in public: the ripped bodice of the hostile takeover, the stock jobber's filth-splattered britches, the soiled undershirt of dodgy bookkeeping, and campaign funding's reeking, horrible socks.

THE NEW BULL MARKET

Michael Kinsley

Slate, July 18, 2002

SO, NOW IT'S THE turn of corporate CEOs to feel the righteous petulance of the American people. In the 1990s the CEO was society's glamorpuss, and politicians were the dawgs. Now people tell pollsters they have lost their faith in corporate officers, and the politicians joyously pile on, measuring their outrage in prison terms for future miscreants and bragging about whose is longer. John Walker Lindh got 20 years this week for joining a terrorist network at war with his country. Lucky for him he didn't try something really bad, like capitalizing an expense item.

It took campaign-spending reform many years to go from an obsession of high-minded scolds and bores to a popular cause to a law of the land. Corporate reform is covering that ground in a few weeks. Republicans have put aside any concerns they might have mentioned once or twice in the past century and a half about overregulation of business, centralizing of power in Washington, and so on, to join the bidding war for new federal constraints on corporations. This issue, so dear to their hearts, is strangely not mentioned at all in the most recent (2000) Republican platform. That document's only reference to "financial markets" is about what a splendid place they would be to put Social Security funds. The Democratic platform touches on some corporate reform issues, but just barely.

President Bush, who spent 56 years on this earth without revealing the slightest passion for corporate reform, now says life will be intolerable if he doesn't have a bill to sign within a couple of weeks. And he has sent signals that he doesn't give much of a hoot what is in it. Bush the born-again reformer even wants to outlaw one of the dubious ways he himself got rich (sweetheart loans from a corporation to buy its own stock).

The politicians are only trying to ride the wake of popular outrage. But this public outrage is also a bit stagey. It seems that average citizens are so emotionally invested in the conventions of financial documents that discovering the cost of stock option grants in a footnote, rather than in the profit-and-loss statement, itself is enough to destroy their faith in the economy. Who knew? And I can't help suspecting—can you?—that the real betrayal people feel is not the dubious bookkeeping or the insider trading or even the outright fraud. It's the downright un-American refusal of share prices to continue soaring. If the Dow were at 15,000, corporations could embroider their financial data all they wanted, turn the embroidery into pillows, and let Martha sell them at Kmart, for all anyone would care.

The abuses have been real, and the reforms are mostly sound, but the connection between the abuses and the reforms is weak. This is all less about solving an actual problem than about a sort of law of political thermodynamics, which holds that every public frenzy produces legislation purporting to address it. Take the proposal—pushed by super-investor Warren Buffett, endorsed by Federal Reserve Chairman Alan Greenspan in congressional testimony on Tuesday, and adopted voluntarily this week by the Coca-Cola company—that stock options should be treated as an expense on corporate books. The argument is twofold. First, as a form of employee compensation, stock option grants are in fact a current expense, and allowing the cost to be hidden or postponed (only on the books, not in real life) makes corporate profits look higher than they really are. And second, this opportunity to mislead investors encourages companies to give their executives more stock options, which gives those executives an unhealthy interest in pushing up the company's stock price.

The basic accounting complaint is legitimate, but odd. All major companies do disclose their stock option grants, even if they don't factor them into their profit-and-loss calculations as they should. There may be two or three investors somewhere who examine the P&L with care and never glance at the fine print. Most folks never look at any of this stuff but rely on professionals who (we presume) read it all and are free to recalculate as necessary. It does not seem possible that enough people could be actively misled about options to affect a company's share price.

Another problem with all this is that stock options are worthless unless the price of a share is going up. (A stock option is the right to buy a share of stock at a set price—usually the market price at the time it is issued.) If we are in a long-term bear market, stock options will be worthless or close to it and will not affect executive behavior for good or ill. In fact, as Greenspan pointed out, when the market is not rising, many fewer options are issued. Meanwhile, if the bull returns, investors are no longer going to complain.

For more than a decade until the past few weeks, the conventional wisdom was that stock options are a good thing because they align the interests of corporate executives with those of their shareholders. Is that no longer true? As shareholders, most investors still prefer to see a company's share price going up, and it is not obvious why they should be enthusiastic for legislation to dim the enthusiasm of the people who run the company about that same goal. The argument must be that options cause executives to do things that hype share prices in the short run but hurt them in the long run, or that options tempt them to corrupt behavior that no decent shareholder would wish to profit from. But I cannot see how options give executives a greater incentive for short-term or corrupt behavior than shareholders would want them to have. If anything, the differences between options and normal shares—option vesting periods, holding requirements, and so on—encourage executives to think longer-term than the ordinary shareholder, who paid full price yesterday and can sell tomorrow, might wish.

In short the abuses these reforms address, if anything, drove stock prices up, but what really bothers people is that they came back down again. Politicians promising to solve that problem are making the same mistake they purport to correct: grabbing a short-term advantage that will cost them dearly in the longer run.

IN PRAISE OF CORPORATE CORRUPTION BOOM

Michael Lewis

Bloomberg News, July 12, 2002

BERKELEY, CALIFORNIA — when George W. Bush went to Wall Street and delivered his speech about corporate reform in front of a banner that read "Corporate Responsibility," I thought: it doesn't get any better than this. It was as if Bill Clinton had flown to Las Vegas to deliver a speech in front of a banner that read "Sexual Abstinence."

But I was wrong. It did get better. Tipped off by a friend, I went to the C-Span Web site and watched the tape of Monday's hearings of the House Financial Services Committee. The committee, previously known mainly as a good place to attract campaign funds from Wall Street, dragged before it for a public whipping the cast of World-Com Inc.

There, as Jack Grubman and Bernie Ebbers stared stoically into the middle distance, California's Maxine Waters referred to the corrupt research reports of a Wall Street investment bank she called "Salomon Barney Frank." And she was reading from a prepared statement.

In the current political climate, it doesn't really matter whether a politician is able to distinguish between Smith Barney and Barney Frank, or to know that EBITDA is not a brand of beer. President Bush doesn't need to recognize that his own putatively successful business career was nothing more than a series of elaborately orchestrated bribes. All that matters is that he is deeply outraged by the people who most recently betrayed capitalism.

BRIGHT SIDE OF GLOOM

That is one good thing to be said on behalf of business corruption: it gives our politicians a rare chance to shine, morals-wise. But it is not the only good thing.

What is being lost in the fog of moral outrage is just how much good may come of its cause. We are all very angry at Ebbers and Enron Corp.'s Kenneth Lay and the Great Kozlowski of Tyco International Ltd. fame, and maybe we should be. But we should be a little grateful to them, too.

The first and most important consequence of these men's alleged deceit is to instill greater investor trust in the markets.

Of course, we are meant to be living right now through a great crisis in investor confidence. Investors' lack of confidence is offered up as the cause of every stock market sell-off. The restoration of confidence has become both a mantra and a reason for being for many otherwise unemployable people.

FUTURE, NOT PAST

Forget for a moment that a better explanation for each stock market plunge is that the market is still pretty rich by historical standards, and historical standards are now back in fashion. Would it not seem likely that investors, even foreign ones who speak poor English, are more concerned about how companies will be governed in the future than how they've been governed in the past?

Anyone who was willing to dump his capital into a black box like Enron will no doubt be more than willing—nay, grateful—to dump even more capital into the newly chastened, slightly more transparent American corporation.

I don't know about you, but every day I feel a bit better about owning General Electric Co. A year ago I had only a vague idea of what they were up to. I relied, mistakenly, on others to watch them for me. Now I know that others are watching them for me and are picking them apart in ways they never imagined.

That is another, related benefit of business corruption: it lets the American investor off the hook for years of sloth.

ACCOMPLICE TO VICTIM

Just now we are busy forgetting that most of what the crooks did, they did to mollify big investors, who agreed to turn a blind eye to whatever the hell was actually going on inside the business for the sake of appearances, and, thus, share prices.

The presence of actual corruption transforms the investor from accomplice to victim. This is probably a good thing for the spirit of capitalism. If the American investor ever was forced to examine his own behavior, he might become genuinely demoralized. And that would not do.

A final benefit of the corruption boom is to remind CEOs—maybe even inform a few for the first time—that they cannot remove themselves from the larger society.

Those of us who have been puzzled for years by the cult of the CEO, and watched in horror as people who were meant to lead others in a cause greater than themselves instead took as much loot as they could for themselves, wondered when, if ever, the process would reverse itself. It just did.

A new correlation has been established in the American mind, between CEOs who pay themselves tens of millions of dollars each year, and CEOs who cook their books and evade sales taxes and send their wives onto television to lie about how much money they still have.

In the future, a healthy new suspicion shall arise whenever any CEO pays himself tens of millions of dollars. The old rule of CEO pay was: the more you pay yourself, the more valuable you must be to the company. The new rule of CEO pay is: the more you pay yourself, the more you will be watched.

After all, any CEO who is actually worth $25 million a year should be responsible enough, and decent enough, not to take it.

BIG BUSINESS'S BAD BEHAVIOR: HOW (AND HOW NOT) TO STOP IT

Irwin M. Stelzer

The Weekly Standard, July 22, 2002

NO SENSIBLE PERSON CAN quarrel with what the president told the Wall Street biggies he addressed last week. Crooks should be forced to disgorge their ill-gotten gains, and should go to jail for extended periods. Enforcement agencies should be given adequate resources. Corporate executives should be held responsible for the accuracy of what they tell shareholders, disclose their compensation in annual reports "prominently and in plain English," and explain why their "compensation package is in the best interest of the company." Board members should be independent and "ask tough questions." Shareholders should speak up. Most important, chief executive officers should create a "moral tone" that ensures the company's top managers behave in accordance with the highest ethical standards.

The quarrel comes not with what the president said, but with what he didn't say. In the game of matching his laundry list of reforms against the inevitably longer list generated by the Daschle-Leahy-Sarbanes-Gephardt crowd, the president inevitably loses, as last week's unanimous vote of Senate Republicans for the Democrats' bill proves. Longer sounds better if you're just compiling a laundry list of items aimed at punishing politically unpopular corporate bad guys. Only if there is a conceptual framework within which specific reforms can be created and defended is there any hope that a sensible corporate governance system will emerge from the congressional legislation factory.

Start with the fact that it is important to distinguish the role of gov-

ernment from that of the private-sector institutions that monitor corporate America. The latter can be relied upon to act when the integrity of
the system is threatened, not because these private sector players are a
bunch of goodie-two-shoes, but for the more reliable reason that honest
markets and accurate profit reporting are in their interest. Just as gam-
blers won't put their bets down when they know a wheel to be rigged, so
investors won't put their money into shares if prices can be manipulated
by inflated profit reporting or special treatment of insiders.

Hence we have a stream of quite sensible reforms proposed by the
Business Roundtable and the New York Stock Exchange, some going
beyond those being pushed by the president. And we have companies
scrambling to adopt governance rules and accounting practices that will
reassure investors that the game is not rigged against them. No CEO
wants to see his company's stock battered by investors who fear that
share values will evaporate as profits are restated to eliminate the imagi-
native counting of revenues (claim them now, before the customer pays
or even considers paying) and of costs (capitalize rather than expense
every outlay, regardless of the life of the item purchased). Plummeting
share prices are dangerous to the careers of chief executives.

But, as the president recognized when he called for higher ethical
standards, self-interest cannot be relied upon to produce honest business dealings unless that self-interest includes what Adam Smith called
a "desire to be both respected and respectable," and such esteem is seen
to flow not from "wealth and greatness" but from "wisdom and virtue."
Which may be what Bush had in mind when he said that we need "men
and women of character, who know the difference between ambition
and destructive greed" to lead our major corporations. And it may be
what he had in mind when, immediately after delivering his talk, he
returned to Washington to award the Presidential Medal of Freedom—
America's highest civilian honor—not to the nation's richest (Intel
founder Gordon Moore may have been the one exception), but instead
to folks who have enriched our national life with their sharp iconoclasm
(Irving Kristol), gentle humor (Bill Cosby), and quiet devotion to family
and good causes (Nancy Reagan).

Still, neither self-interested reform nor a new emphasis on business
ethics can be relied upon to save capitalism from the capitalists. Immediately after the president's speech the White House was bombarded

with calls from CEOs protesting his demand that they disclose their compensation packages in easily accessible terms. I well recall the reaction when, several years ago, I made a similar suggestion at a think-tank-sponsored meeting of top business and government officials. One captain of industry replied that he would not tell his shareholders how much he earns lest he encourage kidnappers (as if they would only become aware of his affluence if he revealed it in his company's annual report).

Nor did anything the president said persuade the accountants to call off their lobbyists, who continue to oppose reforms that would make their devotion to the accuracy of their audit statements unambivalent. Or convince CEOs of Silicon Valley and other high-tech companies to bow to Alan Greenspan's call for them to report their share options as the expenses they most certainly are. Again, I recall a discussion that followed a similar proposal I made several years ago. One CEO said that he couldn't place a value on these options for purposes of reporting to shareholders, even though he could value those same options for the purpose of deducting their cost from his profits for tax purposes. Another claimed that if he treated options as an expense, he would wipe out his entire reported earnings, an argument, I suppose, for refusing to account for almost any expense that constitutes a threat to reported profits—what might be called the WorldCom excuse. (For the economy as a whole, experts estimate that expensing of options would reduce aggregate corporate profits by about 8 percent.) Note that the issue is not whether companies, especially start-ups, should be allowed to use options to attract talented staff, but whether they should have to treat this compensation as an expense when reporting profits. As Greenspan points out, refusing to deduct the cost of options diverts capital and other resources from truly profitable to only apparently profitable firms.

This opposition of important segments of the business and accounting communities to reform means that government must take on the burden of revising the institutional framework within which business operates—setting the rules of the game that will allow markets to do their job of allocating human and financial capital to its highest and best uses. As Milton Friedman, no fan of big government, has written, society needs rules and an umpire "to enforce compliance with rules on the part of those few who would otherwise not play the game."

To keep rules to a Friedmanesque minimum, we need a conceptual framework for reform rather than competing laundry lists. The first step is to understand the limits of criminal sanctions. Yes, it makes sense for the Senate to insist, as it did unanimously last week, that the crimes perpetrated by some corporate managers and accountants be defined as precisely as possible. Yes, criminal sanctions can be used to make life miserable for those caught with their fingers in the till and to deter from evildoing those for whom Adam Smith's "desire to be respectable and to be respected" is insufficient inducement to decent behavior. But, as law professors David Skeel and William Stuntz recently pointed out in *The New York Times*, "Criminal laws lead people to focus on what is legal instead of what is right. . . . In today's world, executives are more likely to ask what they can get away with legally than what's fair and honest." The Senate was pleased with itself for toughening the laws under which executives will operate, but criminalizing bad behavior is no guarantee of future good behavior—behavior that is not merely indictment-avoiding, but is efficiency- and wealth-enhancing.

Instead, policymakers should turn to that trusty guideline, "Get the incentives right." The problems we are facing stem from the fact that we have provided the four guardians of shareholder interests—auditors, analysts, directors, and corporate managers—with the wrong incentives.

Auditors know that success or failure in their profession depends not so much on the accuracy and realism of their audits, as on their ability to conduct themselves so as not to imperil the flow of consulting fees to their firms. Enron paid Arthur Andersen as much or more in consulting than in auditing fees; Andersen's $12 million in consulting fees from WorldCom dwarfed its $4 million audit fee. It would have taken a brave auditor indeed to fly in the face of these clear incentives and tell Enron's management that placing some item off-balance-sheet might be technically legal, but would obscure the company's true financial condition, or to insist on access to documents that might have revealed WorldCom's recording of current expenses as capital investments. Rather than rely on such strength of character, some 70 percent of the directors surveyed by McKinsey & Co. now say they will in the future oppose the granting of such contracts, a policy that Arthur Levitt, Bill Clinton's SEC chairman, was unable to push through over the massed opposition of the accountants' lobbyists. All of which makes Bush's silence on this subject rather odd, and the Senate Democrats' insistence on a broader prohibition on consulting than is contained in the House Republicans' bill more likely to get the auditors' incentives lined up with shareholder interests.

Once those incentives are in place, other provisions of the House and Senate bills become unnecessary. Both bills call for still more regulation of auditors, and create still another regulatory body to set and oversee accounting standards. One need not be an apologist for the accounting profession to suggest that such a move would merely continue the failed practice of attempting to control auditors by closely supervising them. There is no reason to believe that such supervision will be any more successful in the future than it has been in the past, especially since in the end auditors are required only to say that they followed often complex and arcane rules that necessarily involve the exercise of judgment.

Instead of such ongoing regulation, including half-measures that merely restrict auditors from engaging in some specified form of consulting activity, let's get the incentives right by complete, mandated separation of the audit and consulting businesses, as John McCain proposes. Lead the CPAs not into temptation, and reliance on porous Chinese walls becomes unnecessary. Auditors will compete for business on the basis of their ability to provide a product that gives investors confidence in the transparency and accuracy of the company accounts, with the uplifting effect that will have on the prices of their clients' shares. (Audit firms are unlikely to compete on price, since the risks associated with the audit business have risen. There are only four major firms, and rotation of auditors on something like the five-year basis favored by Senate Democrats, although necessary to prevent over-identification between client and auditor, is a classic cartel market-sharing arrangement—all legal, in this case.)

Analysts are another group who now face perverse incentives. Investors may have been naive to believe that these students of income statements, balance sheets, and other economic data would provide honest advice about a company's financial condition and prospects. But they had a right to such a belief, since the commissions they pay their brokers are supposed to be in return for such advice. Along comes New York State Attorney General Eliot Spitzer and revelations that some of these supposed agents of the shareholders' interests are recommending stocks they know to be "shitty" in order to win investment banking business for their partners and increased compensation for themselves. All of this in the presence of Chinese walls erected to separate bankers from analysts. It took no Joshua-plus-trumpet to bring these walls down; the prospect of hefty banking fees was quite enough. Jack Grubman, the Salomon Smith Barney (a division of Citigroup) analyst famous for his enthusiastic recommendations of WorldCom stock, last week told the House Financial Services Committee, "No one can sit here on Wall Street and deny to anybody on this committee that banking is not a consideration in the compensation of analysts of a full-service firm." Forget the double negative: Grubman was conceding that part of his salary, which reached $20 million per year, came from the $140 million in underwriting fees that his firm received from WorldCom over the past five years.

Again, get the incentives right. One way, now preferred on Wall Street, is to write contracts that make analysts' compensation independent of the fees flowing into the investment banking divisions of the large firms. But just how analysts can prosper if the banking division isn't earning enough to pay the rent is unclear. Besides, unless analysts suddenly become willing to issue "sell" recommendations just when their investment banking partners are pitching a company for business, this proposed reform is unlikely to be effective, especially after the current heat is off and congressional attention turns to other matters. True or not, bankers believe that CEOs, being human (yes, most are), are likely to take into account what a firm's analysts are saying about their stock when selecting an investment banker. It would be an unusual CEO, indeed, who would cheerfully receive an investment banker after reading in the morning papers that the banker's analyst-partner had just downgraded his company's stock from a "buy" to a "sell." Many investment bankers—not all, but many—will find ways to persuade their partner-analysts to be team players. Banking fees are large enough to give them an enormous incentive to do just that.

So, let's get the incentives right and mandate a separation of the investment banking and stock-picking businesses, another McCain proposal. Analysts would then have an unambiguous incentive to make the best "buy" and "sell" recommendations they possibly can, so as to build reputations that will attract investors to them. And investors will get something in return for their commission dollars—honest advice from men and women expert in the analysis of corporate financial data, competing with one another to attract clients by creating a track record of picking winners.

Which brings us to directors. Again, we have a case of skewed incentives. Directors are hired by managers to protect shareholders from, er, those same managers. To make sure the directors remain friendly, executives often shower them with perks and consulting fees, the continuation of which depend on the goodwill of the CEOs they are supposed to be supervising. It is the rare director who chooses to feast on the hand that feeds him, not merely because he is venal, but because the courtesies lavished upon him genuinely persuade him that the CEO is a decent chap, deserving of every million he is paid.

To get the incentives right, directors must be selected by vigorously participating shareholders, most especially institutional shareholders, from a slate of demonstrably independent people who, although well-compensated, have reputations worth protecting. Nominations for that slate should come from sources other than the company management, to avoid a you-sit-on-my-compensation-committee-and-I'll-sit-on-yours selection process. The directors should not accept anything within the gift of the CEO; their directors' fees should be compensation enough, and high enough to provide an incentive to accumulate a record that will persuade shareholders to reelect them at reasonably regular periodic intervals—perhaps throwing in term limits to make sure that directors and management don't develop too cozy a relationship.

Finally, we come to the CEOs and top managers. How to create incentives to induce managers to act in the interests of the shareholders who own the business has bedeviled students of corporate governance ever since 1932, when Adolph A. Berle Jr. and Gardiner C. Means published their classic *The Modern Corporation and Private Property*, detailing the potential for managerial abuse created by the separation of ownership from control of large corporations. Managers placing self-interest above the interests of owners were immune to retaliation by far-flung and essentially powerless shareholders. That situation was partially corrected when Mike Milken and his debt-financed corporate raiders snatched control of many companies from the worst abusers of shareholders' interests, grounded fleets of corporate jets, sold off hunting lodges, and generally sweated the fat out of expenses—a wonderful example of markets working to correct abuses that seemed beyond the reach of regulators.

But nowadays there aren't many people who want to be like Mike, so it is incumbent on policymakers to get managers' incentives right. President Bush's proposal for publication of compensation arrangements in an accessible format would be a step in the right direction, its effectiveness attested to by the howls of outrage it produced from some CEOs. Truly independent boards, created along the lines described above, would be another advance, since compensation committees not beholden to corporate management are more likely to relate pay to performance than the supine committees that now exist on some boards. Add in the requirement that options be treated as profit-reducing expenses—another McCain proposal that so horrified senators that it has for now been derailed—and you will have a new parsimony that will keep salaries to levels commensurate with effort and performance. Under such a regime, executives would have a clear incentive to spend their time creating efficiencies and new markets, rather than figuring out how to cash in options, and how to persuade their boards to revalue options if poor company performance has driven the stock price below the price at which the options may be exercised, rewarding executives whether or not they have delivered long-term value for shareholders.

This may sound like an awful lot of regulation. But it is of a special, self-liquidating sort. If we adopt policies that get the incentives of all the players right, government can then get out of the way so that the various actors can do their thing—audit, advise on investments, monitor management performance in the interests of owners, and manage the company in a world in which managers' interests coincide with those of shareholders. The right kind of regulation can be a model of minimal—and effective—government.

SYSTEM FAILURE

Joseph Nocera

Fortune, June 24, 2002

GOLDMAN SACHS CEO HANK Paulson is not a touchy-feely guy. Even by Wall Street standards, he's fairly buttoned down. But the daily drumbeat of news about horrifying corporate behavior would get to any-one—and it's clearly getting to Paulson. "In my lifetime, American busi-ness has never been under such scrutiny, and to be blunt, much of it deserved," he said in a recent speech. To *Fortune* he added, "You pick up the paper, and you want to cry."

You sure do. Every day, it seems, a new scandal bursts into public view. Bankrupt Kmart is under SEC investigation for allegedly cooking the books. Adelphia's founding family is forced to resign in disgrace after it's revealed that members used the company as their own personal piggy bank, dipping into corporate funds to subsidize the Buffalo Sabres hockey team, among other things. Former telecom behemoths World-Com, Qwest, and Global Crossing are all being investigated. Edison Schools gets spanked by the SEC for booking revenues that the com-pany never actually saw. Dynegy CEO Chuck Watson denies that his company used special-purpose entities to disguise debt à la Enron— until *The Wall Street Journal* reports that, lo and behold, the company does have one, called Project Alpha. (Watson has just stepped down.) Most recently, of course, Tyco CEO Dennis Kozlowski resigns after informing his board that he is under investigation for evading sales tax on expensive artwork he purchased. Kozlowski has since been indicted—but even before the most recent disclosures, Tyco's stock was pummeled by the widespread suspicion that it used accounting tricks to boost revenues (a claim the company has consistently denied).

Phony earnings, inflated revenues, conflicted Wall Street analysts, directors asleep at the switch—this isn't just a few bad apples we're talking about here. This, my friends, is a systemic breakdown. Nearly every known check on corporate behavior—moral, regulatory, you name it—fell by the wayside, replaced by the stupendous greed that marked the end of the bubble. And that has created a crisis of investor confidence the likes of which hasn't been seen since—well, since the Great Depression.

Even Harvey Pitt and Bill Lerach, who are poles apart on most issues, agree on this point. "I'm really afraid that investor psychology in this country has suffered a very serious blow," says the controversial Lerach, the plaintiffs attorney best known as the lead counsel representing Enron's beleaguered shareholders. SEC Chairman Pitt, who made his name defending big corporations, concurs: "It would be hard to overstate the need to remedy the loss of confidence," he said at a recent conference at Stanford Law School. "Restoring public confidence is the No. 1 goal on our agenda."

Declining investor confidence is not the only reason the stock market is hurting, of course. (The S&P 500 is down 10% so far this year, while the Nasdaq has fallen 20%.) For one thing, the world is an unsettling place right now, with Pakistan and India busy saber rattling, the Mideast in turmoil—and the threat of more terrorist attacks on U.S. soil very much in the air. For another, stocks remain high by historical standards: Even with a 20% drop since its peak in March 2000, the price/earnings ratio for the S&P 500 is still 29, compared with the norm of 16.

Despite the constant reports of misconduct, investors can't cast all the blame for the market's troubles on the actions of CEOs and Wall Street analysts—much as they might like to. There was a time not too long ago when everyone, it seemed, was day trading during lunch breaks. As Gail Dudack, chief strategist for SunGard Institutional Brokerage, puts it, "A stock market bubble requires the cooperation of everyone."

Still, the unending revelations—and the high likelihood that there are more to come—have underscored the extent to which the system has gone awry. That has taken a toll on investors' psyches. According to a Pew Forum survey conducted in late March, Americans now think more highly of Washington politicians than they do of business executives. (Yes, it's that bad.) A monthly survey of "investor optimism" conducted by UBS and Gallup shows that the mood among investors today is almost as grim as it was after Sept. 11—and has sunk by nearly half since the giddy days of late 1999 and early 2000. Similarly, the average daily trading volume at Charles Schwab & Co.—another good barometer of investor confidence—is down 54% from the height of the bull market. "People deeply believed, as an article of faith, in the integrity of the system and the markets," Morgan Stanley strategist Barton Biggs wrote recently. "Sure, it may at times have seemed like a casino, but at least it was an honest casino. Now many people are questioning that basic assumption. Are they players in a loser's game?" Investing, notes Vanguard founder John C. Bogle, "is an act of faith." Without that faith—that reported numbers reflect reality, that companies are being run honestly, that Wall Street is playing it straight, and that investors aren't being hoodwinked—our capital markets simply can't function.

Throughout history, bubbles have been followed by crashes—which in turn have been followed by new laws and new rules designed to curb the excesses of the era just ended. After the South Sea bubble in 1720, points out Columbia University law professor John Coffee, the formation of new corporations was banned for more than 100 years. In the wake of the 1929 Crash—and the subsequent discovery that insiders had used their positions to skim millions from the market—dramatic reforms were enacted, including the creation of the SEC, the passage of the Glass-Steagall Act separating banks from investment houses, and the outlawing of short-selling by corporate officers.

Is the situation today as dire as it was in 1929? Of course not. But it is serious—serious enough that real reform is once again needed to restore confidence in the system. Already there has been a flood of proposals, which range from the good to the not-so-good. For instance, the New York Stock Exchange's recently announced plan to strengthen boards of directors has been widely lauded—praise, we believe, that is quite deserved (see item 5). If enacted, the NYSE reforms will help prod boards to finally act in the interest of shareholders—which, after all, is supposed to be their job. Similarly, the SEC's decision to crack down on Edison Schools sends an enormously important signal. Money that was going to pay, say, teachers' salaries was being booked by the company as revenue—even though the money never actually flowed through Edison. Believe it or not, Edison's accounting abided by Generally Accepted Accounting Principles, or GAAP. In going after Edison, the SEC was saying that simply staying within GAAP is no longer good enough—not if the spirit of the rules is being violated, as was clearly the case with Edison.

On the other hand, the tepidness of some other reform ideas is disheartening. Sure, New York attorney general Eliot Spitzer extracted $100 million from Merrill Lynch for its analysts' abuses, but he didn't do anything to change the system that allows analysts to participate in investment-banking deals. And Harvey Pitt's "solution" to the analyst problem—that analysts be forced to sign a statement saying their pay was not contingent on how they rated a particular stock—would be laughable if it weren't so tragic. Meanwhile, one of the NYSE's most notable proposals—that option grants be approved by shareholders—is already being opposed by the Business Roundtable. Don't America's business leaders understand how corrosive their egregious pay packages are to fundamental faith in the system? This sends precisely the wrong signal.

What follows is our own package of reforms for cleaning up the system and restoring investor confidence. We do not claim that they are the most politically palatable ideas, or the most likely to be adopted in the short term. In some cases—as with our proposed reforms for Wall Street analysts and IPOs—they're quite radical. To which we say: So be it. There are times that cry out for radical reform. We are living in one of those times.

I. EARNINGS—TRUST BUT VERIFY

When it comes to reporting earnings, U.S. companies have about as much credibility these days as the judges of Olympic figure skating. So how do you begin to restore investor confidence post-Enron, post-Tyco, post-you-name-it? By having companies state profits in a way that is more meaningful and less subject to manipulation. It's not as hard as it sounds.

First, get rid of the absolute funniest numbers—the so-called pro forma earnings companies use to divert attention from their real results. We're talking about things like adjusted earnings, operating earnings, cash earnings, and EBITDA (earnings before interest, tax, depreciation, and amortization). If companies want to tout such random, unaudited, watch-me-pull-a-rabbit-out-of-my-hat figures in their press releases, well, fine. But investors should immediately be able to compare these figures with full financial statements prepared in accordance with Generally Accepted Accounting Principles (GAAP) rather than have to wait 45 days or more for the company's SEC filing.

True, GAAP earnings aren't perfect. They, too, can—and must—be improved. Right now, for instance, they don't reflect the real cost of stock options. It's past time to make this happen, no matter how much Silicon Valley screams.

Next, stop the abuse of restructuring charges. The cost of things like plant closings and layoffs is just part of doing business and should count as an operating expense, not as a special one-time charge. Plus, companies too often set up a reserve to cover restructuring costs, then later quietly shift some of that money back into profits. If that happens, investors ought to know about it. The SEC should make sure they do.

Another favorite accounting trick that has to go: the use of overfunded pension plans to boost income. Standard & Poor's, in its newly formulated "core earnings" measure, excludes pension income altogether, while including any pension costs. That's not a bad solution, since pension expenses are real, but a company can get its hands on pension income only by dissolving the plan, distributing benefits, and then paying ridiculously high taxes on the remaining money. At the very least companies should be forced to recognize the actual gains and losses of their pension plans—not simply estimate them based on prior years' returns.

None of this will make one iota of difference unless companies adhere to the spirit of accounting rules, not just the letter. Here's one way to help make sure that happens: Donn Vickrey, executive vice president of Camelback Research Alliance, thinks auditors shouldn't just sign off on clients' financial statements. They should also have to grade the quality of their earnings. A company that was ultraconservative in its accounting would get an A, while one that arguably complied with GAAP but used aggressive accounting tricks would receive a D. "Companies would then be under pressure to not just make their numbers but also get the highest-quality ratings," Vickrey says. Sure, auditing firms might then be under pressure to inflate grades. But earnings will never mean anything anyway if auditors remain pushovers.   JEREMY KAHN

2. REBUILD THE CHINESE WALL

Here's the single most important fact about securities research at the big Wall Street firms: It loses money. Lots of money. According to David Trone at Prudential Financial, the typical giant brokerage firm spends $1 billion a year on research. But big institutional investors—the clients—only pay about $500 million in trading commissions in return for research. (Historically research has been paid for with trading commissions.) And if you want to understand why research became so corrupted during the late, great bubble—and so tied to investment banking—that's the reason. By serving as an adjunct of their firm's investment bankers, research analysts were, in effect, attaching themselves to a huge profit center. Participation in banking deals is why analysts felt justified commanding seven-figure salaries—and why bankers (and companies for that matter) felt justified in demanding that analysts say only nice things in their research reports to investors. As a respected research analyst puts it, "Corporations are indirectly subsidizing research on themselves because they pay the banking fees that pay for what is called objective research."

When analysts first started participating openly in dealmaking some 30-odd years ago, they were said to have "jumped the wall"—a reference, of course, to the Chinese wall that was supposed to separate analysts from investment bankers. Today nobody uses that phrase. Why would they? There is no Chinese wall anymore.

We should know by now that research with integrity is simply not possible without a Chinese wall. But the most common reform proposal being kicked around—that researchers should not be paid directly for their investment-banking work—doesn't go nearly far enough in resurrecting it. It's way too easy to get around. Still, there is a surprisingly simple fix: Enact a regulation that forbids analysts from being involved in banking deals, period.

Think about it for a second: Why are analysts involved in deals in the first place? The standard answer you get from Wall Street is that they are there to protect investors. They are supposed to "vet" deals on behalf of the investing public—and if they think an IPO doesn't pass the smell test, they are supposed to have the power to force the firm to pass on it. But we all know that is not how it works in reality—if it ever did. In fact, analysts serve as a marketing tool, implicitly (and sometimes explicitly) promising favorable coverage if their firm is allowed to underwrite the deal.

Under our proposal, investment bankers will have to do their own vetting, something they're perfectly capable of handling, thank you very much. Having been shut out of the banking process, the analyst will be able to evaluate the company only after it has gone public—when he can make his own decision about whether to cover it. Indeed, shut out of banking, analysts will once again serve only one master: the investor.

How will analysts earn their seven-figure salaries—and how will the big firms make money on research? We don't know—but we don't really care. Fixing their broken business model is the brokerage industry's problem, not ours. It's possible that analysts will have to take big pay cuts. More likely brokerage firms will have to make a choice: Either openly subsidize research—on the grounds that it offers value to the firm's clients—or shut down their research operations and leave serious securities analysis to dedicated research boutiques like Sanford Bernstein or Charles Schwab, which is trying to set up a system to provide objective research for small investors. Either way we'll be better off than we are now, getting research we can't trust from analysts mired in conflicts of interest. **DAVID RYNECKI**

3. LET THE SEC EAT WHAT IT KILLS

For months it has been the underlying question—surfacing with the Enron collapse, and again with Global Crossing, and again with Kmart, and again with the scandal over Wall Street research: Where the heck is the SEC? Where is the watchdog?

The answer, certainly, is MIA.

As any careful newspaper reader can tell you, the Securities and Exchange Commission has launched one probe after another in recent months. (Indeed, the rate of new investigations from January to March was double that of the first quarter of 2001.) But the agency's enforcement staff is stretched so thin that many of the investigations are likely to fall by the wayside. It sounds like a parable from Sun Tzu: An army that is everywhere is an army nowhere.

Consider the SEC's mandate as sheriff of Wall Street. The agency by law is charged with reviewing the financial filings of 17,000 public companies, overseeing a universe of mutual funds that has grown more than fourfold (in assets) in the past decade, vetting every brokerage firm, ensuring the proper operation of the exchanges, being vigilant against countless potential market manipulations, insider trading, and accounting transgressions—and investigating whenever anything goes wrong. Yet as the $12 trillion stock market becomes ever more complex, the SEC hasn't been given enough resources even to read annual reports. Seriously. One of the agency's chief accountants admitted in a speech last year that only one in 15 annual reports was reviewed in 2000. Take your guess on Enron.

How many lawyers, you ask, does the SEC have to study the disclosure documents of 17,000 public companies? About 100, says Laura S. Unger, the commission's former acting chairwoman. The number of senior forensic accountants in the enforcement division—the kind of experts who can decipher Enron's balance sheets—is far fewer than that. And as if that isn't bad enough, staffers are leaving in droves. The reason is a familiar one: money. Forget about how poor civil service pay is compared with that of the private sector. The SEC's attorneys and examiners are paid 25% to 40% less than those of even comparable federal agencies, like the FDIC and the Office of the Comptroller.

Employee turnover is now at 30%—double the rate for the rest of the government. Which means that in three years or so, virtually the whole staff will be replaced. President Bush actually signed into law a bill that would give SEC regulators pay parity with their federal counterparts, but then Congress didn't bother to fund the raise in its annual appropriations. In the meantime the SEC is left with worse vacancy rates than the Ramallah Hilton.

The strangest part of the story, though, is that the money is already there. Remember those corporate filings? Well, the SEC took in more than $2 billion in processing fees last year—almost five times its entire annual budget. A single company's registration fee, such as that for Regal Entertainment ($31,740), which went public in May, could nearly pay the annual salary for a junior examiner. These dollars, according to the Securities Act of 1933, are supposed to recover the costs related to securities registration processes, "including enforcement activities, policy and rulemaking activities, administration, legal services, and international regulatory activities." They don't. Congress diverts the money to other uses instead. Think of it as an expensive toll bridge in disrepair—and the dollars we drivers are handing over for roadway paving and safety inspections are being used for something else entirely, like the National Archives (which, by the way, is growing its staff at twice the rate of the SEC).

"Investors and corporate filers are paying way over and above the cost of regulation, and they're not getting it," says Unger. "Congress seems to see the money as an entitlement." A recent law (the same one, in fact, that authorized pay parity) will bring the fees sharply down starting in October, but even so there is plenty of money to fund a comprehensive regulatory program—one that brings in enough stock cops to make Wall Street safe for investors again. The cost of not funding the SEC is more disasters like Enron. You do the math. CLIFTON LEAF

4. PAY CEOS, YEAH—BUT NOT SO MUCH

Before they stumbled, they cashed in. Enron's Jeff Skilling made $112 million off his stock options in the three years before his company collapsed. Tyco's Dennis Kozlowski cashed in $240 million over three years before he got the boot. Joe Nacchio, who's still in charge at Qwest but has left investors billions poorer, made $232 million off options in three years.

If you're looking for reasons corporate America is in such ill repute, this kind of over-the-top CEO piggishness is a big one. Investors and in some cases employees lost everything, while the architects of their pain laughed all the way to the bank.

The funny thing is, we asked for it. "Pay for performance" was what investors wanted—and to a significant extent, got: For the first time in memory, CEOs' cash compensation actually dropped in 2001, by 2.8%, according to Mercer Human Resource Consulting. The value of top executives' stock and options holdings in many cases dropped by a lot more than that.

But while CEO pay has become more variable—and study after study has shown it to be more closely linked to company performance than it used to be—it has also grown unspeakably generous. Fifteen years ago the highest-paid CEO in the land was Chrysler's Lee Iacocca, who took home $20 million. Last year's No. 1, Larry Ellison of Oracle, made $706 million.

There are a lot of complicated, difficult-to-change reasons for this. Some are addressed in the next item, on corporate governance. Some may be insoluble. In any case, we're probably due an acrimonious national debate over just what a CEO is worth. But for now, here's a straightforward suggestion: Force companies to stop pretending that the stock options they give their executives are free.

It's probably safe to say that Oracle's board would never have paid Larry Ellison $706 million in cash or any other form that would have to show up on the company's earnings statement. All that money (Ellison didn't get a salary last year) came from exercising stock options that the company had given him in earlier years. And because of the current screwed-up accounting for stock options, Oracle's earnings statement says that Ellison's bonanza didn't cost the company a cent.

Options are by far the biggest component of CEO pay these days. Virtually all of the most eye-popping CEO bonanzas have come from options exercises. While it is sometimes argued that options are popular because they link the interests of executives with those of shareholders, there are other, possibly better ways to do that—outright grants of stock, for instance—that don't get used nearly as much as options because they have to be expensed.

Do the markets really have trouble seeing through this kind of financial gimmickry? Are boards really so influenced by an accounting loophole? In a word, yes. "Anybody who fights the reported-earnings obsession does so at their own peril," says compensation guru Ira Kay of the consulting firm Watson Wyatt. So let's make companies charge the estimated value of the options they give out against their earnings, and see if the options hogs are up to the fight. JUSTIN FOX

5. FIRE THE CHAIRMAN OF THE BORED

Normally, if you ask Nell Minow what's wrong with corporate boards, you get an earful. As a longtime shareholder activist and founder of the *Corporate Library*, an on-line newsletter covering corporate governance, Minow has been one of the most vocal and acerbic critics of American boardrooms. But earlier this month she was uncharacteristically chipper on the subject. "Today I'm just going to be happy," she demurred when asked to go over her usual gripes about boards.

What had Minow in such a good mood? A 29-page report released by the New York Stock Exchange on June 6, proposing sweeping reforms to the rules governing the boards of its listed companies. The reforms won't go into effect until later this summer, when the NYSE's own board is expected to approve them. Once that happens, companies trading on the Big Board will have to adopt them—or risk being delisted. "I never thought I'd see this from the New York Stock Exchange," says Minow.

It's easy to see why she's so ecstatic. The report calls for nearly everything Minow and other shareholder activists have been clamoring for—from a shareholder vote on stock option grants to annual performance evaluations of directors to the requirement that each board publish a code of ethics. The big one, though, concerns the independence of boards.

As Enron and its ilk have shown, too often directors aren't really independent. Even so-called outsiders end up having some ties to the CEO. "On the surface Enron's board looked independent," says Jay Lorsch, a governance professor at the Harvard Business School. "But everybody on that board was selected by Ken Lay." And when the CEO dominates, the rest of the board is often too cowed to question his leadership. "Right now in many board meetings there is no dialogue," a prominent board consultant told *Fortune*. "Directors will just sit and watch the presentations. At the end they nod and say, 'Great.'"

The Big Board plans to change all that. Under its proposal, a majority of directors would have to be outsiders. Real outsiders. That means no ex-employees (they won't count as outsiders until they've been gone five years) or anyone whose livelihood in any way depends on the company. In addition, outsiders will have to meet regularly without management present. This alone will have a huge impact—after all, it's a lot easier to criticize a CEO behind his back than to his face.

Of course, the NYSE's proposals are no cure-all. There are plenty of reforms that it missed—like preventing directors from selling the company's stock until after they've resigned, or rooting out underqualified directors like ex-Dodger manager Tommy Lasorda, who sits on troubled Lone Star Steakhouse's board. (Believe it or not, O.J. Simpson was once on Infinity Broadcasting's audit committee.)

In the end, though, all the rules in the world won't change a thing until directors realize that ultimately they've got to reform themselves. They have to go beyond the rules: They have to ask better, tougher questions, be more skeptical and critical of management, and never forget that their No. 1 job is to watch out for us, the shareholders, not their buddy, the CEO. "Boards are like murder suspects: They need motive and opportunity," says Minow. Now they've been given both. Let's hope they do the right thing.   **KATRINA BROOKER**

6. PUT THE "PUBLIC" BACK IN IPO

The new symbols of Wall Street sleaze are so-called celebrity analysts, hapless promoters like Henry Blodget and Jack Grubman who talked investors into buying all sorts of tech stocks they knew, or should have known, were dogs. But to a certain extent they're really just a sideshow. The main source of corruption in America's financial markets is the sordid, antiquated world of initial public offerings.

It's the ultimate kickback business: Wall Street firms set offering prices for start-ups far below their real value, then offer the cheap shares to their best customers—mutual and hedge funds—in exchange for inflated commissions. The funds then make a killing when the shares invariably zoom on the first day of trading.

Nice for them. Nice for Wall Street. But it's an awfully raw deal for the start-ups—and for the rest of us. During the tech bubble, underpricing became outrageous. In 1999 and 2000, new companies raised $121 billion through IPOs, but shares soared so high the first day that they left $62 billion on the table, money they could have used for R&D

or building brands. In addition, start-ups must pay a 7% fee that Wall Street refuses to negotiate. The upshot: For every dollar start-ups raised in 1999 and 2000, they paid 58 cents in a combination of fees and forgone proceeds. Meanwhile, according to Jay Ritter, a professor at the University of Florida, the grateful funds repaid Wall Street with at least $6 billion in inflated commissions over that period.

The biggest losers, of course, are small investors. On average they get only 20% of any IPO before the offering. "The perception is that the rich milk goes to the fat cats," says Glen Meakem, CEO of FreeMarkets, a Net auction company that went public in 1999. During the tech bubble, big bankers like CSFB's Frank Quattrone even set aside cheap shares for a select group of entrepreneurs and venture capitalists, an ingenious way to woo future IPO business.

Why do the issuers put up with Wall Street's abuse? The reason is twofold. First, gilded names like Goldman Sachs and Morgan Stanley provide a comfort factor, ensuring that the deals run smoothly. Second, going with a top house guarantees that a prestigious analyst will tout your stock. Until recently that's been critical to entrepreneurs eager to market their stock to powerful institutions.

Obviously, given the taint on Wall Street, such endorsements are worth far less to companies today—and that opens the possibility of reform. It should come in two forms. First, the SEC should ban all officers of start-ups and their venture capitalists from accepting any other firm's IPO shares from investment banks within a year of their own company's filing to go public. Second, issuers should finally show a little courage and destroy the old system.

Here's their weapon: Since 1998, W.R. Hambrecht & Co. has been auctioning IPOs on the Internet. Though Hambrecht has done only seven deals so far, its model is a good deal fairer than Wall Street's. Small investors get to bid alongside the institutions. The shares go to the highest bidder, and—voilà—the IPO slush fund, that big pool of money that feeds all the corruption, evaporates.

Founder Bill Hambrecht predicts that the breakthrough will take an unusual route. "Issuers will start demanding that a Merrill or a Goldman do IPO auctions, threatening to use us if they don't agree." And who knows? One or two high-profile auctions may just be enough to break the system, smashing the mystique that only the old way can ensure a smooth offering. Over to you, start-ups. SHAWN TULLY

7. SHAREHOLDERS SHOULD ACT LIKE OWNERS

A mere 75 mutual funds, pensions, and other institutional shareholders control $6.3 trillion worth of stock—or some 44% of the market. With power like that, real reform is only a proxy vote away.

Permissions Acknowledgments